How To Buy Real Estate In Mexico

A Simple Guide To Buying Property In Mexico

By Dennis John Peyton

Second Edition

Law Mexico Publishing, San Diego, California

HOW TO BUY REAL ESTATE IN MEXICO
A Simple Guide To Buying Property In Mexico
By Dennis John Peyton Second Edition

Published By: Law Mexico Publishing
San Diego, California

Toll Free Telephone: 1-800-Law Mexico

Send correspondence to:
Law Mexico Publishing
539 Telegraph Canyon Road #787
Chula Vista, CA 91910-6497
Telephone (619) 482-8244

Library of Congress Cataloging in Publication Date
Peyton, Dennis John
How To Buy Real Estate In Mexico: A Simple Guide To Buying
Property In Mexico / By
Dennis John Peyton. 2nd. ed.
ISBN 1-885328-26-5: $24.95 Softcover

A mi esposa Marcela

PURPOSE OF THIS BOOK

The purpose of this book is to alert you to some the basic concepts of a successful real estate transaction in Mexico. It is not intended to be a complete discussion of the subject, and nothing contained herein should be construed as constituting legal advice.

Examples given to illustrate concepts and systems are considered representative of Federal law, but with thirty two states and the federal district in Mexico, each possibly having different laws, precise interpretation must come from the reader's own Mexican attorney.

"This publication is designed to provide accurate and authoritative information in regard to the subject matter covered. It is sold with the understanding that the publisher is not engaged in rendering legal services. If legal advice or other expert assistance is required, the service of a competent professional person should be sought."

From a Declaration of Principles jointly adopted by the Committee of the American Bar Association and a Committee of Publishers and Associations.

TABLE OF CONTENTS

Chapter 4:Title Documents And Recording 4-1

Chapter 5: People Involved In The Real Estate Industry 5-1

Chapter 9: Property and Property Rights....9-1

Chapter 10: Classification of Real Property Rights 10-1

Chapter 11: Property Ownership and Possession

Chapter 12: Property Acquisition

CHAPTER 13: CO-OWNERSHIP................................ 13-1

CHAPTER 14: CONDOMINIUM OWNERSHIP........... 14-1

CHAPTER 1

NEW FOR 1997

THIS CHAPTER EXAMINES SOME OF THE CHANGES THAT HAVE TAKEN PLACE IN THE REAL ESTATE INDUSTRY IN MEXICO SINCE THE PUBLICATION OF THE FIRST EDITION OF THIS BOOK.

PROPOSED NOM-112-SCFI-1995: INFORMATION REQUIREMENTS FOR RENDERING REAL ESTATE SERVICES.

INTRODUCTION

In March of 1996 the federal government published proposed regulations or, as they are known in Mexico, standards or "NOMs," which address for the first time how the real estate industry in Mexico may be regulated. Even though these regulations have not been passed into law they are still very important because they clearly show that the government is making efforts to impose stricter controls on the real estate industry. It is reasonable to expect that some kind of similar regulations will become law. For this reason the provisions of this NOM should be taken into consideration and voluntarily enforced by all real estate professionals in Mexico.

OBJECTIVE

The main objective of the NOM is to establish the minimum requirements for commercial information that must be provided to consumers or be contained in form contracts used by real estate agents, contractors, developers and promoters who are engaged in the commercialization of real estate.

SCOPE OF APPLICATION:

The NOM is applicable for all persons or legal entities in Mexico that are engaged in the business of rendering real estate services. It is also applicable for those who are engaged in the business of subdividing and developing real estate, construction, the promotion and sale of new real estate, or the sale of real estate under construction.

The NOM explicitly states that commercial information provided to consumers is subject to the provisions of this regulation. Also subject to the regulation are adhesion contracts for rendering real estate related services, preliminary sales agreements, promissory agreements, or any other agreements which involve real estate transactions.

An adhesion contract is defined as a standardized contract form offered to consumers of goods and services on a "take it or leave it" basis. It does not afford the consumer realistic opportunity to bargain and the conditions are such that the consumer cannot obtain the desired services except by consenting to use such a contract.

Essentially, this means that all listing agreements for the sale of real estate, any form contracts for making an offer on real estate, or any other type of agreement leading to the final sale of real estate is regulated by these provisions.

DEFINITIONS

The following definitions are provided to facilitate the application of the NOM.

> **Real estate service provider**: Any individual or legal entity who, either alone or through others, is habitually or periodically dedicated to offering real estate services, in exchange for a fee; the same criteria is used for any individual who is dedicated to the sale of real estate.
> **Real estate services:** Any activity associated with the project design, construction, subdivision, buying and selling, appraisal, leasing or property management, and all related consultation associated with real estate rendered by a real estate service provider.
> **Consumer:** Any individual or legal entity who requires and obtains, as the end user, real estate services or real estate.
> **Model or adhesion contracts:** A document drafted unilaterally by a real estate service provider to establish terms and conditions, in uniform documents, applicable to real estate services or the sale of real estate.
> **Real estate:** Anything that cannot be moved from one place to another without altering, in some manner, its form or substance,

which is dedicated to certain uses: housing, commerce, industry, tourism and urban development.

> **Hidden defects**: Defects or imperfections in real estate construction or installations not immediately apparent and which are not identified prior to or in a contract.

GENERAL PROVISIONS

The cost, professional fees and the price for both the sale of real estate as well as real estate services should be paid in Mexican pesos if there is any question regarding currency for payment. The law allows for the determination of the amount in foreign currency but the actual payment can always be made in pesos. This is usually done by allowing payment at the exchange rate on the day of payment. However, payment must be accepted in pesos even when the parties agreed to an amount in foreign currency.

All contracts entered into within Mexican territory must establish a place of payment somewhere in Mexico. Foreigners who maintain residency outside of Mexico may agree to an additional place of payment outside of Mexico provided that it is clearly defined in the corresponding real estate contract.

Contracts used by real estate service providers for real estate services and the sale of real estate must be registered with the consumer protection agency and available to consumers for review before they are signed. This is to make sure that the consumer can make a fully informed decision when choosing a real estate service provider or buying real estate. Along the same lines, any advertising associated with the promotion of real estate services or the sale of real estate must also abide by the provisions of the Consumer Protection Law.

Section 5.5 explicitly states that sales of real estate and condominiums in tourist areas, particularly when the consumers are foreigners, must abide by the provisions of this NOM. Additionally, it requires real estate service providers to register with the National Registry of Tourism.

INFORMATION TO BE INCLUDED IN MODEL CONTRACTS FOR REAL ESTATE SERVICES

Any model or adhesion contracts used by real estate service providers for real estate services must contain specific minimum requirements:

1. They must be written in Spanish. The contract may be provided in other languages, but a Spanish version must also be provided.

2. All currency amounts must be in Mexican pesos. Foreign currency amounts may be used but only when it is stated that payments may be made in pesos at the exchange rate applicable on the date and at the place where the payment is made.

3. The contract must contain the consumer protection filing number.

4. The contract must contain the service provider's filing number furnished by the National Register of Service Providers, which is operated by the consumer protection agency. If the provider is not registered, the contract must indicate this.

5. It must contain a description of the service contract. When the service contract is for development, design and construction, the service provider must furnish the technical characteristics as well as a description of the building materials.

6. The contract must include the service provider's name, company or firm name, address and tax identification number.

7. It must include the consumer's name, address and, when possible, the tax identification number.

8. The contract must contain the folio or reference number of the contract entered into by the service provider and the consumer.

9. The contract must establish the amount of the fees paid to the service provider or describe how the fees are calculated. If the fees are not fixed, the contract must include the amount that is used as the basis for calculating the fees.

10. The contract must describe how the service providers fees are to be paid.

11. It must include a description of the rights and obligations of both the service provider and the consumer.

12. It must establish the penalties agreed to, which are applicable in cases of non-compliance by the service provider or the consumer.

13. The contract must include the guarantees of compliance offered by the service provider to the consumer.

14. It must describe the procedures for contract cancellation and the consequences of the cancellation for both the consumer and the service provider.

15. The contract must establish the date the real estate services are initiated and the amount of time for which the services shall be contracted.

16. The contract must designate the place and date of the contract.

17. It must describe the expenses that must be reimbursed and the method of payment.

18. The contract must include a description of how the services are to be carried out.

19. The contract must contain a description of how disputes are to be resolved.

REQUIRED INFORMATION FOR THE SALE OF REAL ESTATE

Prior to signing any contracts the service provider must physically show the property to the consumer. In the case of pre-construction sales, the service provider must show the consumer a model home and the construction plans and scale model, and he must provide certain information:

1. The service provider must provide title documents for the property.

2. The service provider must show the legal capacity of the seller and the authorization of the service provider to promote the sale of the property.

3. The provider must indicate the current status of the property's water utility payments and property tax payments.

4. In the case of new homes, the service provider must furnish the authorizations, licenses or permits issued by the corresponding competent authorities, for the following:
   ➢ construction, with technical specifications;
   ➢ security;
   ➢ land use designation;
   ➢ class of materials used in the construction;
   ➢ basic utilities, water, electric power, gas, and sewer;
   ➢ and all others required by law.

5. The service provider must arrange for availability of structural, architectural, and installation plans, or, if these are not available, a report of the structural conditions of the home or building. If neither is available, this fact should be stated.

6. The service provider must furnish documents indicating the characteristics of the property, such as size, surface area with construction, type of buildings and fixtures, parking facilities, common use areas shared with other properties and percentage of undivided rights to the common use areas, utilities and the general physical condition of the property.

7. The service provider must provide documentation of any additional benefits offered by the service provider such as special furnishings or other "extras" which are not normally included.

8. The provider must disclose the payment options available to the consumer. In the event that the consumer is given financing it must be done in accordance with the consumer protection laws. If financing is made available, the service provider must state the type of credit, interest rate and whether it is variable. He must indicate whether a mortgage or trust guarantee is available, and, if so, how it shall be implemented.

9. When available, the service provider should indicate the procedures for modification or re-negotiation of the payment option, the conditions that have to be met and the economic implications for both the consumer as well as the service provider.

10. The service provider must disclose any additional expenses which are paid by the consumer in addition to the purchase price, such as taxes, notary fees, investigation fees, appraisals, etc., as well as any other costs related to additional improvements not included in the normal sales package.

11. The service provider must furnish a document concerning the rights of either party to cancel the contract.

MINIMUM INFORMATION REQUIRED FOR CONTRACTS USED FOR THE SALE OF REAL ESTATE

The minimum required information that must be contained in the model contracts used by real estate agents for the sale of real estate is as follows:

General information

1. There must be a description of the property in Spanish. It may be provided in other languages, but only when a Spanish version is also provided.

2. All currency amounts must be in Mexican pesos. Foreign currency amounts may also be used but only when it is stated that payments

may be made in pesos at the exchange rate applicable on the date and at the place where the payment is made.

3. The contract must provide the consumer protection agency's Registration filing number for the contract.

4. The purpose of the contract or commercial operation must be stated.

5. The name, company or firm name, address and federal tax identification number of the agent must be furnished.

6. In cases involving legal representatives, that representative's legal capacity to act as an agent should be stated.

7. The contract should include the name, address and, when possible, federal tax identification number of the consumer.

8. The contract should include the folio or reference number of the contract between the service provider and the consumer.

9. The contract should indicate the place and date the contract was entered into.

Specific information

1. The model contract should contain the address or physical location of the property.

2. The contract must include a description of the characteristics of the property, such as size, surface area with construction, number of baths, parking facilities, visitor parking, extra improvements included in the sales price, common use areas shared with other properties and percentage of undivided rights to the common use areas, utilities and the general physical condition of the property.

3. The contract must include the property's title history as filed in the public registry.

4. The contract must indicate the form of payment agreed to based on the legally required information which must be provided prior to the execution of the contract, and, when necessary, the frequency of payments.

5. In the event of financing, the contract should indicate the number and type of promissory notes or other negotiable instruments subscribed by the consumer in relation to payments of earnest money deposits and the sales price, including interest and payments to principle.

6. The contract should describe the financial benefits to the consumer of prepaying any financing.

7. The contract must describe the procedure the consumer must carry out to make payments.

8. A model contract must contain a statement of fees and expenses that must be paid by the consumer to government or private agencies at the moment delivery of possession of the property is taken.

9. A contract must indicate the manner by which late payment interests are to be paid, including how they are calculated and when they are applicable.

10. When necessary, the contract should include the name and address of the person or legal entity acting as joint and several debtor.

11. The contract should disclose the rights and obligations of the parties in closing the transaction and subsequent recording with a public notary and filing with the public registry.

12. The contract must include the promise of the parties to have the model contract correctly drafted and recorded before a public notary chosen by the consumer, or, in absence of any selection by the consumer, both parties may mutually agree to use a notary.

13. The contract must describe any contract penalties, which are proportionally applied to both the consumer and the agent/provider in case of noncompliance.

14. The contract must describe the guarantees offered to the consumer that the property shall be delivered within the term agreed to in the contract.

15. The contract must stipulate the obligation of the provider to cure hidden defects and to guarantee the consumer's quiet enjoyment in the case of eviction or dispossession.

16. The contract must describe any additional benefits or "extras" offered to the consumer.

17. The contract must indicate the right that either party has to cancel the transaction in accordance with the law.

INFORMATION REQUIRED AT DELIVERY--ACCEPTANCE OF THE PROPERTY

The provider must give the consumer a manual or instruction guide upon the delivery-acceptance that includes the minimum required maintenance for the exterior, the structure itself as well as for any appliances or other furnishings. When so agreed, the provider should also give the consumer structural, architectural and installation plans, or, in their absence, a written statement describing the structural conditions of the property. This is provided in accordance with the required information to be made available to the consumer prior to the execution of the sales agreement as stated above in Required Information for the Sale of Real Estate.

In cases involving new condominium property, the information required in the preceding paragraph is made available to the manager or president of the condominium owners at their first meeting. This does not, however, eliminate each condominium owner's right to a copy of the same information, provided that he pays the expense for making such copies.

ENFORCEMENT AND INSPECTION

The consumer protection agency has the right to take action against violations of this NOM and any complaints are filed with the nearest office.

1997 FOREIGN INVESTMENT LAW AMENDMENTS

ACQUISITION OF REAL ESTATE

In December of 1996 the Mexican government published various amendments to the Foreign Investment Law. The Second Title, Chapter One, ACQUISITION OF REAL PROPERTY, EXPLOITATION OF MINES AND WATERS AND TRUSTS, had the following amendments.

Article 10 was changed to clarify that Mexican corporations owned by foreigners may acquire ownership of real property located in the restricted zone, intended for non-residential activities, provided that the acquisition is registered with the Ministry of Foreign Relations within 60 working days following the date on which the acquisition is made. This was an important change because prior the amendment it was not clear exactly when the registration has to be completed. It also made it very clear that no authorization of any sort was required of foreign investors before the acquisition.

Effective form the end of January 1997, foreigners who want to acquire real estate outside the restricted zone, or who want to obtain concessions for the exploration or exploitation of mines and waters, must first agree to the provisions of the calvo clause (see Chapter 2) by presenting a written statement to Ministry of Foreign Relations, and then obtain a permit to carry out the transaction.

This formality is necessary in order to comply with the Mexican Constitution, however, it is not intended to be anything other than routine. For this reason the amendment states that when the real estate to be acquired is in a municipality located totally outside the restricted zone or when they are trying to obtain a concession for the exploitation of mines and waters in national territory, the permit shall be granted automatically if the refusal of the Ministry of Foreign Relations is not published in the Diario Oficial of the Federation within the five working days following the date of the filing of the application.

Additionally the amendment also gives the Ministry the discretion to decide when foreigners will not require a permit and must only file a written statement agreeing to the calvo clause, in order to acquire real estate. Given these provisions, it is not likely that any such permits shall ever be denied.

TRUSTS ON REAL PROPERTY IN THE RESTRICTED ZONE

Chapter two was modified to reduce the term the Ministry has to grant trust permits from 30 to 5 days. Any petition for a permit must be decided by the Ministry within the 5 working days following the date of its presentation before the office in Mexico City. The term of 30 days is still en effect if the application for the permit was made in the state delegations of the office of the Ministry. Once those periods expire without a decision being issued, the respective petition shall be considered as approved.

NEW TRUST PERMITTING POLICY

STATE OFFICES AUTHORIZED

On October 28, 1996 the Mexican government published several provisions aimed at deregulating the involvement of the Ministry of Foreign Relations in various permitting processes. In accordance with the National Development Plan 1995-200, the Mexican government has undertaken the task of deregulating and simplifying administrative procedures to streamline current regulations and eliminate unnecessary governmental discretion and excessive bureaucracy. This was done by delegating more authority to the state offices throughout Mexico and cutting back the amount of time the Ministry has to issue permits.

The following changes were made regarding the permitting processes required before the Ministry of Foreign Relations:

➢ Permits for real estate trusts in the restricted zone: permits are now valid indefinitely. This eliminates the 90 day requirement that the trust permit had to be used by setting up a trust before a notary otherwise a new permit would have to be applied for. This is a very important change. There should no longer be any reason not get a trust permit when entering into a real estate transaction. One reason many buyers did not get a permit was due to the fact that they were making installment payments over a long period of time. Under the old regulations, given the 90 day use requirement, the buyer and the seller would wait until the last payment was made and then apply for a trust permit. Now the permit can be applied for when the contract is entered into and thereby protecting the buyer and guaranteeing that he or she will not have worry out being denied a permit in the future.

➢ Permits for the assignment of trust rights for real estate in the restricted zone: the same holds true as in the case of trust permits. The 90 day use requirement has been eliminated.

➢ Permits for the modification of restricted zone trust agreements: a copy of the trust's permit is no longer required to carry out the contract modifications.

➢ Permits for the acquisition of real estate by foreign individuals and foreign companies: State offices of the Ministry are now authorized to determine whether applications should be approved. This should simplify and shorten the permitting process.

➢ Permits for concessions allowing foreign individuals and foreign companies to obtain water and mining rights: State offices of the Ministry are now authorized to grant approval.

NO INVESTMENT REQUIREMENTS

The new policy used at the Ministry of Foreign Relations for issuing trust permits is: if the application is for real estate under 2,000 square meters that is going to be used for residential purposes no minimum investment requirements apply.

In other words, when purchasing residential property under 2,000 square meters the buyer will not have to commit to making a certain amount of investment in improvements. With this change it is safe to say that permits for these properties should be issued without delay and without exception. The whole permitting process should take no longer than a week or two at the very most if the application is made in Mexico City, and four to five weeks if the application is made at a state office.

In applications for properties larger than 2,000 square meters, the applicant will have to provide more information depending on the size of the property. It should be noted, however, that the Ministry has denied only 6 permits since 1994.

CHAPTER 2

BEFORE BUYING

THIS CHAPTER ADDRESSES SOME OF THE INFORMATION A PROSPECTIVE BUYER
SHOULD KNOW BEFORE CONSIDERING ANY PROPERTY. BASIC INFORMATION
CONCERNING APPLICABLE LAWS, FOREIGN INVESTORS, AND THE RESTRICTED ZONE
GIVES THE POTENTIAL BUYER THE LEGAL BACKGROUND NEEDED TO UNDERSTAND
THE BASIC LEGAL FRAMWORK

INTRODUCTION

Before investing in real estate in Mexico, a potential buyer should first get a clear understanding of the legal requirements necessary to secure their rights in the property and know how to properly carry out the transaction. Although the most basic elements of Mexican real estate transactions are the same as in the United States, there are some differences of which a buyer should be aware. Chapter Two, "Before Buying," identifies some of these differences, starting with the concepts of foreign investment and foreigners under Mexican Law. The sections on "Kinds of Property" and "People Involved in the Real Estate Industry" are intended to give potential buyers a general idea of how real estate is divided and identified under Mexican Law and alternatives available to them.

Chapter Six, "Steps To Take When Buying Property," looks at a general approach for buying most types of property in Mexico. These steps are applicable to any transactions involving raw land, houses, or condominiums. The different types of contracts that are used in real estate transactions are discussed as well as the procedures required to complete the transaction.

This book gives potential foreign buyers the fundamental principles and procedures that apply to Mexican real estate transactions. Most of the book deals with foreigners who want to buy coastal and beachfront property, which, as discussed later, is in the restricted zone.

The second part of the book is a brief overview of the Mexican Legal System and laws pertaining to foreign investment and highlights those areas that pertain to real estate transactions involving foreigners. This book is as detailed as possible in addressing many of the problems a foreigner may encounter in Mexico.

APPLICABLE LAWS

The legal foundation for real estate law in Mexico starts with the Federal Constitution. Each state in Mexico has its own Civil Code, which is usually the same as the Civil Code for the Federal District in the provisions concerning real estate. Nevertheless, check the Civil Code of the state in which you intend to purchase to make sure that there have not been any changes.

Consult a Mexican attorney to make sure that any of the state or municipal laws do not conflict with the federal provisions. This book is only intended to give a broad summary of the most general provisions. Most of these provisions are reflected in the various state legislation, but a competent Mexican real estate attorney can assure that there are no surprises.

The most basic laws applying to real estate transactions are:

➤ The Mexican Constitution and international treaties
➤ The Foreign Investment Law and its regulations
➤ The Civil Code
➤ The General Law of National Properties
➤ Federal Zone Regulations
➤ Condominium Law
➤ Tax Laws: Income Tax Law, Acquisition Tax Law
➤ The General Law of Negotiable Instrument
➤ Commercial Code
➤ Public Registry Regulations
➤ Notary Law and Federal Law of Public Brokerage
➤ Agrarian Law
➤ Corporation Law

FOREIGNERS AND FOREIGN INVESTORS

First of all, what is a foreigner and what is considered foreign investment in Mexico? Articles 30 and 33 of the Mexican Constitution specify that foreigners are those who are not Mexican by birth or naturalization.

An individual qualifies as Mexican by birth by meeting any one of three conditions:

➤ The individual was born in Mexico, regardless of parents' nationality.
➤ The individual was born outside of Mexico and at least one parent is Mexican.
➤ The individual was born on a Mexican airplane or ship.

An individual qualifies as Mexican by naturalization by meeting one of two conditions:

➤ The individual obtains a letter of naturalization from the Ministry of Foreign Affairs.
➤ The individual marries a Mexican national and establishes residency within Mexico.

Article 33 also stipulates that all foreigners are protected under the civil rights provisions of the Constitution. What this means is that foreigners are afforded the same treatment under the law as Mexican nationals while they are in Mexico.

The Mexican Foreign Investment Law, which was published on December 27, 1993, and reformed on December 24, 1996, defines the terms "foreign investment" and "foreign investor:"

FOREIGN INVESTMENT

➤ the participation of foreign investors, in any proportion, in the capital stock of Mexican companies;
➤ that which is made by Mexican companies with a foreign capital majority;
➤ the participation of foreign investors in the activities and acts provided for in the Foreign Investment Law.

FOREIGN INVESTOR

> an individual or legal person of a nationality other than Mexican
and foreign entities without juridical personality.

THE RESTRICTED ZONE AND "FIDEICOMISOS"

In an attempt to avoid some of the problems Mexico had to deal
with in the past with regard to its territorial rights, the 1917 Mexican
Constitution enacted restrictions on property ownership by foreigners.
In essence, the law declares that the Mexican nation has original
ownership to all land and water in Mexico, as well as minerals, salts,
ore deposits, natural gas and oil; but that such ownership may be
assigned to individuals.

The Mexican Constitution prohibits direct ownership of real estate
by foreigners in what has come to be known as the "**restricted zone.**"
The restricted zone encompasses all land located within 100 kilometers
(about 62 miles) of any Mexican border, and within 50 kilometers
(about 31 miles) of any Mexican coastline. However, in order to
permit foreign investment in these areas, the Mexican government
created the *"fideicomiso,"* (FEE-DAY-E-CO-ME-SO) which is,
roughly translated, a real estate trust. Essentially, this type of trust is
similar to trusts set up in the United States, but a Mexican bank must
be designated as the trustee and, as such, has title to the property and
is the owner of record. The Mexican Government created the
"fideicomiso" to reconcile the problems involved in developing the
restricted zone and to attract foreign capital. This enabled foreigners,
as beneficiaries of the trusts, to enjoy unrestricted use of land located
in the restricted zone without violating the law.

A *"fideicomiso"* is a trust agreement created for the benefit of a
foreign buyer, executed between a Mexican bank and the seller of
property in the restricted zone. Foreign buyers cannot own real estate
in the restricted zone due to Constitutional restrictions. The bank acts
on behalf of the foreign buyer, taking title to real property. The bank,
as trustee, buys the property for the foreigner, then has a fiduciary
obligation to follow instructions given by the foreigner who is the trust
beneficiary. The trust beneficiary retains and enjoys all the rights of
ownership while the bank holds title to the property. The foreigner is
entitled to use, enjoy, and even sell the property that is held in trust at
its market value to any eligible buyer.

In summary, the following parties are involved in a real estate trust:

➢ **The seller of the property, or trustor** *(el fideicomitente)* who irrevocably transfers title to the property to the bank.

➢ **The bank, which acts as trustee** *(el fiduciario)* and holds title to the property and is obligated to administer the property only for the benefit of the buyer or beneficiary.

➢ **The buyer, or beneficiary** *(el fideicomisario)* who is entitled to use, enjoy, lease, or sell the property held in the real estate trust without limitation whatsoever.

TERMS AND CONDITIONS FOR OWNERSHIP BY FOREIGNERS

The Foreign Investment Law, published in December of 1993, and reformed on December 24, 1996, extends the term of real estate trusts to 50 years and allows for foreign owned Mexican corporations to hold property in fee simple in the restricted zone.

Article 10 of the law states:

> In accordance with that which is provided by Section I of Article 27 of the Mexican Constitution, Mexican corporations with foreigners exclusion clause or which have executed the agreement to which said precept refers, may acquire ownership of real property in national territory.

Article 27-I of the Constitution states that legal capacity to acquire ownership of lands and waters in Mexico is governed by the following provision: "only Mexicans by birth and Mexican companies have the right to acquire ownership of lands, waters and their easements, or to obtain concessions for the exploitation of mines or waters."

The Mexican government may grant these rights to foreigners, provided that they:

> ...agree before the Ministry of Foreign Affairs to consider themselves as nationals and not to invoke the protection of their governments in matters relating thereto; under penalty, in case of noncompliance with this agreement, of forfeiture of the property they had acquired to the benefit of the nation.

This is known as the "**Calvo Clause**."

The theory behind this concept is generally attributed to Dr. Carlos Calvo, a lawyer from Argentina, who spoke out against the use of diplomatic or armed intervention as a legitimate means of resolving private international pecuniary contract disputes. The basic principles became known as the "**Calvo Doctrine**" and for a time were used by many Latin American countries in reference to the responsibility of the State and the legal status of foreigners. Mexico is one of the only countries currently applying a form of this doctrine.

In Mexico, the Calvo Clause was developed out of this doctrine and is included in the Mexican Constitution as a general principle of law. It establishes an obligation for foreigners to consider themselves as Mexicans and not invoke the protection of their nations' governments in real estate transactions.

In order to allow foreigners to enter into the agreement contained in the Calvo Clause, Mexico requires all foreigners to apply for and obtain a permit from the Ministry of Foreign Affairs prior to contracting to acquire real estate in Mexico. This is currently done by the trustee/bank at the time a real estate trust is set-up.

Given the changes made for 1997 in the foreign investment Law, and the fact that a buyer can now apply for and obtain a trust permit in a matter of days, it is always better to secure the trust permit from the Ministry of Foreign Affairs before entering into any contract

Article 10 of the Foreign Investment Law, as reformed in December of 1996, states that for **Mexican companies** whose by-laws include the agreement contained in the Calvo Clause (Article 27, Section 1), the following shall apply:

➢ They may acquire ownership of real property located in the restricted zone, intended for **non-residential activities**, duly registering said acquisition with the Ministry of Foreign Affairs within 60 days following the acquisition; and,
➢ They may acquire real property in the restricted zone, intended for residential purposes, in accordance with the provisions of the chapter on real estate trusts in the restricted zone.

In other words, a foreign owned Mexican corporation may own property in the restricted zone, and not be required to hold the property in trust, provided that the property is going to be used for non-residential activities.

The key term here is "non-residential activities." Since the first edition of this book was published, the Ministry of Foreign Affairs has clarified the question as to what actually constitutes a non-residential activity. In a strict sense, if an activity were commercial in nature, by law it would not be residential. In other words, if you buy property to be used in a business venture, by definition, it is not being used for residential activities. This may seem obvious, but it is an important distinction under Mexican Law when trying to resolve conflict of law issues.

A high level official at the Ministry of Foreign Affairs makes it clear, when interviewed for this book, that non-residential activities refers to any commercial or industrial activity. **"Residential activities"** refers to any activity that ends with the property being used for residences, or a place in which people live. Therefore, in the case of a residential development, the developer is involved in a non-residential activity because he is in the business of building and selling residential real estate. On the other hand, a person buying property from the developer is involved in a strictly residential activity with no business or commercial aspects whatsoever.

The focus of this book is primarily the purchase of residential property in its various forms, so the importance of the interpretation of what constitutes residential activities will not have much impact on the foreign homebuyer in Mexico. Most people are buying property for a second home rather than for a business. The developer will have the trust already in place when the residential units are sold, or the buyers of the units will have to apply for an individual trust for each unit as they are sold. In the first case, a master trust would have to be place, allowing the developer to assign the rights to property held in trust to the buyer.

It is important to point out that master trusts are no longer used in Mexico. The Ministry of Foreign Affairs eliminated master trusts because of the problems that they created. As a result, except for developments that obtained master trusts before 1994, the seller or developer must apply for an individual trust for each real estate transaction.

Article 13 of the Foreign Investment Law extends the duration of trusts to a maximum of 50 years and clarifies that they can be renewed. This provision also applies to trusts already in existence, but to take advantage of the new term you must apply for the new term before the Ministry of Foreign Affairs.

The bank, as trustee, must get a permit from the Ministry of Foreign Affairs to establish a real estate trust and acquire rights on real property located within the restricted zone. The purpose of the trust is to allow the trust's beneficiary the use and exploitation of the property without constituting real property rights. The beneficiaries of the trust *(fideicomisarios)* may be:

➤ Mexican corporations with foreign investment
➤ Foreign individuals or legal entities

The law defines "use" and "exploitation" as the right to use or possess the property, including its fruits, products, or any revenue that results from its operation and exploitation by third parties or from the bank/trustee.

The law does not clarify how trust permits will be issued. Article 14 of the law states that the Ministry shall decide on issuing the permits "...considering the economic and social benefit, which the realization of such operations imply for the nation." The basic criteria used to determine such benefits are likely to change somewhat with the publication of the new foreign investment regulations. However, it is reasonable to anticipate that some of the unwritten rules used by the Mexican government in the area of real estate trusts will be included in the new foreign investment regulations. It is also possible that some of the confusing elements will be eliminated. It is important to understand the application of the current regulations, even if they are going to be replaced, as well as some of the unwritten policies the government has used in the past, to better understand what criteria will be used by the Ministry in the future.

The Ministry of Foreign Affairs must grant any petition for a trust permit that complies with the stipulated requirements within 5 working days following the date of its presentation to the Ministry's central office in Mexico City. It must be granted in 30 days if the application is submitted to one of the Ministry's state offices. The Ministry of Foreign Affairs must confirm the registration of any property acquired by foreign-owned Mexican corporations a maximum period of 15 days following the filing of the petition. In both cases, if the maximum period passes with no action by the Ministry, the trust permit or registration are considered authorized.

There is a common misconception among foreigners investing in Mexico that once the trust expires, the beneficiary loses all rights and benefits of the sale of the property held in trust. This is not the case. On the contrary, the beneficiary has a contractual right under the trust agreement with the Mexican bank to all benefits that may result from the use or sale of that property, even though he does not hold title to the property. Under Mexican Law, the bank, as trustee, has a fiduciary obligation to respect the rights of the beneficiary.

A real estate trust is not a lease. The beneficiary can instruct the bank to sell or lease the property at any time. The beneficiary can develop and use the property to his liking and benefit, within the provisions of the law. Generally, the law allows most activities engaged in by foreigners.

OUTSIDE OF THE RESTRICTED ZONE

Foreigners may buy property outside of the restricted zone, in fee simple, with authorization from the Ministry of Foreign Affairs. This change took place in 1989 when the Foreign Investment Regulations were passed, and was subsequently clarified in the most current amendments to the Foreign Investment Law for 1997.

The 1997 amendments still use the word "permit" when referring to the authorization granted by the Ministry of Foreign Affairs to allow foreigners to buy real estate outside of the restricted zone. Strictly speaking, this is not a permit but an agreement—the foreign buyer of property outside the restricted zone agrees to the Calvo Clause with the Ministry of Foreign Affairs. The permit issued by the Ministry is an official documentation that such an agreement exists.

There are no circumstances in which the Mexican government would deny authorization of a real estate acquisition by a foreigner outside the restricted zone based on the nationality of the buyer. The only reason any authorization is required is to assure that the Calvo Clause is executed—not to approve or allow the sale of real estate to foreigners. The Ministry has no right to deny consent for a real estate transaction based solely on the fact that the buyer is not Mexican. This simply means that the buyer must notify the Ministry of Foreign Affairs that he agrees to the conditions included in the Calvo Clause. The Ministry issues a document of recognition and a notary may finish the transaction. This requirement stems from Article 27 of the Constitution, which states that legal capacity to acquire ownership of national lands and waters is governed by the following general provisions:

- ➢ In principle, only Mexicans by birth or naturalization and Mexican companies have the right to acquire ownership of lands, waters and their easements and concessions.
- ➢ The Mexican government may grant this right to foreigners provided they agree before the Ministry of Foreign Affairs to consider themselves as nationals. They must also agree not to invoke the protection of their governments in matters relating to their property or water rights, under penalty, in case of noncompliance, of forfeiture of the property or water rights they have acquired to the benefit of the nation. (Calvo clause.)
- ➢ Under no circumstances may foreigners acquire direct ownership of lands or waters within a zone of one hundred kilometers along the borders and of fifty kilometers along the beaches of the country.

CHAPTER 3

KINDS OF PROPERTY

THIS CHAPTER EXPLAINS THE CHACTERISTICS OF THE DIFFERENT KINDS OF
PROPERTY A POTENTIAL BUYER WILL ENCOUNTER IN MEXICO INCLUDING PRIVATE
PROPERTY, TIME-SHARES, PUBLIC PROPERTY AND EJIDO PROPERTY.

INTRODUCTION

Mexican Law refers to real estate in many different ways. The following terms are important when determining the classification of property in Mexico:

"Fincas:" refers to all real estate, independent of its location. This would include all lands as well as any construction on the land.

"Finca Rústica:" refers to all real estate located outside of the limits *(perímetro)* of cities, in other words, rural property.

"Finca Urbana:" refers to real estate located inside the limits *(perímetro)* of cities, or urban property.

"Terreno:" translates as "land" in its most general use.

Real estate in Mexico is divided into many categories. The basic classifications are private, public, and social property. Social property in Mexico refers to real estate that is set aside for the benefit of the society. *Ejido* properties (defined and discussed fully later in the book) fall into this category. With the 1992 changes to the Mexican Constitution, *ejido* property has emerged as a new alternative for foreign investors. In any event, a buyer must determine what category of property he is dealing with before making the final decision to buy.

The following sections will explain the different kinds of property a prospective buyer will encounter in Mexico.

PRIVATE PROPERTY

Private property is the most common category involved in real estate transactions in Mexico. In short, private property is all property that is registered as such in the public registry of property.

The public registry of property *(el registro público de la propiedad)* is where all real estate transactions are recorded. The registry is open to the public and people working there are obligated to allow any interested party to read the entries filed. They must also provide certified copies of the entries or statements that are recorded there, as well as certificates stating that there are no entries with respect to a specific property.

The seller of the property should provide a copy of his title documents *(escrituras públicas)* which are the recorded documents showing a real estate transaction is in the public record. As in the United States, recording gives **constructive notice** of a document's existence and therefore is binding before all third parties of good faith. Typically, the title documents will have a stamp on the last page. This stamp assures that the transaction by which the seller acquired title to the property has been recorded with the public registry of property. It also gives the buyer all the necessary filing information. If this stamp is missing from the last page of the title documents, it is possible that the seller has some problem with his title to the property. In such cases, the transaction should be postponed or canceled until the alleged owner can prove ownership.

If the seller is unable to produce documents which prove the property has been registered in the public registry, it can mean either that the property is not private property or that the seller does not have title to the property. As discussed later in this chapter, public property cannot be sold—certainly not by an individual. If the buyer chooses to proceed though the seller cannot produce proof of ownership, the buyer must use extreme caution.

Private property is treated the same in or out of the restricted zone. The only difference is the limitation discussed above regarding ownership by foreigners.

In this book, private property is divided into four types: unimproved property; improved property/single family homes; condominiums; and time-shares. Development property is intentionally omitted because it is the subject of another book, and because most people are likely to buy one of the four types of properties listed above.

When a foreigner purchases property in the restricted zone for residential purposes, it must be held in trust. This is true whether the property is unimproved or improved, whether it is a condominium unit or a house. There have been cases where foreigners believed that since they had bought condominiums, they did not need a real estate trust. If the property is a condominium, that does not eliminate the need for a real estate trust.

UNIMPROVED PROPERTY

Unimproved property refers to real property that has received no development, construction, or site preparation. This type of property is commonly known as **raw land** because it does not have any added improvements such as landscaping, drainage, streets, utilities, or structures.

Unimproved property in the restricted zone is sometimes a problem for foreign buyers. It is difficult to obtain a trust permit from the Ministry of Foreign Affairs when the property is not improved. In the past, the Ministry issued trust permits for almost any property regardless of its location and improvements. More recently, however, they have indicated that it is better if the property is part of a larger development.

The Mexican government is more inclined to grant trust permits for unimproved property in larger developments rather than for isolated lots in areas with little or no other development. The intent is to encourage a more uniform and planned development of Mexico. For this reason, when looking at unimproved property, a prospective buyer must first determine whether there will be problems obtaining a trust permit from the Ministry of Foreign Affairs.

A buyer should contact the trust department of any Mexican bank in the area where the property is located. Usually, they can indicate how difficult it will be. A buyer should get this information personally. The owners or real estate agents often will not mention that there are problems with the trust permit. The chapter on **Promissory**

Agreements takes a closer look at procedures buyers can follow to protect themselves in these, and other, situations.

A buyer should also determine if the unimproved property is held under **co-ownership** *(copropiedad)*. In many cases, property has been passed down through the family for years but the proper formalities were never carried out. The transactions may never have been recorded, or, when the transaction was executed, the parties did not want to pay the taxes and expenses involved in formalizing the arrangement.

It is not always apparent to the foreign investor that the property is not owned solely by the seller. There are no legal safeguards to protect the unknowing investor from buying an undivided interest in the property. There are legal ways to remedy the situation, but it is always better to avoid litigation, especially in a foreign country.

A buyer should always ask if the owner holds title to the property individually. If the property is held under co-ownership, the title documents will indicate that the seller has an undivided interest in the property. In Spanish the most common term to indicate this is *"proindiviso"*.

The **certificate of no encumbrances** issued by the public registry will indicate that the title to property is held under co-ownership. This certificate is a statement issued by the public registry detailing the status of any registered property. The certificate of no encumbrances is required by the Public Notary to record any real estate transaction.

If the seller has an undivided interest in the property to be purchased, he must first get the consent of the other co-owners to subdivide his parcel out of the property in order to sell it. If this is not done, the sale is not valid. The buyer is then forced to take action against the seller to recover his money. The buyer cannot sue for the title to the property because the seller did not have the right to sell the property. Therefore, the buyer cannot show that he ever held legal title to the property.

A buyer should also determine if the property is *"ejido"* **property**. *Ejido* **property** is explained in more detail later in this chapter. For now, there is one important thing a prospective buyer should remember: if the property is not recorded with the public registry of property, then don't buy it! It's that simple. Neither *ejido* property nor public property can be registered in the public registry of property.

There are many areas in Mexico where there are little or no **utilities** such as water, sewer, gas, electricity, and telephones. This is particularly true in rural areas such as Baja California Sur. If water is not available, a buyer must get assurance from the owner of the property that a well can be sunk.

"Servidumbres" or **easements.** If a buyer and seller have agreed that the seller will grant the buyer an easement of any kind, this fact should be included in the **promissory agreement** and the final sales agreement. If the property is already subject to any easements, the seller should make it known but a buyer is wise to ask. The second section of the book has more on types of easements and related questions.

IMPROVED PROPERTY/SINGLE FAMILY HOMES AND CONDOMINIUMS

This section will take a look at buying **single family housing,** including **condominiums.** Single family housing shall refer to any type of residential structure designed to include one dwelling. Units may share walls and other structural components but generally have separate access to the outside and do not share plumbing and heating equipment. Examples include:

➢ Condominiums
➢ Detached housing units
➢ Town houses
➢ Beach houses

The second section of this book contains a detailed explanation of the legal provisions dealing with condominiums which is important to know before buying any property. The following is intended as a summary of the most essential considerations to be aware of when buying a condominium.

If the property is in the restricted zone the foreigner must have his real property rights held in trust. All other aspects are the same for properties inside and outside the restricted zone.

In legal terms, condominium ownership is defined as real property with vertical, horizontal, or mixed construction that is susceptible to individual ownership but belonging to various owners, with common areas which are co-owned and undivided.

Condominium properties are very common in Mexico, especially in resort and tourist developments. This is because condominium properties are self-contained and therefore they are not open to public access. This may be a very important consideration when purchasing property.

Unlike subdivisions *(fraccionamientos)* where the municipality provides the roads, in condominium properties, the developers and ultimately the condominium owners lay out and maintain the roads. Since the roads are private property many condominium properties also have a gated entrance with security personnel. In normal subdivisions this is not possible because their streets are public.

A common misconception is that the word condominium refers to a type of architecture. Most often people think of apartment buildings or townhouses. However, the type of architecture used has nothing to do with condominium ownership. Condominiums are properties that are divided into sections which are individually owned by various owners and sections which are co-owned, or collectively owned.

Because many of the resort developments are looking to achieve an exclusive high scale look and feel, they are often set up under a condominium ownership system. Typically, the property will be divided into individually owned lots while all the common areas, sidewalks, and streets are co-owned by all the condominium owners. For this reason, the sale of a condominium property is very similar to the sale of an individually owned home or lot. The difference is that when a buyer purchases a home in a condominium property, that buyer is also buying an undivided right to all the common areas, sidewalks, and streets of the property.

When buying a condominium property, the promissory agreement should include a copy of the public title documents that indicate that the property has been registered as a condominium property. Usually the seller will not include a copy of this document but if the purchaser asks for it, the seller must provide a copy. A buyer can always verify the information at the Public Registry of Property *(Registro Público de la Propiedad),* where condominium ownership documents must be filed. The condominium documents serve as title to the property and allow the individual condominium units to be sold separately and registered as such in the Public Registry of Property.

The law requires that any contract used for the acquisition of ownership of condominium property must contain the information listed below. The contract must also state that the interested buyer was given a copy of the condominium regulations certified by a public notary.

1. The contract must contain the layout, dimensions and property lines of the condominium property which clearly indicate individual ownership areas from co-owned areas.

2. There must be written proof that the condominium declaration from the government was obtained as well as all of the necessary building permits.

3. The contract must contain a general description of the construction and quality of building materials.

4. The contract should have descriptions of each apartment, dwelling, house or premise, including parking areas.

5. The contract must describe the value of each apartment, dwelling, house or premise and the percentage that each represents in the total value of the whole condominium project.

6. The contract must describe the general use of the condominium as a whole and the particular use of each apartment, dwelling, house or premise.

7. The contract must establish the use and characteristics of common areas.

8. The contract must stipulate the terms and conditions of the performance bond for the construction contract and defects. The government determines the amount and the term of the bond when it issues the building permit.

9. There must be a description of the conditions under which any of the above may be modified.

10. Certified copies of a general survey and plans for each apartment, dwelling, house or premise, and common areas must be attached as an exhibit to the notarized document.

11. The above mentioned regulations of the condominium.

This and any other documents should be delivered to the administrator of the condominium project who is legally responsible for carrying out its provisions.

Any new condominium owner should know much of the above information. A buyer must be sure he receives a copy of the condominium's title documents regardless of the excuses given for not providing them.

The following sections apply to all types of properties, including condominium properties.

New Homes

When buying a new home a purchaser needs to ask the following questions:

➢ Is the property already held in a real estate trust?
➢ If the property is not held in a real estate trust, does the property form part of a larger recognized development?
➢ Does a homeowners association regulate the property?

Property Held In Trust

If the property is already held in trust, most likely the developer is the beneficiary of the trust and will merely assign the rights to the property to the buyer. To do this, the bank, as trustee, must get authorization from the Ministry of Foreign Affairs. This process is a mere formality and shouldn't take more than a few weeks to a month to finalize.

Once the bank gets the authorization to assign the beneficial rights in the trust to the buyer, the bank will notify a public notary or broker. The notary or broker then prepares the documents in order to execute the assignment of rights to the buyer. Most of the time these documents are executed in Spanish only. It is important that all the information included in the assignment contract is correct. Sometimes, due to confusion or lack of communication between the buyer and the bank, the contract information gets mixed-up. This can be disastrous, costing thousands of dollars to correct. Therefore, a foreign buyer should have an attorney help with the process, or he should have the documents that are prepared by the public notary translated and then review them carefully.

If the attorney does not include a translation of the title documents signed before the public notary or broker, the buyer should have a translation done by an official translator before signing the Spanish version. An official translator, *"perito traductor"* is licensed to translate documents by the Superior Court of Justice and their translations are essential should disputes occur later.

Property Not Held in Trust

Over the years the Mexican government has increased its requirements of foreign investors who apply for real estate trust permits. Most recently the Ministry of Foreign Affairs denied nearly all 1993 trust applications for most of Baja California. Currently, the Ministry is granting trust permits for new individual trusts, provided that the property for which the trust is being requested is part of a larger and recognized development project.

The Ministry of Foreign Affairs has the discretionary power to grant permits for real estate trusts. When the new Foreign Investment Regulations are published, it is expected to set guidelines that clearly indicate when a permit will be issued and what will be required to get one.

In the meantime, prospective buyers will have to meet the Ministry's unofficial conditions for getting a trust. As mentioned earlier, the permit process can vary depending on where the property is located. Properties outside the Baja California peninsula are subject to less red tape. To a certain degree, properties in the northern border zone are also a problem but, with time, this will change.

As a general rule, if the property is located in an area where there are other developments, a prospective buyer will get a trust permit. However, in remote areas, like much of Baja California, where there is little or no development, it is difficult, even impossible, to get a trust permit.

The Mexican government is not as willing as in years past to allow a single isolated property to be put into a real estate trust. There are three reasons for this:

➤ The government would like to see uniform, well-thought-out developments. They would like to avoid situations where a development will have trailer homes next to a row of expensive homes, and small homesteads out in the middle of nowhere.

> ➤ The government feels that small isolated sprinklings of real estate investments are not in the interests of Mexico.
> ➤ The government would like to eliminate the element of speculation from the real estate industry. In other words, they would like to see only investments which lead to real developments, instead of having someone buy property, hold on to it, and sell it for a profit down the road.

If a buyer wishes to purchase property that is not already held in trust, he should have tentative approval for the trust before any serious money is exchanged.

TIME-SHARE PROPERTIES

On November 30, 1993, the Secretary of Commerce and Industrial Development published federal standards for time-share services. All time-share operators in Mexico were required to register their time-share contracts by April 1, 1994.

These standards, known as *Normas Oficiales Mexicanas (NOM)*, are minimal standards for consumer protection and are enforceable throughout Mexico. They are intended to protect consumers from unscrupulous practices by requiring time-share operators to give potential buyers enough information to make a rational decision when buying a time-share. There may also be state time-share legislation, which will make additional demands on the time-share operator; however, the federal standards, or NOM, cannot be ignored or diminished by the state legislation. The old time-share regulations published in 1989 are no longer in effect. However, the federal NOM cites them as a biographical reference, and they may be used as a prototype for local legislation. There is a summary of the regulations in the appendix.

A time-share purchase is not a real estate purchase. The buyer does not buy any real property rights; rather, he is buying the right to use the real estate for a specific time period. Given the importance that time-share properties represent in the overall real estate market, however, this section will briefly touch on the most important information a buyer should know before buying an interest in a time-share.

PARTIES INVOLVED AND TYPES OF TIME-SHARES

All time-share operators in Mexico are regulated by the time-share NOM. The information and advertising used by time-share operators must be clear and it must not generate error or confusion. The time-share NOM defines two parties who may be involved in the sale of time-share services as:

➤ **The Time-share Operator:** The person or legal entity who, by means of a contract, is obligated to provide time-share services. Even when the time-share operator contracts a third party to furnish the time-share services, the operator is solely responsible for the services rendered.

➤ **The Promoter:** The person or legal entity who represents the time-share operator and promotes or executes the sale or presale of the time-share services.

The activity involved in a time-share service is defined as: any act that puts at the disposition of one person or group of persons the use, enjoyment and other rights to a property or any part of the same, in a variable unit of a determined class. This right of usage, etc., is for periods previously agreed upon, and is accomplished through the payment of a certain amount, but does not transfer ownership of the time-share's movable and real property.

The NOM also distinguishes between time-share services involving finished developments and unfinished time-share developments as follows:

➤ **Sale:** Any legal act through which it is agreed that a time-share service shall be provided in regard to a specific real estate development which is in operation, or to a part of the same which is offered to the public and which **is totally built and in operation**.

➤ **Pre-sale:** Any legal act through which it is agreed that a time-share service shall be provided in a real estate development that is not yet finished, nor operating.

REQUIREMENTS FOR PROVIDING TIME-SHARE SERVICES.

The sale or pre-sale of time-share services that are sold directly by the time-share operator or through a promoter, may only be carried out by first filing with the Secretary of Commerce and Industrial

Development (SECOFI). The following requirements must be fulfilled by the time-share operator and filed with SECOFI:

The Sale of Finished Developments (Sales):

➤ The time-share operator must be domiciled in Mexico or have a representative, a branch office or affiliate with a domicile in Mexico.

➤ The operator must provide proof that the property has been allocated for providing time-share services. These requirements should be set out by local legislation. If there isn't such legislation, the time-share provider should record a statement before a public notary that the property is to be used for time-share, or have the same included in a publicly recorded real estate trust agreement. In both cases, filing with the Public Registry of Property will be considered adequate proof.

➤ The operator must provide proof that an insurance policy has been taken out to cover total or partial destruction of the time-share's property. The insurance should cover reconstruction and reparation, as well as coverage of the users and their belongings. This insurance should never have coverage less than coverage required for hotel services.

➤ The reasons for fees or dues to be paid by the time-share users must be clearly specified.

➤ A copy of the time-share's internal regulations must accompany the notification.

The Sale of Unfinished Developments (Presales):

Except in those cases where the local laws already make provisions, the following is required:

➤ The operator must obtain a building permit for the time-share development, as well as an alternative use guarantee or a joint liability guarantee by another company.

➤ The operator must obtain an insurance policy covering total or partial destruction of the time-share's property. The insurance should cover reconstruction and reparation.

➤ The operator must comply with points 1, 2, 4 and 5 for the sale of finished developments listed above.

The dedicated use of real estate allocated for time-share services may not be changed until the time-share term has lapsed, or as indicated by law. Changes that may affect the time-share installations negatively are subject to discussion by the users so that by their votes and opinions the changes may or may not be made.

CONTRACTS USED BY TIME-SHARES

The model contracts between time-shares and potential users must be registered with the Consumer Protection Board, and should be written in Spanish. A contract may be registered in another language but only if the time-share operator provides a foreign language version that is prepared by an official translator. The translator must certify that the foreign language version is exactly the same as the original Spanish document. Such translated contracts should also include a clause stating that the time-share operator accepts sole responsibility for any discrepancies which may exist between the contract in Spanish and the foreign language version.

All time-share contracts must include the following information and comply with the following stipulations:

1. The contract must include the name and address of the time-share operator.

2. It must contain the address where the time-share service is provided.

3. It must describe the obligation of the time-share operator to fulfill the time-share users' rights to use and enjoy the properties, including the periods of usage and the characteristics of the personal property and the real estate used for the time-share services.

4. It must disclose the costs of maintenance for the first year in cases involving the sale of finished developments, and how the changes in these costs will be determined in subsequent years. In the case of pre-sales, or the sale of unfinished developments, the contract should include the criteria and mechanisms to determine the costs for the first year, and how the changes in these costs will be determined in subsequent periods.

5. The contract must establish the acquisition price of the time-share.

6. The time-share contract must describe the exchange options with the other time-share providers and whether such exchanges will generate any additional costs. In such cases, the contract should indicate that the development is registered in an exchange program

carried out by a third party and is subject to an affiliation contract, which implies additional costs.

7. The contract must contain a clearly expressed statement that it is the responsibility of the time-share operator to immediately provide lodging of a similar category and quality, in the vicinity of the time-share establishment, when the user is unable to utilize the services agreed to through the fault of the time-share operator. If the time-share operator is unable to meet this obligation for reasons not within his control, he must pay the user, within five days, all the expenses the user incurred traveling to and from the time-share.

8. The contract must include a description of the insurance covering the time-share property if it is a finished development. In pre-sale of unfinished developments, the contract should include the specification of the bond or guarantee taken out to cover the time-share property.

9. It must describe the calculations used to determine interest when the time-share user is paying on a credit account.

10. It must explain the process users should follow when they want to sell or assign their rights in the time-share. The contract should state whether the sale or assignment will result in any charges, and how those charges will be calculated.

11. The contract must contain a statement which indicates that, when the contract requires payments in foreign currency, the payments may be made in pesos at the exchange rate current at the place and time of payment. All the contracts that are executed within Mexican territory must establish that the place of payment is Mexico. However, residents of foreign countries may agree to liquidate their payments outside of Mexico, if the contract allows.

12. The contract must describe the process users should follow to notify the Consumer Protection Board and the time-share users when important changes are considered that may affect the time-share installations negatively. The users, by their votes and opinions, could then influence the proposed changes.

13. It must disclose the penalties that the time-share operator and user will suffer in case of cancellation or breach of contract, as well as the method of calculation and application of such penalties upon the termination of the contract.

14. The contract must contain a clause that specifies the term within which the consumer may cancel the time-share service without losing payments already made. Such terms may not be less than five working days starting from the first working day after the day the contract was signed. All refunds should be made within the fifteen days following the cancellation of the contract. Such cancellation should be submitted in writing at the place where the agreement was executed or at the domicile of the time-share operator or the representative of the company indicated in the contract.

PUBLIC PROPERTY

When buying property in Mexico a purchaser needs to know where private property ends and public property begins. This is particularly true in coastal properties where the federal zone exists. Traditionally, public property is broken down into two categories: common use public property, and property for public service. Public areas of particular interest to foreign buyers are the federal zone, islands, and water rights.

FEDERAL ZONE

The "federal zone" refers to that part of federally owned beachfront property that extends out from the beach. The Mexican nation owns this property and it cannot be sold or owned by Mexicans or foreigners.

The correct and full term for this land is *"La zona ferderal marítimo terrestre,"* which translates from the Spanish as "the federal maritime land zone." A buyer must know where the federal zone ends and the lot for sale begins when buying beachfront property. It is not likely that someone will try to sell property in the federal zone, but it has happened.

The federal zone consists of the first **20 meters of beachfront property on firm, adjoining and traversable ground** measured from the high tide line in horizontal areas with a continuous slope of no more than 30 degrees. Therefore, if there are any hills, cliffs, or similar natural land elevations, the federal zone is measured from the first point where the slope is no more than 30 degrees. This measurement must be made for thirty consecutive days when there are no hurricanes, cyclones, or high winds.

The law states that the federal zone and beaches are public and may be equally enjoyed by everyone with the following restrictions:

➤ The government specifies the areas, schedules and conditions under which no vehicles can be used, and any other activities that shall endanger the users of the beaches, according to the master control program.

➤ The government forbids any construction and installation of elements and buildings that obstruct free passage are forbidden, except those that are approved by the government according to the rules of urban development and the environmental protection laws. When the property adjoins the federal zone, trust permits now require the beneficiary to retain any established public access to the federal zone.

➤ Any acts that pollute the public areas are prohibited.

In addition to the above restrictions, the law provides for permits and concessions for the use and enjoyment of the federal zone. This chapter will examine concessions and permits later.

ISLANDS

There are 1,034 islands within Mexican territorial waters. Most of these islands are just small specks in the ocean, while a few, namely Cozumel, Islas Marias, and Isla Del Carmen, are considerably bigger.

All islands within Mexican territorial waters are regulated by the provisions of the Mexican Constitution and they all fall under the jurisdiction of the federal government. Islands that were under the jurisdiction of a Mexican state before 1917 are the exception. The civil, penal, and administrative laws of the Federal District are applicable in Mexican islands, and the federal tribunals closest to the island have jurisdiction.

Like real property on the mainland, the real property rights over land and water on islands originally belongs to the Mexican nation. The Mexican government can transfer ownership of such land and water to individuals.

The Ministry of the Interior *(Secretaría de Gobernación)* administrates all islands within Mexican territory.

WATER RIGHTS

Water rights in Mexico are divided into two categories:

➤ Continental waters make up all water within Mexican territory other than maritime or ocean waters.
➤ Maritime waters refer to oceans or seas.

This section will examine continental water rights rather than maritime water rights. Most people buying property in Mexico are not likely to have use of maritime waters. Given that Mexico does not have, in remote areas, the same infrastructure providing water availability as does the United States; access to water is often the determining factor when purchasing real estate.

Article 27 of the Mexican Constitution states the following:

> Ownership of the lands and waters within the boundaries of the national territory is vested originally in the nation, which has had, and has, the right to transfer title thereof to private persons, thereby constituting private property.

Water in Mexico is part of the public domain. In other words, the Mexican nation owns the water. It cannot be sold for any reason. Public law regulates all rights to water and the nation's ownership is inalienable and imprescriptible.

Basically, the Mexican nation owns all inland fresh water sources. Article 27 of the Constitution lists the following as "properties of the nation:"

➤ Interior marine waters;
➤ Waters of lagoons and estuaries permanently or intermittently connected with the sea;
➤ Waters of natural inland lakes which are directly connected with streams having a constant flow;
➤ Waters of rivers and their direct or indirect tributaries, from the point in their source where the first permanent, intermittent, or torrential waters begin, to their mouth in the sea, lake, lagoon, or estuary forming a part of the public domain;
➤ Waters of constant or intermittent streams and their direct or indirect tributaries, whenever the bed of the stream, throughout the whole or a part of its length, serves as a boundary of the national

territory or of two states, or if it flows from one state to another or crosses the boundary line of the Republic;

➢ Waters of lakes, lagoons or estuaries whose basins, zones, or shores are crossed by the boundary lines of two or more states or by the boundary line of the Republic and a neighboring country; or when river banks serve as a boundary between the states of the Republic and a neighboring country;

➢ Waters of springs that issue from beaches, maritime areas, the beds, basins, or shores of lakes, lagoons, or estuaries in the national domain, and waters extracted from mines and the channels, beds, or shores of interior lakes and streams.

The owner of a property can bring underground waters to the surface by **sinking a well** or by any other artificial means. The property owner can then utilize the underground waters, however, since it involves the use of national property, the owner must get a concession from the government. The government can regulate, and even prohibit, the extraction and utilization of underground and public domain waters if the rights of third parties are affected, or in order to protect the public interest.

The end of Article 27 of the Constitution states that any waters (exclusive of those described above as national waters) are to be considered an integral part of the property through which they flow. In other words, the water rights are incorporated into the real property rights of the owner of the property. The waters must be located in one parcel of property; if they are located in two or more properties, their use is considered a matter of public use, and subject to laws enacted by the States.

By definition, lakes and lagoons are considered national waters. Anything smaller, such as a creek or a pond may fall into the non-national water category. In these cases only the owner of the property may exploit the water in question. The owner cannot sell the water rights without selling the property or vice versa.

The Federal government can grant concessions to individuals or to companies that are organized in accordance with Mexican Laws, to exploit, use, or enjoy national waters. The next section examines concessions.

The following general provisions govern legal capacity to acquire ownership of national lands and waters:

> In principle, only Mexicans by birth or naturalization and Mexican companies have the right to own lands, waters and their easements and concessions.
> The Mexican government may grant this right to foreigners provided they agree before the Ministry of Foreign Affairs to consider themselves as nationals. They must also agree not to invoke the protection of their governments in matters relating to their property or water rights, under penalty, in case of noncompliance, of forfeiture of the property or water rights they have acquired, to the benefit of the nation. This is known as the Calvo clause.
> Under no circumstances may foreigners acquire direct ownership of lands or waters within one hundred kilometers of the borders and within fifty kilometers of the beaches of the country.

Concessions: Water Use and the Federal Zone

There are two kinds of concessions that are important to a potential buyer:

> Concessions for the exploitation, use, or enjoyment of national waters.
> Concessions for the exploitation, use, or enjoyment of the federal zone.

Chapter Six examines these two kinds of concessions individually; this section takes a brief look at concessions in general.

A concession is an administrative act by which the government temporally grants individuals or legal entities the right to carry out a service or to exploit and enjoy national property.

The Mexican Constitution provides for concessions and states that all concessions must be granted in accordance with the provisions of the law. They may only be granted within the legal limitations and conditions that assure efficiency in the administration or exploitation of the object of the concession. The concession must not conflict with public interests. Concessions should not be granted based on the whim of the official in charge of granting them; rather, the person receiving the concession, the concessionaire, must meet certain criteria. Also, the concessionaire may not violate the rights of others or those of the general public in his exploitation of the object of the concession.

There are three possible parties involved in concessions:

1. **The granting authority**: the part of the municipal, state, or federal public administration.

2. **The concessionaire**: the person or legal entity given title to the concession.

3. **The user**: the people who use the service offered by the concessionaire. This only applies to service concessions.

Legal Capacity of a Concessionaire

The Mexican Constitution limits the capacity of foreigners to acquire rights to land and water concessions unless they agree to the inclusion of the Calvo clause just as they do when a foreigner wishes to purchase national lands and waters. Similarly, there are certain laws that require that the concessionaire be a Mexican national or a Mexican corporation with no foreign investment.

Foreigners, who hold federal zone concessions and national water concessions, have no other limitation than the Calvo Clause. They must consider themselves as nationals and they cannot, under penalty, invoke the protection of their governments in matters relating to concession rights. In case of noncompliance, they forfeit the rights they have acquired to the benefit of the nation.

EJIDO PROPERTY

AMENDMENTS TO ARTICLE 27 OF THE CONSTITUTION

In January of 1992 a very important decree was published in the Official Gazette (*Diario Oficial De La Federación*) stating that Article 27 of the Mexican Constitution was amended. The most important changes to Article 27, as far as real estate is concerned, have to do with the possibility of selling "*ejido*" property.

Before examining the amendments to Article 27, this section will quickly review the background of *ejidos*, the definition of an *ejido*, and the legal regulation of *ejidos*.

The Mexican Revolution inspired the idea for the *ejidos*. One of the main objectives of the revolution, reflected in the revolutionary 1917 Mexican Constitution, was to break up large tracts of privately owned land, "*latifundidios*," into smaller holdings and return the land to the peasants. The *ejidos* were agricultural land grants. The new Mexican government issued grants to use federally owned property to farming and ranching cooperatives, whose membership was largely peasant. Members of the *ejidos* were entitled to use and work the land to their benefit but they did not own the property. The government issued the peasants a limited title to the land; the peasant could not sell the land or use it for collateral. The peasant had to continue to work the land or the title would be revoked. The idea was to help the peasant farmers at that time get a start in life, and at the same time, bring about an equitable distribution and use of property. With the Amendment to Article 27, it appears that after nearly 75 years, the dreams of the peasant may become a reality.

REGULATION OF *EJIDOS* BEFORE 1992

Until the new Agrarian Law was passed in February of 1992 *ejidos* were regulated by the Agrarian Reform Law, which strictly prohibited the sale or even the lease of *ejido* property. Article 52 of the Agrarian Reform Law states the following:

> The rights acquired by *ejidos* over agrarian property shall be inalienable, imprescriptible, non-attachable, and non-transferable, and therefore, one may not, in any case or form whatsoever, dispose of, cede, assign, lease, mortgage, or encumber, (such rights) in whole or in part. All operations, acts or contracts executed or that seek to do the same in violation of this provision are null and void.

In other words, a foreigner presently living in Mexico on land leased from an *ejido* before 1992 is doing so illegally.

The new Agrarian Law allows for the lease of *ejido* properties under certain circumstances. However, if a Lessee leased from an *ejido* before the law was changed, he will need to execute a new agreement with the *ejido* for the agreement to be legal. Later, this chapter takes a closer look at leasing *ejido* property.

So, what does all this mean for the foreign investor in Mexico? The answer to this question depends on whether the foreign investor is presently leasing from an *ejido*, or is just interested in purchasing property in Mexico. For anyone interested in purchasing property in Mexico, the changes to Article 27 could be the best news to hit the Mexican real estate market.

The amendments to Article 27 clearly provide for the leasing and sale of *ejido* property in subsection VII. The following is a portion of that subsection:

...The law... shall regulate the rights of every *ejido* member in relation to his parcel of *ejido* property by establishing the procedures by which they may form partnerships among themselves, with the State, or with third parties, and for the granting of the use of their properties... as well as establish the requirements and procedures by which the *ejidos* may grant its members ownership to their parcel of *ejido* property.

It is clear that *ejido* property may now be sold, and that the *ejido* shall have the right to determine how its property is parceled off and made available for sale.

To better understand these changes one needs to remember that previously *ejidos* did not own their property, rather they only had the right to use federally owned property. Now, with the amendments to Article 27, not only does the law recognize the *ejidos'* property rights, but it also provides for the possibility that individual members of the *ejido* may sell their parcels of the *ejido* property.

An *ejido* can be described as a form of corporation in order to clarify the above possibilities. The *ejido* is not exactly the same as a corporation, but it is very similar. For example, an *ejido* is a legal entity governed by something much like a shareholder meeting and administrated by a board consisting of a president, a secretary and a treasurer. Each member of the *ejido* has voting rights with regard to the use of the property owned by the *ejido*. However, unless the *ejido* property has been legally parceled off to an individual member, all the property is owned by the *ejido* as a distinct legal entity separate from its members.

It is now possible for an individual member of the *ejido* to acquire property rights over a parcel of the *ejido* property. Under the provisions of the amendment, the *ejido* members, meeting as the governing body of the *ejido*, are empowered to grant the property rights for each individual member's parcel of land.

AGRARIAN LAW OF 1992

With the changes to the Constitution and the publication of the Agrarian Law, *ejidos* now own the land granted to them under the provisions of the old law. Article 9 of the law states that *ejidos* own all real property granted to them as well as any property that they may have acquired title to by any other means.

The individual members of the *ejido* can acquire property rights over a parcel of the *ejido* property. Under the provisions of the amendment, the *Asamblea de Ejidatarios*, as the governing body of the *ejido*, is empowered to grant each individual member property rights over his parcel of land.

The real property of the *ejidos* is divided into three categories:

1. Individual parcels

2. Property for common use

3. Property for community development

Property for community development is intended to meet the needs of the *ejido* community for urban development. Property for common use is that which is not specifically designated by the *Asamblea de Ejidatarios* for community property or individual parcels. Individual parcels are those for which parcel certificates have been issued to individual *ejido* members and sanctioned by the National Agrarian Registry.

INDIVIDUAL *EJIDO* PARCELS

Each member of an *ejido* may not have title to parcels of more than five percent of the *ejido*'s property, or a parcel that is larger than a small land holding, or a *"pequeña propiedad."* These range from 100 to 800 hectors, depending upon the type of property.

Once an *ejido* member legally acquires his parcel certificate he has the right to determine how his parcel shall be used. Neither the *ejido*'s *Asamblea* nor the *Comisariado* may use or restrict the use of parceled properties.

Each parcel owner may lease his property or contribute the use of his property to partnerships or corporations, without prior authorization of the *ejido*'s *Asamblea*. Article 81 of the law states that "when the majority of the parcels of an *ejido* have been delineated and assigned... the *Asamblea* may resolve that the *ejido* members may assume direct ownership over said parcels..."

Once the *Asamblea* adopts the resolution to convey ownership to individual *ejido* members, the members are then free to petition for the cancellation of their respective parcels in the National Agrarian Registry. A deed for the property is issued which would then be filed with the Public Registry of Property (*Registro Público de la Propiedad*). From the moment the deed for the parcel is filed with the

Public Registry of Property, that property considered private property and may be bought and sold as any other private property.

Many *ejido* members already have parcel certificates and many more are in the process of obtaining them. It is a slow process but, in time, there is going to be substantially more property on the market. Since this property was not available before 1992, it is possible that its arrival could drastically change the current real estate market.

JOINT VENTURES WITH *EJIDOS*

Article 73 of the law defines common use properties *(tierras de uso comun)* as those which "...constitute the economic support of the *ejido* community..." and consist of the properties which have not been specifically reserved by the *Asamblea* for urban development or individual parcels.

The use and exploitation of common use properties is regulated by the *ejido*'s internal regulations and cannot be assigned or attached except for the cases provided for in Article 75 of the law.

Article 75 of the law states that in cases of manifest benefit to the *ejido*, it may transfer ownership of common use properties to partnerships or companies in which the *ejido* or its members participate. In other words, *ejidos* may now enter into joint venture corporations in which their capital contributions consist of property. This is an important change from the old law, which strictly prohibited such transactions.

Title to the property in these cases is assigned to the corporation, and the *ejido* no longer owns the property in question. However, the law does state that in the event that the corporation is liquidated, the *ejido* would have a preferential right to receive property as their share of the assets. Therefore, under the provisions of the law, investors can enter into a joint venture corporation to develop *ejido* properties. In many areas of Baja California, where tourist development is booming, the possibilities are endless. Because the investors do not have to purchase the property, they can dedicate more funds to developing.

The value of the shares acquired by the *ejido* or its members in relation to the contribution of property shall be equal to that established by the Appraisal Commission of National Property, *"Comisión de Avalúos de Bienes Nacionales"* or by any credit institution. So it is possible, for example, that an *ejido* could contribute property worth $300,000, while the other investors contribute $700,000, which brings total capital contributions of the corporation to $1,000,000. In that case, the *ejido* would hold 30% of the shares and the other shareholders would hold 70%.

In projects that do not involve agriculture, such as tourist developments, there are no restrictions on how much the *ejido* must hold in the capital of the corporation. In essence, the transaction is treated the same as any other real estate transaction with regard to the application of the Foreign Investment Laws and the restrictions on foreign ownership.

Although the Agrarian authorities are still involved in the procedures necessary to assign common use *ejido* property to a joint venture corporation, their participation is limited to simply issuing an opinion on the feasibility and soundness of the proposal in question. Unlike the provisions of the old law, the provisions of the new law no longer require that the Agrarian authorities intervene to sanction transactions between third parties and *ejidos*. Consequently, the procedures for assignment can be completed fairly quickly.

LEASING *EJIDO* PROPERTY

Article 45 of the law states that common use property and individual parcels may be the objects of any contract that entails the use of the property. Such contracts are limited to a term of thirty years and may be renewed.

Prior authorization of the *Asamblea* is required to lease common use property. Individual parcels do not require authorization to contract provided the corresponding parcel certificate has been duly issued and registered.

CHAPTER 4

TITLE DOCUMENTS AND RECORDING
THIS CHAPTER ADDRESSES HOW TO IDENTIFY TITLE DOCUMENTS AND WHERE AND HOW REAL ESTATE DOCUMENTS ARE RECORDED IN MEXICO.

TITLE AND DEED

It very easy for a foreigner to get confused when involved in a Mexican real estate transaction considering how much is done in Spanish. For this reason, it is important to make certain that when a seller provides a document, it is what the seller believes it to be. Many times neither the buyer nor the seller can read or understand Spanish, or at least not to the level that is required to read and understand legal documents. This can lead to disaster if the buyer does not take care. A prospective buyer must not assume that every document is what it is said to be. The most important document in any real estate transaction is the title document because it is by means of this document the ownership to real estate is conveyed.

Title, in its most common definitions, is broken down to:

➢ the coincidence of all the elements that constitute the fullest legal right to control and dispose of property or a claim.
➢ the aggregate evidence that gives rise to a legal right of possession or control.
➢ the instrument, such as a deed, that constitutes this evidence.

Black's Law Dictionary defines "title:"

The formal right of ownership of property. Title is the means whereby the owner of lands has the just possession of his property; the union of all the elements which constitute ownership; the rights to ownership in land; also, the evidence of such ownership.

A "deed" is defined as a conveyance of realty; a writing signed by the grantor, whereby title to realty is transferred from one to another. In Spanish a deed translates as *"escrituras."* When the deed has been recorded with a notary public and filed with the Public Registry of Property the deed becomes *"escrituras públicas."*

Mexican law requires certain acts, including title deeds, be in writing to be valid. The document used may be private or public. It is a public deed if the document was executed before notary public in Mexico or in the Mexican embassy or one of its consulates abroad. Mexican law recognizes title deeds conveyed by private documents but only as evidence that the parties to the contract consented to enter into an agreement. Such agreements are not valid when used to the detriment of a third party. In other words, even though a real estate sale executed through a private agreement is valid between the buyer and the seller, it is not enforceable against the claim of a person who recorded and filed their deed to the same property with the Public Registry.

The general rule under Mexican contract law is that the parties to a contract may agree to anything provided that it is not against the law. No specific formalities are required for the validity of agreements, except as expressly required by law. The law requires that real estate title deeds be recorded with a public notary and filed with the public registry. Failure to comply with theses requirements can, but does not necessarily, result in an invalid contract. In such cases either party to the contract may demand from the other that the required formalities be carried out to validate the contract.

Normally, and almost without exception, a seller has the title deed to the property in the form of a public deed, or *escritura públicas,* and is able to provide a copy of the deed to the seller. Since the information contained in the deed is public information, that is to say, it is available to anyone at the public registry; there is no reason for the seller to refuse to provide a buyer with a copy.

Therefore in any real estate transaction in Mexico, the buyer should always request a copy of the **public deed** *("escrituras públicas")* to verify:

> The chain of title
> The **metes and bounds** of the property
> The property's public registry filing information

The **chain of title** refers to the history of ownership of the property. The buyer's attorney usually takes care of this. It should include the names of at least three previous owners. A buyer can have a **title search** done and, in some cases, get **title insurance** from a number of different "land title companies" but it is usually very expensive and only available when buying property in a large development.

The **metes and bounds,** or *"medidas y colindancias"* of the property describe the **boundary lines** of the property beginning from the north and then proceeding to the east, south, and west. The description of each boundary line will also include the description or name of the owner of the abutting properties.

The easiest way to obtain the **public property filing information** is by making a copy of the registration stamp on the last page of the title document. If this information is missing, chances are that the seller does not have title to the property. If a public notary has recorded the seller's title documents, as is required by law, the notary's name and address is on the cover of the first page. If the stamp is missing, the buyer should contact the notary and request that the documents be filed with the public registry. However, it may be that the transaction was never recorded—the seller may have acquired the property through a private agreement. A buyer must insist that the seller first have the transaction recorded before a public notary **BEFORE** the buyer takes any further actions concerning the property.

It must be emphasized that a buyer must make sure this is done before continuing with any other negotiations. There is a tendency for anxious buyers to get carried away with the deal. Real estate agents may insist that the property will be sold if a buyer does not make that down payment, but a prospective buyer must ignore such tactics. If there is no problem with the property, the seller can get his documents in order in a fairly short time.

RECORDING AND THE PUBLIC REGISTRY

One of the biggest concerns when purchasing real estate is whether the buyer is getting valid title and if he will have to deal with a conflicting claim at some time in the future. There is a general principle of law that applies to claims to real estate which states that "first in time is first in law." What this means is that if two people have an equal claim to real estate, the first one to be legally recognized as the owner has the better claim to the property, and therefore is entitled to the property. But how does the law determine who was first to be recognized as the owner of the property?

This is why real estate transactions are recorded. The principal function of recording real estate transactions is to give the buyer a way to verify whether there has been an earlier transaction which, in some way, limits or undermines the sellers legal right to sell the real estate that the buyer is interested in acquiring. If the earlier transaction is not recorded, a good faith buyer purchasing the property afterwards **gains priority** if his purchase is recorded. This simply means that the law considers the second buyer as first in time, and, therefore, first in law.

In Mexico real estate transactions are recorded and filed at the Public Registry of Property. Each municipality usually has an office of the Public Registry of Property and each office is normally not affiliated with a central office. Some states have adopted a centralized system as is currently being used in Mexico City. Those states, such as Baja California, Tamaulipas and Morelos, to name a few, centralize all the Public Registries of the state through a main office in the state Capitol. There is not a nationally centralized system that encompasses all the offices presently operating throughout Mexico.

Fortunately, most of the offices of the Public Registry of Property operate much the same. The Public Registry of Property is normally divided into four different registers or books:

➤   The First: register of real estate.
➤   The Second: register of personal or moveable property.
➤   The Third: register of corporations, or legal entities.
➤   The Fourth: register of urban planning and land use.

Other Pubic Registries are divided in to two sections: Civil and Commercial. Even though the sections are limited to only two, basically they are the same. The information can still be obtianed in the same manner. Normally most investigation would be made in the Civil section.

When investigating a piece of real estate, the buyer can go to the local office of the Public Registry and request information regarding the property he or she is interested in buying. Most of the registry offices can investigate a particular piece of real estate with only the owners name or the address of the property. In some areas the registry may still not be up to date and it might be more difficult to get information unless more information about the property is provided, such as its current filing information.

The registry will issue "certificates" for several different requests for recorded information. These certificates are intended to document the legal status of real estate recorded and filed with the registry. In this manner the registry is able to keep the public aware of property sales as well as when property has been encumbered in any way.

The Public Registry issues certifications for the following:

➢ **Certificate of inscription**: This is used to confirm whether a property is on file with the registry. As much of the following information should be provided: name of owner, filing information such as filing number, page, volume; date filed, name of the subdivision where the property is located; lot number; block number; and surface area of the property.
➢ **Certificate of no inscription**: This is used to confirm that property is not filed with the registry. The same information as a certificate of inscription should be used, or just the name of the alleged property owner. This certificate is very helpful to prove that property is being offered with false information.
➢ **Certificate of no property**: This is used to confirm that an individual does not have any property filed with the registry in his or her name.
➢ **Certificate of no encumbrances**: This certificate is used in all real estate transactions and is discussed more later in the book.
➢ **Certificate of filing history**: This is used to get a detailed description of the change of title for property filed with the registry.

There is a small fee for these certificates and not all public registry offices will necessarily have all of them. The amount of information needed to get a certificate also varies from one office to another. Most of the offices in small towns will be more likely to require more information to carry out a request. There is also no guarantee that no mistakes will be made by the registry. If there is any doubt as to the reliability of the information obtained form the registry an attorney should be hired to do a complete title search.

In addition to the above certificates, certified copies of information filed with the registry can also be requested. Requests can be made for all or any part of any documents that have been filed with the registry. The advantage of having a copy rather than a certificate is that with a copy more information is made available. Sometimes more than just the fact that a property has been filed with the registry is necessary, in such cases a copy of the document should be requested. To avoid unnecessary expenses just specific information, such as a certain parts of a document or a certain pages can be requested.

CHAPTER 5

PEOPLE INVOLVED IN THE REAL ESTATE INDUSTRY

THIS CHAPTER EXPLAINS THE ROLE PLAYED BY REAL ESTATE COMPANIES, ATTORNEYS, TRUSTEE BANKS, AND PUBLIC NOTARIES IN THE REAL ESTATE INDUSTRY IN MEXICO.

INTRODUCTION

Normally, there are three to four players involved in any real estate transaction in the restricted zone:

➢ A real estate company
➢ The buyer's lawyer
➢ A bank
➢ A public notary

All four are helpful in their respective areas in assisting with real estate transactions. Transactions outside of the restricted zone do not involve a bank since it is not necessary to establish a real estate trust in those areas. Otherwise the transactions are much the same.

REAL ESTATE COMPANIES

When in Mexico do as the Mexicans do? It may sound like a good idea. In reality, when it comes to real estate transactions in Mexico, the expression could be—when in Mexico, try to make it look like the United States.

A foreigner traveling in Mexico is constantly reminded of just who the target real estate buyer is, especially in resort towns. Large billboards, all in English, selling everything from beach bungalows to luxury homes, make it perfectly clear that Mr. and Mrs. USA play a very important role in real estate acquisitions throughout Mexico.

Once involved in a real estate transaction a foreigner might start to think that Spanish isn't the language of Mexico. Advertisements for property are almost exclusively in English. All of the real estate agents speak English and the majority are not Mexican. When it comes time to make an offer on property, the documents provided by the real estate agent are almost inevitably in English without a Spanish translation. For the most part, such use of the English language is unavoidable because many of the buyers do not speak Spanish, or their knowledge of the language is insufficient when it comes to the complexities of real estate transactions.

Because of the similarities of real estate transactions in general, it is easy to assume that the basic terms and principles which are familiar in the United States also hold true in Mexico. This assumption becomes easier to make when United States real estate terminology is adopted for transactions in Mexico. Much of the paperwork is similar, if not exactly the same, as that used in the US. There have even been cases where the paper work used was nothing more than photocopies of real estate documents anyone can buy at the office supply store in San Diego. If a foreign buyer encounters such a situation, he is wise to seek out another real estate company. There are plenty of honest and reputable people in this industry, but there are always a few who are less than honest.

Although, there are many aspects of Mexican real estate transactions that are identical to procedures carried out in the United States, there are many aspects that are completely different. As a rule, a foreigner should assume nothing.

Mexican real estate transactions are not carried out in the same manner as United States real estate transactions. The buyer must retain professionals to assist in the transaction. Mexico has yet to regulate real estate transactions. Real estate agents and brokers are not legally licensed in Mexico. Consequently, a foreign buyer cannot always depend on the normal safeguards that would be applied to real estate transactions in the United States. The old saying "let the buyer beware" is very appropriate. Anyone can set up a real estate company in Mexico. There are no special requirements or brokerage licenses to obtain. A would-be real estate agent merely has to establish a Mexican corporation, obtain a work visa, and he is in business.

This book was written because there is very little information available in English on this subject. Many of the people involved in the real estate industry in Mexico are foreigners who do not speak Spanish, and are completely ignorant about the laws applying to the transactions in which they are involved.

There are good reasons why the real estate industry in the United States is highly regulated. Until the real estate industry is regulated in Mexico, there will always be some real estate companies who prefer that buyers know as little as possible about real estate transactions. After all, a buyer cannot ask questions if he does not have any knowledge of the laws.

Currently there is nothing similar to a **Real Estate Commissioner** or a **Department of Real Estate** in Mexico. Some states are beginning to look at some kind of real estate legislation, but it might be some time before this is a reality. The American Embassy and the American consulates in Mexico are good places to start when trying to determine if a real estate company is reputable. Some of the real estate companies have established quite a reputation for themselves at some of the Consulates.

ATTORNEYS

A Mexican attorney should be involved to draw up contracts and to review the conditions and terms of sale. Additionally, an attorney can do a title search and point out any problems or alternatives a buyer may have. The buyer should always have his or her own attorney rather than using the attorney of the seller or some attorney used by a real estate company free of charge. As the old saying goes, you get what you pay for, and usually if someone's services are offered free of charge you are probably paying for them in some other way.

Legally, only a licensed Mexican attorney should provide advice on the law. If an attorney is licensed in Mexico he should be able to produce a *"cédula profesional."* This document is a registered license to practice law in Mexico and includes a photo of the attorney and his signature. To be sure that an attorney is licensed in Mexico, a foreign buyer should ask to see the attorney's license, or have the attorney's license number included in a retainer agreement before employing any services.

Besides formalizing your real estate transaction, an attorney can be very helpful in saving you money. This is because attorneys are involved in many different transactions and have contacts with banks, notaries, and the Mexican government on a regular basis. Because of this they are aware of the most competitive cost and fees involved in a transaction and can make sure that the buyer is given the best possible prices.

An attorney can also inform the buyer regarding his or her legal options and by doing so can make sure that no opportunities are missed which otherwise could result in more expenses for the buyer at a later date. Examples of this are usually found in tax planning considerations, closing costs which should be paid by the seller, and ways of taking title to the trust rights which make sense for the particular circumstances of a specific buyer. Very often one piece of good advice can save the buyer thousands of dollars in tax savings or other savings when the buyer eventually sells the property.

When looking for an attorney it is important to remember that any Mexican attorney can normally handle a real estate transaction. The buyer is not limited to only the local attorneys where the property is located. All real estate transactions involving a trust are governed by federal law. This means that all such transactions are carried out the same way regardless if the property is in Can Cun or Los Cabos.

Many attorneys in Mexico do not use written agreements or retainer agreements. It is always a good idea to ask for a written agreement which clearly lays out precisely what the attorney will be doing and what the client is going to pay. Some attorneys don't tell their clients how much their fees are until the client already owes a considerable amount of money. To avoid this, always get some kind of written estimate of what the attorney expects his or her fees to be. It is difficult sometimes to calculate the exact amount that the attorney will have to incur in expenses, therefore, very often this will be left open. This should not be a problem if the attorney gives the client an itemized account of the expenses.

Since most transactions can be carried out by any attorney it is always a good idea to shop around to get an idea of the range of services and prices available. Always compare fees of local attorneys with other attorneys in other larger cities. Very often, due to the greater number of attorneys in some of the larger cities, fees will be lower. Some firms also have offices in more than one city, and they may be able to make the whole transaction much easier. Once you have an idea of what the going rate for the services needed don't be afraid to ask the attorney you felt most comfortable with if the price you came up with is acceptable. Very often on small transactions the attorney may be willing to be flexible.

American attorneys are not licensed to practice law in Mexico and should not give advice on Mexican Law. I should clarify, here, that I am referring to individuals who are licensed to practice law in the United States, and not merely individuals who are citizens of that country. There are currently very few Americans who are licensed to practice law in Mexico. The fact that a person is licensed to practice law in the United States in no way allows him or her to practice law in Mexico: Mexican or United States law. The legal systems in the two countries are very different and, besides the fact that anyone who did this would be practicing law without a license and committing a crime, one should question what would motivate them to do this. In spite of all the lawyer jokes, the practice of law in not a hobby, and it is not a very good idea to get legal advice form anyone who is not involved on a full time basis.

THE BANK

If the real estate transaction involves property in the restricted zone a buyer needs to choose a bank to act as a trustee to hold title to the property. Only banks may act as trustees in Mexico. A buyer should get a clear idea of all the alternatives when picking a bank. In time, all banks will be the same in their treatment of trusts and the fees associated with them. Currently, it is still wise to shop around for the best deal.

When considering a bank the following questions should be answered:

➢ How much is the bank's annual fee?
➢ How much does the bank charge for the assignment of rights?
➢ How much is the bank's trust set-up fee?

The bank is responsible for getting the trust permit from the Ministry of Foreign Affairs to establish the real estate trust for the benefit of a foreigner. The permit fee is set by the government and should be the same at every bank. Chapter Six examines the steps to be taken when establishing a real estate trust.

PUBLIC NOTARY

An essential element in any real estate transaction is the participation of a public notary. A public notary in Mexico should not be confused with his counterpart in the US. A Mexican public notary acts as an artificial extension of the government and ensures that all real estate transactions are executed in accordance with the law.

All public notaries are licensed attorneys and are issued a special license to be a notary by the government. They are held accountable for any transactions in which they are involved.   However, they are not responsible for the optional content of the documents presented to them; they only ensure that the transaction is carried out in accordance with the law.   Therefore, it is very important to seek legal advice before any document is signed.

In real estate transactions, a public notary is legally responsible to ensure that all essential legal formalities are observed—such as; correctly identifying the property, the names of the buyer and the seller, and incorporating this information into the title deed. He is not obligated to advise either party to the transaction on legal options available to them, such as stipulations regarding the payment of costs involved in the transaction, or agreements that hold one of the parties responsible for the payment of all tax consequences.

There have been cases where the title documents were drawn up stipulating the buyer was responsible for the payment of capital gains taxes on the property, which should be paid by the seller. The buyer never took the time to fully understand what he was signing.

Transactions carried out before a public notary must be done in Spanish, and the notary should refrain from using any other language in carrying out his duties. If one of the parties does not understand Spanish, an interpreter should be designated. The interpreter must declare before the notary that the translation will be faithful to the original. The parties who do not understand Spanish may appoint the interpreter.

As a preliminary draft or record of a transaction, all documents executed before a public notary are recorded in special books called protocols. These documents, also referred to as notarial instruments, are considered valid proof of execution of a transaction in the event of controversy. However, notarial instruments for real estate transactions must be filed with the public registry of property to be binding before third parties.

CHAPTER 6

STEPS TO TAKE WHEN BUYING PROPERTY

THIS CHAPTER EXAMINES AN EIGHT-STEP PROCESS FOR BUYING REAL ESTATE IN
MEXICO. THE CONTRACTS USED IN REAL ESTATE TRANSACTIONS IN MEXICO ARE
EXAMINED IN DETAIL. THESE CONTRACTS INCLUDE THE OFFER AND ACCEPTANCE,
PROMISSORY AGREEMENTS, AND VARIOUS FORMS OF A SALES AGREEMENT. THE
STEPS ARE PRESENTED IN SEQUENCE. THE SECTIONS EXPLAINING EACH STEP
ADDRESS THE NECESSARY PROCEDURES AND DESCRIBE THE PEOPLE INVOLVED.

INTRODUCTION

Once a prospective buyer decides on a piece of property in Mexico,
the next step is to determine whether the seller has legal title. Although
this seems to be a logical and natural precaution, there have been
instances in which foreigners thought they had acquired real estate only
to find out later that the seller was unable to transfer title because he
didn't own the land.

This chapter will examine some of the legal restrictions confronted
by foreigners when buying real estate in Mexico, as well as the
necessity of a real estate trust. Once the decision is made to acquire
property in Mexico there are some basic considerations to be
examined. The following section examines some of the procedures
involved in property ownership in the restricted zone.

The first thing a buyer must consider is whether the seller of the
property has legal title to the property, and, if so, whether the property
can be legally transferred. Before a buyer can answer these questions,
he must consider how much he knows about the applicable laws and
regulations and whether he is capable of obtaining this information on
his own. He may be better off seeking help and advice of a Mexican
attorney.

A buyer must always remember that he is not in the United States. The rules are not the same! It is easy to assume this, especially when dealing with American real estate agents, sellers, etc. throughout the transaction. The Mexican legal system is not the same as its American equivalent.

This is not to say that in Mexico real estate transactions are totally different or more complicated than those in the U.S. are, but common sense should be exercised. When buying property in Mexico, or any foreign country, a buyer should take the same precautions he would take when buying the same property in the United States. In the United States this procedure is fairly straightforward since real estate transactions are legally regulated. Consequently, in the United States real estate brokers and agents generally handle much of the transaction. Since no such regulations exist in Mexico, a buyer must know who the players are in any real estate transaction, and who to turn to for help and assistance when necessary.

The worst a buyer can do is remain ignorant to the law and procedures involved in real estate transactions in Mexico. Typically the seller is already somewhat knowledgeable in these areas since he has been through a real estate transaction at lease once before in Mexico. However, the buyer should not depend on the seller for information or advice because he has no way of knowing if it is correct. The buyer should always seek the advice of a Mexican attorney to make sure that she clearly understands what is taken place.

REAL ESTATE CONTRACTS

The most common types of real estate contracts in Mexico are the following:

➢ Offer and acceptance *(oferta)*
➢ Promissory agreement (*contrato de promesa*)
➢ Real estate trust agreement *(contrato de fideicomiso)*
➢ Purchase-sales agreement *(contrato de compraventa*)
➢ Purchase-sales agreement with reservation of title *(contrato de compraventa con reserva de dominio)*
➢ Assignment of real estate trusts rights (*contrato de cesion de derechos fideicomisarios*)

Most real estate transactions will have at least two contracts:

> **Offer and acceptance and/or a promissory agreement**: a preliminary agreement containing only the basic information. It is not the instrument by which title to the property is transferred to the buyer.
> **Purchase sales agreement**: the agreement by which title transfers to the buyer. It may take different forms: a reserve title agreement, or a real estate trust agreement.

The Civil Code defines an agreement *(convenio)* as an accord *(acuerdo)* between two or more persons to create, transfer, modify or extinguish obligations. More specifically, the Civil Code defines contracts as agreements that produce or transfer obligations and rights.

LEGAL REQUIREMENTS

In order for contracts to legally exist the following requirements must exist:

> Consent: this is the acceptance or approval of what is agreed to in the contract by buyer and the seller.
> A legal object which is subject-matter of the contract: this refers to the property which must be property that can be sold.

A contract may be judged invalid for any of the following reasons:

> One or both of the parties lacks legal capacity to contract.
> Defects *(vicios)* of consent: this refers to case when one or both of the parties did not properly consent to enter into the agreement due to violence, error, or fraud;
> The contract's object, motive or purpose *(fin)* is illegal;
> The consent given by one or both of the parties is not expressed in the form prescribed by law.

As a general rule, real estate contracts must be recorded before a public notary and, to be binding before third parties, filed with the public registry.

There are three contracts normally involved in a real estate transaction in the restricted zone:

> Offer to Purchase
> Promissory Agreement

➢ Trust Agreement or Deed to the property.

Cases involving property outside of the restricted zone may not require a promissory agreement because there usually is not a delay in getting the deed *(escrituras públicas)* to the property transferred to the buyer. However, in any transaction, outside or within the restricted zone, if the buyer is making payments over an extended period of time, or for any reason the actual transference of title is delayed for more than a few weeks a promissory agreement should be used.

STEP ONE: OFFER AND ACCEPTANCE

Most often the first document a potential buyer sees in a real estate transaction in Mexico is an Offer to Purchase Contract. The contract takes many different forms in Mexico, and has many different names. Some of the most common names given to this contract are:

➢ Offer and Acceptance
➢ Offer to Purchase
➢ Offer to Purchase and Earnest Money Deposit
➢ Earnest Money Deposit

From a legal standpoint, an offer is any proposition which one person makes to another to enter into a contract under certain conditions. The law states that anyone who proposes the execution of a contract to another person, fixing a time for its acceptance, is bound by his offer until the expiration of the time period proposed.

The law recognizes "express" or "tacit" consent when determining when an offer has been accepted. The consent is "expressly" given when it is given verbally, in writing or by unequivocal signs. "Tacit" consent is given when the facts or acts involved in the transaction warrant the presumption of consent, except when by law or agreement the consent must be "expressly" given.

In other words, the fact that an offer and an acceptance were not made in writing does not mean that the parties did not consent to the terms of the sale. This can result in confusion regarding the terms and conditions agreed to by the buyer and the seller. For this reason, a buyer must **make sure both the offer and acceptance are made in writing**.

By writing out the offer and acceptance the parties are more likely to address the main points of the transaction and avoid confusion when it comes time to sign contracts. At this stage in the transaction, a buyer is only proposing that a sales contract or promissory agreement be executed. Not all of the details of the transaction will be addressed; they will be dealt with in the sales contract or promissory agreement, once more detailed information is made available and an investigation of the title to the property is done.

There have been cases where a potential buyer has had his offer accepted by the seller and has given an earnest money deposit to the seller's real estate agent. He finds out later, however, when the contract is drawn up, that there are other conditions of which he is unaware and is unwilling to accept. This is especially true in transactions involving buyers who have no knowledge of how real estate transactions are carried out in Mexico.

The seller or his real estate agent is not necessarily trying to hide anything, but it is often assumed that the buyer knows how the transaction is to be carried out. The real estate agent may not even know what the sales contract or promissory agreement will contain because they are drafted in Spanish by the company's lawyers. To be safe, a buyer must insist that he will not fully consent to the purchase until he is able to review the final agreement in English and verify that the Spanish version contains the same information. The buyer should always request that all agreements be done in both English and Spanish. Both version should be then be reviewed by a Mexican attorney.

If possible, the buyer should request that the property be taken off the market for two weeks so that his lawyer has time to draft the final agreement. For this short amount of time, the seller shouldn't require an earnest money deposit. If he does, it should be refundable. If the seller requires a non-refundable earnest money deposit, the buyer should be sure it is not more than he is willing to lose. Whatever the case may be, everything should be in writing. A buyer must not take the real estate agent's word that his money will be refunded. He must insist that it be in writing and without any conditions. Although most real estate agents can be trusted it is always better to put everything in writing.

How To Execute

Normally the real estate company will have either an Offer To Purchase and Deposit Receipt form for the buyer to fill out, or they will have a boilerplate in their computer that can be modified for each offer. Either the real estate agent or the buyer's attorney will hold earnest money deposits. When small sums of money are involved a real estate agent can hold the deposit. The buyer should have an attorney set up a trust account to hold the deposit when large sums of money are involved. Since attorneys are licensed they are held much more accountable than real estate agents in relations with there clients. The offer must clearly indicate who received the earnest money. It will need to be clear in case the buyer wants a refund.

A prospective buyer must carefully read and clearly understand the offer before signing it, particularly when he has a new real estate agent. If there is something the buyer does not understand, he should have it removed or rewritten. A buyer must not accept the inclusion of anything he does not clearly understand, even if the real estate agent insists that it must be included by law. Common sense should dictate what is or is not included in an agreement. As long as the provisions do not entail breaking the law, any special provisions may be included in the offer or acceptance.

Most of the well-established real estate companies are experienced enough to avoid the pitfalls associated with making offers. By including certain provisions, "escape clauses," in the written offer, one is able to protect the buyer's interests by not releasing any earnest money deposited with them until a written acceptance and, if necessary, a promissory agreement are signed, at which time such deposits become non-refundable.

More often than not the offer to purchase will include provisions for an earnest money deposit. A buyer should take care to clearly understand the provisions regarding the refund of the deposited money. He must make it clear that he wants a written guarantee that his money will be refunded if either a promissory agreement or a final sales agreement isn't executed in a certain amount of time.

An earnest money deposit is typically a deposit made by the buyer to evidence good faith that he is serious about going ahead with the transaction. This is necessary in order for the seller to avoid having his property tied up and possibly miss a sale. For this reason, the seller may require that the money deposited not be refundable.

A foreign buyer may not be aware of exactly what steps need to be taken in a Mexican real estate transaction and therefore may require time to consult with an attorney before agreeing to the exact sales conditions. This is expected and should be made clear from the beginning. In most cases, the parties should agree to include only the most basic conditions in the offer, and should agree to a term of one or two weeks to have the final contracts drawn up. If during this period, the buyer should choose not to buy the property, his deposit should be refunded.

A buyer should not commit to the purchase of the property before having a clear idea of the variables that may affect the transaction. There is always something that the parties didn't consider or didn't write into the offer. This can cause problems and possibly the loss of the deposit. Therefore, if possible, the buyer should insist that he be given a reasonable period of time to investigate the property and consult an attorney before the earnest money deposit becomes non-refundable.

The property will stay on the market until the buyer has received a written acceptance of his offer. The terms and conditions of the buyer's offer do not bind the seller until the seller accepts the offer. However, such acceptance can be considered provisional as long as a promissory agreement has not been executed. Consequently, if the transaction will not be completed in more than a few days, it is in the interests of both the buyer and the seller to execute the promissory agreement as soon as possible once acceptance is received.

In smaller real estate transactions that involve a single parcel or a single family home, the importance of the offer is minimal, and is often reduced to a mere formality by which the real estate agent is able to take the property off the market. However, even if the offer is verbal, a buyer should include the condition that he must see the sales contract or promissory agreement before his offer is final.

Unless the buyer has total confidence in his agent's capabilities, he should have an attorney review the documents before signing them. Most real estate agents have little or no training or education in Mexican real estate transactions. Many also speak little or no Spanish.

Therefore it is always a good idea to get an educated opinion before signing any documents.

Once there is a **written** acceptance to the offer, the buyer's attorney should draw up the sales contract or promissory agreement. Since this agreement is the single most important document the buyer will execute with the seller, and the agreement's contents will determine the terms and conditions of the transaction, the buyer should insist that his attorney assume this responsibility.

The real estate company usually includes a fee in the **"closing costs"** to cover the costs of having the sales contract or promissory agreement drawn up. If this is the case, the buyer can have that amount deducted from the closing costs and hire his own attorney. Often he will pay the same amount, or a little more to hire his own attorney, but, by doing so, he has someone responsible and knowledgeable to represent his interests.

WHEN AND HOW LONG AN OFFER IS VALID

The law recognizes express or tacit consent when determining when an offer has been given and accepted. The consent is expressly given when it is given verbally, in writing or by unequivocal signs. Tacit consent is given when the facts or acts involved in the transaction warrant the presumption of consent, except when by law or agreement the consent must be expressly given. The law states that anyone who proposes the execution of a contract to another person, fixing a time for its acceptance, is bound by his offer until the expiration of the time proposed.

The law also includes other provisions regarding the period of time an offer is binding as follows:

1. When the offer is made to a person present, or by telephone, without fixing a time for acceptance, the person making the offer, the "offerer," must honor the offer only if it is accepted immediately.

2. When the offer is made without a time limit to a person not present, the offerer is bound for three days, plus the time necessary for the mail to be sent to that person and returned to the offerer.

3. The contract is formed at the moment the offerer receives the acceptance of the offer, being bound until then as provided above.

4. The offer, as well as the acceptance, is considered as not made, if it is withdrawn before the other party receives the offer or the acceptance.

5. If at the time of acceptance the offerer has died, without the knowledge of the acceptor, the heirs of the offerer are bound to fulfill the contract.

6. The offerer does not have to honor his offer if the acceptance is not in the exact terms offered; if it involves any modification, it is considered as a new offer subject to the same conditions for acceptance as the original offer.

7. An offer and acceptance by telegraph are effective, if the parties had previously agreed in writing to contract in this manner, and if the originals of the respective telegrams contain the signatures of the parties.

Note that, under the provisions of number 6 above, a counter-offer is legally considered as a new offer. As such, the role of the offerer and acceptor are reversed. This allows the buyer, upon receiving a counter-offer from the seller, the right to withdraw from the transaction completely. In other words, the buyer does not have to honor his first offer. This is very important, especially in complicated real estate transactions with many rounds of negotiations.

ESCROW AND EARNEST MONEY DEPOSITS

Because of the similarities in real estate transactions in general, it is easy to assume that the basic terms and principles with which a buyer is familiar in the US also hold true in Mexico. This assumption becomes easier to make when US real estate terminology is adopted, and much of the paperwork is similar, if not exactly the same, as that used in the US. Without a doubt, there are many aspects of Mexican real estate transactions that are identical to procedures carried out in the United States, but a buyer is much better off to assume nothing.

What is escrow? The Encyclopedic Dictionary of Business Law defines escrow as follows:

> In business or in real property transactions, the delivery of personal property, usually money, to a third person to be held by him until a certain condition agreed upon in advance is met. Upon the occurrence of that event, the escrow property is to be delivered to the party as provided for in the original agreement.

In the United States, an escrow company or a person legally empowered to act as an escrow agent will act in this capacity. In some states, attorneys handle escrow and the activity is commonly known as "settlement." In any case, the individual or company who carries out the escrow or settlement procedures is licensed and empowered by law to do so, and is legally responsible to see that the agreed upon conditions are met before any funds are released.

The word "escrow" is not easily translated into Spanish. One term that is often used is "*arras*." *Arras* is roughly translated as follows: the deposit of a sum of money or property that one contracting party makes with the other contracting party upon the execution of a contract for a specific purpose. Normally the use of *arras* is intended to assure the performance and fulfillment of the terms and conditions of the contract in question.

There is a significant difference between escrow and *arras*, in that, by definition, escrow always involves the services of a third party, which is not the case with *arras*.

The participation of a third party in escrow services in Mexico presents some very serious problems. First of all, when an individual or company offers escrow service, it is assumed that this service is being offered to the public in general. In other words, the individual or company is offering to hold money, normally for their clients or for the public in general, until certain contractual conditions are met, at which time such funds are to be released as payment or fulfillment of the contractual obligations in question.

The use of the word "escrow" or "escrow company" in any real estate transaction in Mexico is deceiving. Any service in Mexico that claims to be anything like an escrow company, without any affiliation to a Mexican bank or credit institution, is suspect.

Escrow services usually refer to legally regulated and authorized companies, or licensed individuals. Real estate "brokers" are not licensed in Mexico and escrow companies do not exist in Mexico. It is possible, however, to establish an escrow company in Mexico, because nowhere in Mexican Law is the **trust**, or **escrow** account, prohibited.

The choice of the word "trust" in this case is interesting and accurate. If it were possible to translate the word "escrow" with all its baggage and depth of meaning, the word in Spanish would be *"fideicomiso."* Two of the largest banks in Mexico, which were consulted on this subject, agreed with this translation.

An escrow account or escrow service must be handled through a *"fideicomiso"* if it is to be similar to those in the US. A *"fideicomiso"* can only be administered by a credit institution in Mexico.

The reason for this is simple. Credit institutions and Mexican banks are legally regulated and authorized to receive and solicit funds from the public. They also have the fiduciary obligations that come with the job, and therefore have the financial backing to guarantee their work, as well as protect the public interest.

Why are escrow services regulated in the U.S.? If just anyone could set up an escrow company, without any regulations or licensing, such services would probably not exist. If they did exist, not many people would use them. They would not inspire much confidence.

Given the nature of the activities carried out by "escrow services" only banks and legally established credit institutions may act as escrow companies in Mexico. There is no alternative. If someone is offering escrow services he is probably doing so because he does not understand what the word escrow means, or because it is a convenient way to simulate real estate transactions from the US and make a foreign buyer more comfortable with the deal.

The best alternative is to use an attorney's client trust account. By doing so, the parties are dealing with a licensed professional regulated by the government. This is preferable to making deposits with unlicensed real estate agents who typically do not set-up a separate account for deposits.

For more information on escrow and Mexican real estate transactions and possible alternatives, see Mr. Leo's article in the appendix.

STEP TWO: PROMISSORY AGREEMENT

It is recommended that a promissory agreement *(contrato de promesa)* be executed as soon as both parties have agreed to the basic conditions for the purchase of the property. **In transactions outside of the restricted zone, this contract is not necessary if both parties**

are ready to execute the sales contract immediately. However, when there is any delay between the execution of the offer and acceptance and the execution of the final notarized sales agreement, it is always better to enter into a promissory agreement.

The three most common forms of this agreement in real estate transactions are:

➢ Promise to execute a sale;
➢ Promise to execute a real estate trust;
➢ Promise to execute an assignment of the beneficial rights of a real estate trust.

The first is used most often in transactions outside of the restricted zone, or for nonresidential properties within the restricted zone. The second and third are commonly used in transactions involving properties in the restricted zone. In fact, until the December 1993 Foreign Investment Law, they were the only alternatives in the restricted zone.

In the restricted zone foreigners may not hold direct title to property and it takes time to get the necessary permits and documentation to transfer title to a real estate trust. The purpose of such a promissory agreement is to allow the parties a sufficient amount of time to obtain the necessary documents required to execute the transaction. It also allows time to fix the basic terms and conditions for sale of the property in a legally binding agreement.

With the recent changes which are in effect for 1997, trust permits are now valid for an unlimited period of time. These changes have made it easier for the buyer to obtain a trust permit quickly without having to worry about it expiring before the trust can be set-up. For this reason the buyer should always insist that a trust permit be applied for before entering into a long term commitment under a promissory agreement.

When a buyer is unable to complete a real estate transaction immediately upon coming to an understanding with the seller on the basic conditions for the sale, the execution of a promissory agreement is imperative. Once the buyer submits a written offer to buy the property, and receives a written acceptance for such an offer, a promissory agreement should be executed.

Under normal circumstances, a real estate company is involved in the transaction, and they will have the necessary documents to complete the offer and acceptance. If a buyer is purchasing property directly from the owner, it is very likely that this first step of offer and acceptance will be omitted. Traditionally, Mexicans execute these transactions by a mere handshake.

The promissory agreement, on the other hand, should never be omitted, regardless of whether the transaction is being handled by a real estate company or directly with the owner of the property. Although the offer to purchase and its acceptance have legal effects, this in itself does not legally bind the parties to carry out the sale of the property in question.

For example, Mr. Jones makes a written offer to buy a certain piece of property from Mr. Caballero, and Mr. Caballero, in turn, gives Mr. Jones a written acceptance of that offer. Mr. Caballero decides later not to sell the property to Mr. Jones; Mr. Caballero may be liable for any damages caused to Mr. Jones by his withdrawing from the transaction. Nevertheless, Mr. Jones has to take legal action to recover any such damages, which involves a considerable amount of time and effort, and the outcome may not be to his total satisfaction.

To avoid these situations, Mexican Law permits the use of preparatory or preliminary agreements known as promissory agreements *(contrato de promesa)*.

Under the legal provisions for a promissory agreement, the law specifies that the parties to an agreement may assume the **obligation to execute a future agreement**. In other words, one or both of the parties to the promissory agreement promise to execute another agreement at some specific time in the future if certain terms and conditions are met. In real estate transactions involving foreigners, the agreement that the parties promise to execute is a real estate trust agreement or sales agreement depending upon where the property is located.

For example, the conditions might be as follows: Mr. Caballero promises to execute a real estate trust agreement in order to sell Mr. Jones his property in Loreto for $10,000, provided that a real estate trust can be established in order for Mr. Jones to obtain beneficial rights. In turn, Mr. Jones promises to execute the same agreement and pay Mr. Caballero the amount specified, provided that the title to the property can be legally transferred to the real estate trust free and clear.

The promissory agreement is similar to a **letter of intent** in that the parties intend to execute a contract sometime in the future, and that it is their intent to carry out a specific action as a condition to reaching some mutual point where the contract can be executed.

A promissory agreement under Mexican Law is different from a letter of intent, or similar agreements in the United States, because the parties to the promissory agreement are bound by its terms to execute an agreement in the future. If the promissor should refuse to execute the agreement as promised, a judge may sign and execute the agreement for him by default. In other words, if a buyer has a promissory agreement with a seller to have some real estate held in trust, and the seller decides not to go through with the deal, the buyer can get a judgment and have the judge execute the necessary documents to have the property legally transferred to the trust without the intervention of the seller.

If a promissory agreement wasn't used the buyers position is much weaker in the event that the seller does not go through with the transaction. No one wants to get into a legal battle, but, when there is no other choice, it is always best to have all the elements of the transaction clearly defined in a written agreement. This is precisely what the buyer gets when a promissory agreement is used.

LEGAL REQUIREMENTS FOR A PROMISSORY AGREEMENT

In order for a promissory agreement to be valid it must meet the following requirements:

➢ The agreement must be in writing.
➢ The parties to the agreement must have legal capacity to contract.
➢ The agreement must include the principle characteristics of the future agreement.
➢ The future agreement must be executed within a specific term.

The parties to any contract must have **legal capacity** to contract. This means that the parties are adults, which in Mexico means 18 years or older, and the parties must have full use and control of their mental faculties.

Foreigners no longer need special visas in order to contract in Mexico. In June of 1990 legislative reforms were passed enabling foreigners to acquire real estate, as well as the rights associated with real estate, without requiring a special visa.

The content of the promissory agreement must include **the basic elements of the future agreement**. This means that the agreement includes the names of the parties, the name of the bank that will act as the trustee, and the price or consideration involved in the transaction. To make sure all bases are covered, a buyer can attach a draft of the future agreement to the promissory agreement. It becomes an exhibit to the contract. That way there is no doubt as to what the basic elements of the future agreement are.

Finally, the contract is limited to a **specific term**. It is best to be precise as to the amount of time the parties have to execute the agreement. For example, the promissory agreement may include a term of one year from the date of its signing for the execution of the final agreement.

In most real estate transactions in Mexico, the real estate company or agent is acting on behalf of the seller. Often they use contracts drawn up by attorneys hired by the seller. Worse yet, some use contracts that were "acquired" from another company and are supposedly good for any transaction. As a result, the agreements entirely favor the seller, or they are flawed to such a degree that if they are ever subject to litigation, the agreements are useless.

Larger developments that have their own sales agents, as well as some of the well-established real estate companies, provide the buyer with promissory agreements and suggest that he review it with his attorney. These agreements can be very complicated because of all the different factors that must be considered, such as master trusts, land held under condominium regulations, and association fees. They are not drawn up to take advantage of the buyer but they are also not written with the buyer's interests in mind.

After the promissory agreement is signed and executed the seller should contact a bank selected by the buyer to start the initial trust application. Since the seller hold title to the property he must consent to having the property transferred to the trust. After this has been done, the buyer is usually responsible for making sure the bank obtains authorization from the Foreign Relations Ministry to set-up a real estate trust.

If the seller has not already done so, the buyer is also responsible for obtaining, or at least paying for, an official appraisal, a certificate of no encumbrances, and a certificate of no tax debt for the property. None of these responsibilities are set by law and the buyer should first request that the seller provide these documents. Usually the buyer assumes such responsibilities in a sellers market. This is very often the case in tourist developments.

Once these documents are obtained, they must be presented to a public notary. At this point the buyer should verify that the notary has all the necessary documents to complete the transaction and subsequently file it at the public registry. If everything is in order, the notary will work with the bank and the buyer's attorney to have the trust documents drawn up and executed at the notary's office.

If a buyer decides to have his real estate agent handle these procedures, he should know how much it will cost beforehand. Very often these services are included in the "closing costs" which the buyer is solely responsible for, and in many cases at a fee higher than an attorney will charge. If a buyer is going to pay the same or more for these services, it is in his interest to hire an attorney who will usually finish the process faster while ensuring that the procedures are being carried out correctly.

The buyer should always confirm who the real estate agent is representing. If the agent is being paid a commission from the seller then he or she is acting as the seller's agent. This is most often the case. There are some real estate agents who represent only buyers but they are few and far between. Therefore it is preferable that the buyer retain a Mexican attorney to make sure that his interests are really represented and the best possible price for the property is negotiated.

Certain words and phrases are often misused in real estate transactions in Mexico, many times at the buyer's expense. A buyer should never accept such broad terms as "closing costs" in any agreement. A buyer should always get a detailed list of what will be included in so called "closing costs" as well as any other blanket descriptions used in contracts to cover several costs or expenses. If there is no legal reason for the buyer to pay a certain cost or expense a request should be made to have the seller pay for it. There is no reason for a buyer to be shy in these matters. Very often the only reason the buyer is stuck with certain cost and expenses is because nothing was ever said to the contrary. Speak and ye shall be heard. If the buyer is uncomfortable or unable to confront the real estate agent or seller on these matters, an attorney should be hired to do so.

SPECIAL CONSIDERATIONS

It is important to understand the purpose of a promissory agreement so as to avoid misusing it and possibly violating the law. A foreign buyer must consider the following if he is thinking about using a promissory agreement.

Is it really an agreement to execute a contract in the future? There have been many cases where the parties choose to use a promissory agreement simply to avoid complying with the law. They call it a promissory agreement, but in reality it's a sales agreement. This is usually done to avoid paying taxes or to gain possession of property in the restricted zone without using a real estate trust.

The promissory agreement should not be used instead of the final agreement. A promissory agreement is only used to bind the parties to the execution of an agreement in the future because they are unable to execute that final agreement immediately.

There are many reasons why the buyer and the seller may not be able to execute the final agreement right away. The most common reason is the property has to be put into a real estate trust or is being held in a real estate trust. Either a trust must be established, which requires the intervention of a bank and a permit from the government, or the rights to the trust must be assigned over to the buyer, which also requires the intervention of a bank and a notification to the government. In both cases it is impossible to establish the trust or assign the beneficial rights in the trust immediately.

Every real estate transaction has some tax consequences. Therefore, it is important to determine exactly when the transaction takes place in order to avoid fines and late tax interest payments. For example, if the tax authorities determine that the sale of the property took place at the time the parties signed a promissory agreement, and not two years later when the real estate trust was established, the parties to the contract are responsible for two years of fines and interest payments. These can be very substantial. If it were determined that the parties intentionally avoided paying their taxes, criminal actions could also be taken against them.

A buyer can avoid these problems if the following rules are followed when deciding if a promissory agreement is the right agreement for the transaction.

A buyer must ensure that the promissory agreement is not a sale in disguise. There are two court decisions that deal with this problem:

> **Rule One:** If the promissory agreement does not contain the exclusive obligation to do something (such as execute another agreement), or if the property is delivered and the price is paid in whole or in part, the agreement is considered a sales agreement. This is regardless of what the parties to the contract call it.
> **Rule Two:** A promissory agreement is valid when the purpose of the contract is to execute an agreement in the future; in other words, the parties to the contract must again give their consent to something other than what they consented to in the promissory agreement.

Some concrete examples will help to explain when a promissory agreement is really a sales agreement.

EXAMPLES

Example 1: Purchase of property in the restricted zone: Mr. Gonzalez has some beachfront property in the restricted zone that Mr. Leo wants to purchase. The parties come to an agreement on the price and are ready to complete the transaction. But, Mr. Leo is a foreigner, and the property is in the restricted zone, so they must obtain a trust permit. Additionally, Mr. Leo will need more tine to make full payment and since this will take about four to six weeks, they decide to execute a promissory agreement so that Mr. Gonzalez can receive most of the purchase price right away. Mr. Leo agrees to do this only if he is given legal possession of the property. They have a promissory agreement drawn up stipulating these conditions.

Example 2: Assignment of beneficial trust rights: Mr. Smith owns a beach front home in Baja California which is held in a real estate trust. Mr. Jones offers to buy the home but can only do so if Mr. Smith agrees to receive half the money upon signing the promissory agreement, and the other half within two years. They agree and have the promissory agreement drawn up. Mr. Smith receives payment and Mr. Jones takes possession of the property.

Example 3: Purchase of property outside of the restricted zone: Mr. Smith owns a home in Guadalajara, which is not held in a real estate trust because it is not in the restricted zone. Mr. Jones offers to buy the home but can only do so if Mr. Smith agrees to receive half the money upon signing the promissory agreement and the other half within two years. They agree and have the promissory agreement drawn up. Mr. Smith receives payment and Mr. Jones takes possession of the property.

EXPLANATION AND SOLUTIONS

Example 1: Purchase of property in the restricted zone. In example 1 above, Mr. Gonzalez is paid in full and Mr. Leo takes possession of the property. This violates Rule Number One above because the property was delivered and the price was paid in full or in part. Additionally, they have also broken Rule Number Two because legally the parties have already consented to the sale of the property. Therefore, there is nothing else for them to consent to regarding a future sale: Mr. Gonzalez has already delivered the property and Mr. Leo has already paid the purchase price.

The easiest solution to this problem is not to pay the purchase price or take delivery of the property until the government issues the trust permit. Often, the parties to the agreement need some assurance that the transaction will be completed so that plans can be made, or so the buyer can warrant paying to obtain a trust permit and establishing the trust.

If the parties feel that payment of the purchase price right away is indispensable, the law allows a deposit clause to be included in the promissory agreement *(depósito)* instead of making a payment. The money paid by the buyer is considered temporarily deposited with the seller and is to be returned to the buyer as agreed to by the parties. Once the trust permit is obtained, the parties then rescind the deposit agreement and apply the money to the payment of the sales price.

If it is not necessary to take delivery of the property when the promissory agreement is executed, then it is best that delivery be taken upon execution of the trust agreement. Normally, it is not necessary for the buyer to take legal possession of the property before the trust agreement is signed. If the seller does not comply with the promissory agreement a judge may do so for him by default.

However, if possession must be taken by the buyer before they trust permit is issued or before the final sales agreement is entered into, the seller should enter into a bailment (*comodato*) or a lease agreement with the buyer. The reason for this is without some kind of an agreement to the contrary, it is assumed that the buyer would be taking ownership of the property. This would be in violation of article 27 of the Mexican Constitution.

A bailment can be defined as the rightful possession of property by one who is not their owner. The bailee (the person holding the property) by virtue of his or her possession, owes a duty of care to the bailor (the owner of the property). In other words, the bailee is responsible for taking care of the property while it is in his or her possession.

In a bailment agreement the seller is allowing the buyer the use of the property free of charge on the condition that the property will be returned to the seller under certain conditions at some time in the future. The bailment would be in effect until the title of the property can be conveyed to the buyer legally. At that time the contract could be rescinded and the final sales agreement could be executed. Since the buyer is only legally entitled to use the property under the bailment, he is not considered the owner, and, therefore, there is no violation to the Constitution.

There has been somewhat of a debate among lawyers in Mexico regarding the use of a bailment agreement for real estate since this type of agreement is usually used for personal or moveable property. However, more recently it has been accepted that its use with real estate is legal.

The other alternative for taking possession of the property is through a lease. With a lease the buyer can make rent payments that can be deducted later form the sales price.

Example 2: Assignment of beneficial trust rights. In example two above, the property is held in a real estate trust, and the seller does not legally own the property. What he does own are the beneficial rights to the real estate trust. Therefore, the seller is selling his rights in the trust rather than the real property itself. Although the outcome is the same as a real estate sale, the procedure is somewhat different.

When selling property that is held in trust, a seller is actually **assigning** his right in the trust to the buyer. Therefore, the promissory agreement is a **promise to assign trust rights**, and the final agreement is an **assignment of trust rights**.

In an assignment of trust rights, the buyer assumes the rights and obligations to the bank/trustee and to the Mexican government that the seller used to have in relation to the property. This means that the buyer must abide by the same terms and conditions that applied to the seller. Such terms and conditions are found in three sources:

➢ The trust permit issued by the Ministry of Foreign Affairs.
➢ The trust agreement which designates the bank as trustee and the buyer as the beneficiary.
➢ Applicable Mexican Law.

All of the buyer's rights are subject to the conditions in the trust permit, because without the trust permit the trust could not be established. Therefore, in order to assign the rights one has in a real estate trust, one must first make sure that the provisions of the trust permit or the trust agreement are not being violated by the assignment.

Currently, the Ministry of Foreign Affairs requires that the bank notify them before an assignment of trust rights is carried out. This is because each new beneficiary must agree to the inclusion of the Calvo clause in the trust agreement. Any assignment of trust rights executed without first notifying the Ministry of Foreign Affairs is in violation of the trust permit and, therefore, against the law.

The trust agreements also require the trust beneficiary to notify the bank of any assignment of the beneficial rights in the trust; otherwise the assignment is null and void. The trust agreement should include the following conditions for an assignment to be valid:

➢ The written consent of the bank.
➢ The fulfillment of all legal formalities required for the assignment.
➢ The payment of all taxes generated by the assignment.
➢ The property held in trust is current in all property taxes.

Example 3: Purchase of property outside of the restricted zone. The parties in example 3 above are actually executing a sales agreement. In these cases, the preferred contract is a **reserve title agreement** *(contrato con reserva de dominio),* which is similar to a **land contract** in the United States. This type of contract is explained in detail in the section on reserve title and installment agreements.

REGISTRATION OF PROMISSORY AGREEMENTS

As a general rule, promissory agreements are not registered at the public registry: a promissory agreement does not affect real property rights over the property being sold. However, some public registries will register promissory agreements when possession of the property is delivered to the future buyer upon the execution of the promissory agreement.

When the promissory agreement cannot be registered it is common and legal to file a lawsuit, without notifying the defendant, to indirectly obtain the registration of the agreement. The end result is similar to *lis pendens* or *lis imaginaria,* which notifies third parties of the existence of the contract and protects the interests of the future buyer.

STEP THREE: TITLE SEARCH

An adequate title search must be done on the property before making the final payment, particularly in remote or underdeveloped areas of Mexico. Sometimes information filed with the public registry is overlooked, even though a certificate of no encumbrances must be issued before the notary will record the transaction.

There are title insurance companies in the United States that cover real estate transactions in Mexico. However, a buyer should still read the policies carefully.

A buyer should hire an Attorney to do the title search. The reason for this is that only an Attorney can give a legal opinion that a buyer can hold him responsible for. A real estate agent should not do the title search. They are usually representing the seller and unlikely to do a careful study of the chain of title, particularly if the agent cannot read Spanish, and if they give the buyer false of incorrect information there is not much recourse. They are not licensed to give legal opinions so I can be very difficult to hold them responsible when one relies on that opinion. This is especially true if the buyer could have hired an attorney and simply chose not to.

STEP FOUR: CERTIFICATE OF NO ENCUMBRANCES

For the public notary to record the purchase sales agreement, he needs to see a certificate of no encumbrances from the public registry and a certificate of no tax liability from the tax authority for the property.

The seller should obtain these certificates at his own expense, although very often the buyer is charged for them. The buyer should ask for copies of these documents before seriously committing to the transaction. Normally, neither the real estate agent nor the seller will bother to get these documents unless the buyer is serious. They will often insist on an earnest money deposit to defray the costs of obtaining the documents.

CERTIFICATE OF NO ENCUMBRANCES

If the seller is unwilling to provide a current certificate of no encumbrances, it can be obtained at the public registry. This is public information, so there is no reason for the registry to deny issuing such a certificate to any interested party.

The certificate of no encumbrances should include the following information:

➤ The number of years back the title search on the property goes.
➤ The surface area of the property, its classification (urban or rural), and a legal description, including whether the property is held under co-ownership.
➤ The metes and bounds of the property.
➤ Property filing information, including the page, volume and section numbers.
➤ The name of the owner and the date of acquisition.
➤ The name of the person who requested the certificate.
➤ The city and state where the certificate was issued.
➤ The time and date the certificate was issued.
➤ The fee paid for the certificate.

➢ The name and signature of the registrar.
➢ The official seal of the public registry.

These certificates contain useful information regarding both the property and the owner. If any of the information from the certificate does not agree with the information provided by the seller, a buyer should take care. If the discrepancies are not eliminated, the buyer should request a refund and look for another piece of property.

CERTIFICATE OF NO TAX LIABILITY

The certificate of no tax liability is used as proof of property tax payment at the time of the transaction. It is intended to show that there are no pending tax payments which may not show up on the certificate of no encumbrances.

The certificate is issued by the head of the property tax department of the general treasury of the municipality where the property is located.

The certificate should contain the following information:

➢ The classification of the property (urban or rural).
➢ The property tax registration number *(clave catastral)*.
➢ The tax appraisal value.
➢ The name of the owner.
➢ The period up to which taxes are paid, and the receipt number and date of the last payment.
➢ The signature of the department head and seal of the municipal treasury.

This certificate is simple to obtain. The seller is usually happy to provide a copy. If there is an outstanding tax payment, it should be paid before continuing with the transaction.

ADDITIONAL DOCUMENTS

Normally the seller of the property will provide the public notary with all the necessary documents need to complete a real estate transaction. This is because the notary will not proceed with the transaction if any document required by law is not provided to him. Since the property is recorded in the name of the seller, it makes sense that he or she should have all the necessary documents which were required when the property was acquired and recorded in the public registry. These documents make up the set that are usually kept together as the title documents.

Most states require the following documents to be presented when filing a real estate transaction at the public registry:

➢ Property survey authorized by the tax real estate registry (*Direccion de Catastro*). This document is normally valid for one year from the date issued.

➢ Property appraisal issued by the State Appraisals Commission, banking institutions, or an authorized appraisal expert. This document is also normally valid for one year from the date issued.

➢ Declaration of real estate acquisition taxes paid when the property was acquired.

➢ Declaration of provisional income tax payment for the transfer of title.

➢ Certificate of no tax liabilities.

➢ In regard to rural land (*predios rusticos*), besides all the above mentioned requirements, a written authorization issued by the Agrarian authority must also be presented. This is to verify that the property is not *ejido* property or in any way subject to the laws that deal with social property. This is done to make sure there are no reasons the property should not be sold as private property.

The buyer is not responsible for the above information and all of these documents should be required by the public notary when the transaction is being recorded and notarized. To avoid delays and possibly confusion it might not be a bad idea to make sure the seller has all of the above documents before closing.

STEP FIVE: PROPERTY APPRAISAL

This section was written by Lic. Jorge Diez de Bonilla, a Corredor Público in Tijuana, Baja California.

In accordance with the law on real estate it is mandatory to produce a topographic survey/plot plan of the land and an official appraisal. This appraisal is done to estimate the commercial value of the property including raw land, lots, houses, subdivisions, federal maritime-terrestrial zone, commercial and industrial units, etc. A *"Corredor Publico"* (an attorney at law licensed by the Federal Execute) may act as an appraiser for the estimation of the commercial value of all kinds of personal and real properties. The Federal Law of Public Brokerage states:

> SECTION 6th. The public broker (*Corredor Publico*) is entitled to... II. Act as an expert appraiser to estimate, quantify and express the value of the properties, service, rights and obligations submitted to his/her option, appointed by a private party or by order of competent authority.

Furthermore, Section 4th of the Regulations for the Federal Fiscal Code appoints *Corredores Publicos* to concur with certain local authorities and Banks for the appraisal of properties for fiscal purposes. There are other federal and local laws establishing the appointment of *Corredores* in the appraisal field.

However, Banks are also authorized to produce appraisals. They use architects, civil engineers, and others duly registered and licensed by the National Bank Commission. The appraisals made in such manner will have some value and enforcement as those made by *Corredores Publicos* in accordance with Sec. 46 XXII of the Law of Credit Institution.

The difference between using *Corredor Publico* or a Bank is that a *Corredor Publico* will often report the fair market value of the property in a prompt and simple manner. He can also certify, as a commercial notary public, appraisals made by other qualified persons. Banks require more time to elaborate the appraisal. Both are legally accepted by government agencies and notaries for the transfer of any property.

STEP SIX: CHOICE PURCHASE-SALES AGREEMENT

As mentioned earlier, the purchase-sales agreement is the contract by which title to the property being sold is actually transferred to the buyer or held in his benefit in the case of real estate trusts or *fideicomisos*. The type of transaction carried out almost always determines the choice of contract. Although all real estate transactions have some common elements, some require special considerations and therefore the agreements will vary.

All of the contracts have one thing in common: the seller wants to sell his property for a certain price and the buyer agrees to purchase the property at that price. The variables involve the amount of time the buyer has to pay the sales price and when the title to the property is actually conveyed to the buyer. This section examines the following types of contracts:

➤ General purchase sales contract.
➤ Reserve title and installment sales agreement.
➤ Irrevocable real estate trust agreement.
➤ Assignment of beneficial trust rights.

In order to determine which contract is best, the following questions need to be answered:

➤ **Where is the property located?** If the property is located in the restricted zone, a **real estate trust agreement** is required. The only exception to this rule is property to be used for non-residential purposes. In such cases, a foreign-owned Mexican corporation is used instead of a real estate trust. See Chapter Two for more information on the use of Mexican corporations for this purpose. If the property is located outside of the restricted zone then a normal **purchase sales contract** is used.
➤ **How will the purchase price be paid?** If the purchase price is going to be paid in installments over a long period of time, a **reserve title agreement** is used.
➤ **Is the property currently held in a real estate trust?** If the property is already held in trust then a contract for the assignment of rights is used. If the property is not currently held in trust a real estate trust agreement is used.

All of the contracts mentioned above include the basic elements of a purchase sales agreement. They all require the immediate or eventual payment of the purchase price and the subsequent transfer of title to the buyer. The following section summarizes the basic provisions applicable to all purchase sales agreements.

General Provisions

When the Contract is Perfected

Generally speaking, purchase-sales agreements *(compraventa)* occur when one of the contracting parties obligates himself to transfer the ownership of property or trust rights, and the other agrees to pay a certain price for such property or rights. In theory, the contract is perfected and binding between the parties as soon as the property and its price are agreed upon, even when the property has not been delivered and the price has yet to be paid. For this reason, it is important that the seller and buyer recognize in writing, as soon as possible, that a formal contract must be drawn up to reflect the details of the sale, and that the parties still have not fully consented to the sale and purchase of the property being sold.

Requirements for an Agreement to Exists and be Valid

All purchase-sales agreements must meet specific requirements to legally exist and to be valid. Such requirements are known as essential elements and elements of validity.

The essential elements of any purchase-sales agreement are:

> **Consent:** acceptance or approval of what is planned or done by another. In a purchase-sales agreement, the seller grants consent by agreeing to transfer title to real property to the buyer. In turn, the buyer grants consent by agreeing to a certain price.
> **Object of the contract:** the purpose, aim, or goal of the contract. In a purchase-sales agreement, the purpose is to transfer title to real property to a buyer and to transfer a certain amount of money to the seller. The indirect object of the contract is the property and the price.

The contract is declared null, having no legal force, if it does not include the price, or if the property does not exist. To legally exist, the property must physically exist and it must be included in objects of commerce. In other words, the property can be seen and identified. To be "included in commerce" means that the property may be sold—it is not federally owned property or affected in any other law or defect that would hinder or prohibit its sale.

There are properties that either by law or by their nature cannot be acquired. Such properties are considered excluded from commerce.

An object is considered excluded from commerce by its nature when an individual cannot possess it exclusively. It is considered excluded from commerce by provision of law when the law declares that the property cannot be reduced to private ownership.

The price can be stipulated as a payment in money or in some other personal or real property as long as such other property has legal value. The price must be fair. The law states that **when someone acquires excessive profit by taking advantage of the ignorance, inexperience, or distressed state of another person, the disadvantaged person has the right to demand that the contract in question be declared null and void; or that there be an equitable reduction of their obligation, plus the payment of damages**.

The elements of validity of a purchase-sales agreement are as follows:

➤ **Legal capacity:** the legal rights the parties have to enter into the contract. Generally, one must be in control of his mental faculties and be an adult. In some real estate transactions, such as those involving properties in the restricted zone, the law also requires that the parties both be Mexican. Foreigners do not have the capacity to enter into a purchase-sales agreement in this instance due to provisions in Article 27 of the Constitution. For this reason a real estate trust is used.

➤ **Legal Form:** All purchase-sales agreements for real estate transactions must be in writing. In order for the transaction to be binding before third parties, the agreement must also be recorded with a public notary and filed with the public registry.

In addition to the limits of legal capacity of foreigners in real estate transactions in the restricted zone, the following should also be considered:

➤ **Legal Capacity in the sale of co-owned property**: In sales of co-owned property, the other co-owners of the property have the right of first refusal when one of the other co-owners wants to sell his undivided share of the property. The law requires that the co-owner notify the other co-owners of sales through a notary or the courts, in order to allow them to exercise their right of first refusal. The legal term for exercising this right is eight days from date of notification or the co-owners lose this right. Any sale made without such notification is null and void and has no legal effect whatsoever. If several co-owners are interested in exercising their right of first refusal, the co-owner with the greater share in the property is given preference. If they have equal shares, the co-owner is designated by lot, unless agreed otherwise.

➤ **Capacity of husband or wife:** A marriage partner must have the consent of the other spouse to enter into a contract to sell real estate if the marriage is designated as under community property *(sociedad conyugal).*

➤ **Capacity of Parents of children:** Parents of children who are under their parental power must get consent from the courts to sell property owned by the children.

PAYMENT AND INTEREST FOR LATE PAYMENT

The buyer must pay the sales price according to the terms and within the time stipulated in his agreement with the seller. If the agreement makes no specific indication, it is assumed that the payment will be made in cash. If the buyer delays payment he may be required to pay **interest at the legal rate** (9% annually) on the amount due. In all cases involving interest payments, the parties may use a higher percentage as long as it is not excessive.

LUMP SUM SALES

Generally, if one or more pieces of real property is sold for a lump sum *(precio alzado)*, without determining its parts or measuring the properties involved, neither of the parties to the agreement may rescind the contract based on a deficit or excess upon the delivery of the property. A lump sum payment refers to a transaction in which a single sum of money serves as complete payment for several distinct parcels of real estate. These are also known as *ad corpus* sales. The basic idea is that the buyer and the seller agree to the sale of the property or properties "as is" without being held to a specific calculation or measurement.

PAYMENT OF TRANSACTION OR CLOSING COSTS

The law states that the parties shall each pay one-half of the costs of the instruments of sale and registry unless otherwise agreed. These costs are normally notary fees and public registry filing fees. The law does not specifically mention other costs; therefore, each party is responsible for his transaction costs, such as legal fees and the like. However, by mutual consent, these costs and any other fees and expenses may be designated the responsibility of one of the parties. For example, in a "seller's market" the buyer may agree to pay all transaction costs.

MULTIPLE SALES ON A SINGLE PROPERTY

If the same seller sells a property to several buyers, the following provisions are observed:

➤ If the sale involves **personal property,** *(bienes muebles)* the first sale will prevail over those that were carried out later. If the time of the transaction cannot be determined, the sale executed by the person who is in possession of the property shall prevail.
➤ If the sale involves **real property**, the sale first registered with the public registry will prevail. If none has been registered, the above rules covering personal property apply.

PRIORITY AND GOOD FAITH ACQUISITIONS

There is a fundamental rule: a **person can only sell property that he owns.** The sale of property that is owned by another person is void unless the person selling the property is representing the owner. If the sale resulted from fraud or bad faith, the seller is liable for damages and losses caused by the sale.

On the other hand, if the buyer acquired the property in good faith, the provisions relating to the public registry must be taken into account. These provisions state that a record of a transaction in the public registry protects the rights acquired in good faith by a third party, even if the right of the party executing them is later annulled or rescinded.

The only exceptions to this rule are:

➤ When the cause of the nullity appears clearly in the same registry.
➤ When the contract used required no payment to change hands in the transaction.
➤ When the executed contracts are in violation of the law.

However, if the seller acquires ownership of the property by any legal title before dispossession takes place, the contract is validated.

SALE OF PROPERTY UNDER LITIGATION

Property under litigation may be sold. However, the law requires that the seller of such property tell the buyer of the existence of the litigation. If the seller does not inform the buyer, the seller is liable for damages and losses if the buyer suffers dispossession. If the buyer is informed of the litigation on the property at the time of purchase, and is subsequently deprived of title due to the outcome of the litigation, the seller is not responsible for damages and losses the buyer incurs.

PERSONAL RESTRICTIONS ON CERTAIN BUYERS

The law prohibits certain people from buying property due to their personal legal relationship to the seller. The following fall into this category:

➤ Magistrates, judges, the district attorney, official defenders, lawyers, prosecutors and experts cannot buy the property affected by litigation in which they take part, nor can they be assignees of rights relating to such property. The exceptions to this rule are hereditary property in which they are co-heirs or properties where the property rights belong to them.

➤ Children subject to parental rights *(patria potestad)* can only sell to their parents property which, according to the law, they have acquired by their own labors.

➤ Owners of an undivided property cannot sell their respective share without notifying the other co-owners so that they may exercise the right of first refusal to buy the property.

➤ Experts *(peritos)* and brokers *(corredores)* cannot buy property in the sale of which they have intervened.

➤ The following persons may not purchase the property which they have been entrusted to sell or administrate: guardians and curators; agents; testamentary executors and those appointed in case of intestacy; inspectors appointed by the testator or by the heirs; representatives, administrators and inspectors in case of absence; public employees.

Any sales made in violation of the above provisions, whether made directly or through another person, are void.

OBLIGATIONS OF THE SELLER

The law provides for three basic obligations of the seller:

> To deliver the property sold to the buyer;
> To guarantee the quality of the property;
> To guarantee his title.

The extent of these obligations is determined by the purchase-sales contract. The last obligation refers to the seller's obligation to compensate the buyer in the event the buyer is disturbed in his right to quiet enjoyment of purchased property through foreclosure or similar proceedings.

DELIVERY OF THE PROPERTY

The Civil Code identifies delivery as **real, juridical or virtual delivery.** Real or actual delivery consists of conveying material possession of the property to the buyer, or of assigning the title documents, in cases concerning the sale of trust rights, to the buyer.

Juridical, or "constructive delivery" as it is known in the United States, occurs when, without actual delivery, the law considers the property as having been received by the buyer. This means that the seller has made the property available to the buyer for his use and enjoyment. From the moment that the buyer accepts the property at his disposition, he is regarded as having virtually received it, and if the seller retains it in his possession he has only the rights and obligations of a depository.

The seller is not obligated to deliver the property if the buyer has not paid for it, unless a designated time of payment is provided in the contract. The seller is not obligated to deliver property if, during such time, the buyer becomes insolvent, thus endangering the payment unless the buyer posts a bond to guarantee payment when due. Proof of insolvency must be such that there is imminent danger that the seller will not receive payment.

As a general rule, the property is delivered in the condition it was in at the time the contract was completed. This rule is warranted because the buyer is considered the owner of the property from the moment the contract is completed. For this reason, the two events—contract completion and property delivery—often coincide. In cases where improvements have yet to be completed, the contract should state that such improvements must be made before delivery is taken.

OBLIGATIONS OF THE BUYER

The principle obligation of the buyer is to comply with the terms of the purchase-sales contract, most importantly, the obligation to pay the seller in the place, time and form agreed upon. If no place and time are set in the contract, the law requires that payment be made at the time and place of delivery. In case of doubt as to which party should deliver first, the property and money should both be deposited with a third party.

The law requires the buyer to pay interest between the time of delivery and the time of payment in the following cases:

➢ When the parties so agree.
➢ When the buyer receives benefit from the property in the form of produce or income before he has fulfilled his obligation of payment as stipulated in the purchase-sales contract. The law compensates the seller because the buyer has received benefit from the property without paying for it. In cases of installment sales without stipulation for interest, the buyer is not liable for interest, even if he has received the benefit from the property. The law assumes that the parties took the term of the contract into consideration when setting the price.
➢ When a term for payment is granted after the execution of the purchase-sales contract, the buyer must pay interest from the date the contract was executed unless otherwise agreed.
➢ When the buyer is in default in fixed term payments.

GENERAL PURCHASE-SALES AGREEMENT

A purchase-sales agreement is the contract by which title to real estate is conveyed. If the value of the real estate sale does not exceed the equivalent of three hundred and sixty-five times the minimum salary in effect in the Federal District at the moment of the operation, the parties may execute the sale in a private agreement. In this case, two people must witness the signatures of the seller and the buyer, and then their signatures are ratified before a notary public, a Justice of the Peace, or the Public Registry. Most real estate transactions exceed this limit. The rule is only intended as a general method of procedure because the actual amount is set by the Civil Code of the state where the property is located.

Regardless of the provisions of the state Civil Code, the use of a private agreement is not recommended. The transaction should always be done before a notary. The buyer will need to eventually record and file the transaction anyway, if the transaction is to be binding before third parties. Therefore, it is never worth taking a chance by not recording the transaction no matter what the seller or the real estate agent may say.

If the parties celebrating the contract cannot write, another person with legal capacity may sign in their name at their request, with the exception of the witnesses of the transaction. The fingerprint *(huella digital)* of the party who did not sign is then impressed on the document.

Typically, the notary public who records the purchase-sale agreement also draws up the agreement. If there are any particular provisions that need to be included, an English translation of the agreement should be done. In any event, if the buyer does not speak Spanish it is almost always worth having an English translation done of the agreement. Such translations should be done by a *perito traductor*, or the translation should be reviewed or done by a Mexican attorney.

RESERVE TITLE AND INSTALLMENT SALES CONTRACTS

In a reserve title agreement the seller reserves title or ownership to the property until payment is made in full, however, the buyer is allowed to take possession, and may use and enjoy the property while payments are being made. More often than not reserve title agreements will include installment payments. The advantages of using this type of contract are twofold:

➢ It can be registered at the Public Registry, therefore it is binding before third parties.
➢ The seller may not sell the property as long as the buyer is in compliance with the agreement. This usually means that the buyer is current in his payments to the seller.

In a reserve title agreement the obligations of the parties are subject to a **suspensive condition**, which, in other words, is a condition which prevents a contract form going into operation until it has been fulfilled. This type of condition is the opposite of a **resolutory condition** which is that which, when accomplished, operates the revocation of the obligation, placing matters in the same state as though the obligation had not existed.

In a reserve title agreement this means that the obligations to convey title take effect from the day on which they were contracted, but they cannot be enforced until a certain event takes place. In a reserve title contract, this event is usually the final payment to the seller from the buyer.

During the period of the installment payments, the buyer is considered the conditional owner of the property. As long as the buyer complies with the conditions of the agreement, title is transferred on the date full payment is made, as in any other real estate sale. However, if payment is not made, then the buyer is considered a lessee for the time he held the property.

When the property is sold under a reserve title agreement, the agreement is enforceable against third persons only if it is registered in the Public Registry.

Sales agreements in which the buyer makes **installment payments** (*abonos*) are subject to the following rules:

➢ In sales of real property it may be stipulated that the seller may rescind the contract if the buyer fails to pay one or more installments. However, in order for the rescission to be effective against third parties who have acquired the property from the buyer in spite of the installment sales contract, the contract must be registered in the public registry.
➢ In the sale of personal property which can be positively identified, the same clause for rescission may be stipulated, and it is also only effective against third parties acquiring the property when the contract has been registered in the public registry.
➢ In case of personal property which cannot be positively identified, and therefore cannot be registered, the parties may stipulate that the contract may be rescinded upon failure to pay the sales price, but this clause is not enforceable against third persons acquiring the property in good faith.

If the sale is rescinded, the buyer and seller must make reciprocal restitution of whatever has been received. However, when the seller has delivered the property sold to the buyer, the seller may require the buyer to pay rent for the period of time the buyer had possession of the property. The amount of rent is predetermined either by the parties in the contract or by experts, if the contract does not include such provisions or if the rent stipulated in the contract is excessive. The seller is also entitled to payment for any damages the property has suffered. If the buyer has paid part of the price, he may be entitled to legal interest (9% annually) on the amount paid. Any agreements imposing obligations on the buyer more onerous than those expressed shall be void.

In installment contracts, the buyer may withhold payment if he is disturbed or justly fears disturbance in his possession, until the seller guarantees the buyer's possession. On the other hand, unjustified failure to make payment entitles the seller to sue for the rescission of the installment contract.

IRREVOCABLE REAL ESTATE TRUST AGREEMENT

The irrevocable real estate trust agreement, or *el fideicomiso*, is the most common way to take title to property in the restricted zone. For a review of what constitutes the restricted zone and parties involved in a real estate trust agreement see Chapter Two, and Condominiums in the restricted zone in Chapter Fourteen.

TRUST PERMIT PROCESS

A Mexican bank must obtain a trust permit from the Ministry of Foreign Affairs to set up an irrevocable real estate trust. The buyer and the seller must provide the bank/trustee with the following information:

➤ Name, address and nationality of trustor(s) (This is the person who is selling the property).
➤ Name, address and nationality of beneficiary(ies).
➤ Title documents for the property to be held in trust. Most often producing a recorded and registered deed to the property *(escrituras)* accomplishes this. These documents also include a legal description of the property as well as its location, surface area, and metes and bounds. The bank/trustee may not require that the seller or the buyer produce the deed to the property but rather only a legal description of the property, its location, surface area, and metes and bounds; however, a buyer at this point in the transaction should already have a copy of the *deed.* If not, he

should get one immediately. The trust permit process should not proceed until a current copy of the *deed* is obtained and the buyer is satisfied that there are no problems with the title to the property.

➤ A survey of the property *(croquis)*.

➤ The distance the property is located from the federal zone. If the property adjoins the federal zone, trust permits now require the beneficiary to allow access to the federal zone via any established public access.

➤ A letter of intent indicating the amount that will be invested in improving the property.

With the above information the bank/trustee can apply for a trust permit. The application also includes the following conditions:

➤ The intended use of the property. In this case, the intended use is residential. If the property is not to be used for residential purposes, a buyer should consider using a Mexican corporation to hold the property instead of a real estate trust. See Chapter Two for more information.

➤ The beneficiary agrees to the inclusion of the *clausula calvo*. This means that they will consider themselves as Mexican with regard to the rights they have in the property and not invoke the intervention of their government with regard to those rights.

➤ If the beneficiary assigns the trust rights contained in the real estate trust, the bank/trustee must obtain authorization from the Ministry of Foreign Affairs for the new beneficiaries of the trust.

➤ The beneficiaries must notify the bank/trustee of compliance with the purpose of the trust and any other conditions agreed to in the trust agreement. The bank/trustee informs the Ministry of Foreign Affairs of such compliance.

➤ The bank/trustee must notify the Ministry of Foreign Affairs of any cancellation of a trust within 90 working days.

➤ The beneficiaries and the bank/trustee agree that any violation of the conditions contained in the trust permit may result in the cancellation and liquidation of the trust within 180 days of notification.

➤ If the trust beneficiary instructs the bank/trustee to lease the property held in trust to foreigners or Mexican corporations with foreign participation, prior authorization must be obtained from the Ministry of Foreign Affairs.

> The duration of the trust is that established by the Foreign Investment Law (50 years) and it can be renewed before the term of the contract lapses.
> The Ministry of Foreign Affairs reserves the right to verify compliance with the conditions agreed to in the trust permit.
> The use of the trust permit implies the unconditional acceptance of its terms and conditions.

All banks/trustees require a trust permit fee depending on the duration of the trust. This fee is paid to the government and is periodically adjusted. The fees are paid in new pesos. The table below uses dollars because the dollar amounts usually stay about the same over time. The approximate permit fees to the government are as follows:

> Fifty year permit: $2,500 US
> Twenty year permit: $1,800 US
> Ten year permit: $1,000

It is hard to say which type is best. Many believe that the use of trusts in the restricted zone will be eliminated within ten years.

Another governmental fee that is required is the foreign investment registration. This is a one time fee which is about $300 US.

DRAFTING AND EXECUTION OF THE TRUST AGREEMENT

Once the bank/trustee obtains the trust permit from the Ministry of Foreign Affairs, an irrevocable real estate trust agreement is drawn up, usually by the bank/trustee or the public notary who works with the bank/trustee. The parties are then notified to execute the agreement before the public notary.

The following will be required for the notary to begin the recording process:

1. Title documents for the property to be held in trust.

2. A certificate of no tax liability.

3. A certificate of no encumbrances.

4. Topographic studies of the property.

5. An appraisal of the property.

The seller provides items 1 through 4. A bank appraiser or a public broker completes item 5.

The contractual relations for executing the trust agreement are between the seller of the property as trustor and the bank as trustee. The beneficiary of the trust is represented by the bank/trustee and does not execute the trust agreement. However, the principle rights and obligations of the beneficiary—the person buying the property, are contained in the trust agreement. For this reason it is important that the buyer understand what is contained in the agreement before the bank/trustee and the seller sign it. The buyer is the one who will have to live with the terms and conditions of the trust agreement.

Once the seller signs the trust agreement, title to the property is conveyed to the bank as trustee. Since there is not much in the law concerning trust agreements, most of the buyer's rights and obligations are laid out in the trust agreement. As in any contractual relationship, it is always better to make any changes or adjustments before the contract is executed.

Since a trust agreement is a contract, many of its terms and conditions can be modified. Unfortunately, many do not take the time to find out what the agreement contains. Most of the banks do not offer an English translation of the trust agreement, and the typical buyer believes it is beyond his comprehension and so chooses not to delve into the mysteries of the contract.

A buyer should always get a translation of the contract done or he should have a Mexican attorney review it. Most Mexican contracts, including a trust agreement, are pretty straightforward and easy to understand. A buyer who takes the time to review the contract, is not only able to get the most favorable bank fees but also has a better understanding of what he can and cannot do with the property held in trust.

Most trust agreements are essentially the same, although there may be some slight changes from one bank/trustee to another. The following is intended to apprise a buyer of the most common elements of the trust agreement and the alternatives available.

The bank that is acting as trustee should be able to provide a copy of the trust permit and a sample trust agreement for review. Some banks are starting to make sample English versions available but more often there is only a Spanish copy. A Mexican attorney working with a buyer may be able to have an English translation done for a minimal fee, or even include the translation in the legal fee for setting up the trust.

It is important to obtain copies of both the trust permit and the trust agreement itself, since these two documents include almost all of the buyer's rights and obligations. The final recorded version of the trust agreement will probably not look the same as the copies obtained from the bank/trustee but it will contain the same information. The text of the trust permit is copied to the final recorded trust agreement, and the actual clauses of the agreement are the same as what the bank/trustee provided.

SPECIAL CONSIDERATIONS FOR THE TRUST AGREEMENT

The information contained in the trust permit cannot be changed. It should be similar to the outline above. The trust agreement itself, as with any contract, may be modified. The part of the agreement that reads *"CLAUSULAS"* is where the clauses of the contract start. If there are other sections before this section, this is not a cause for concern; those sections are for filing purposes and declarations regarding background information on the property.

OBJECT, CONSIDERATION AND WARRANTIES

Usually, the first few clauses deal with the purpose of the trust, the consideration, or the amount paid for the property, and warranties against hidden defects. These clauses should state that the trust is irrevocable and that the real estate held in trust is conveyed without any reservation or limitation.

The trustor/seller is also responsible by law for any hidden defects of title relative to the real estate in trust, and binds himself to pay any indebtedness affecting the real estate in trust previous to the date of the trust agreement.

The consideration *(contraprestación)* should be the full amount paid for the property. There have been many transactions recorded with a sales price lower than what was actually paid, supposedly to save on tax payments. This is tax evasion and should not be accepted for any reason. In such cases, the buyer is considered a party to defrauding the Mexican tax authorities.

It is foolish to run such a risk considering that the benefit to the buyer is very small since the buyer only pays a 2% acquisition tax. The buyer usually ends up paying these taxes anyway when he sells the property due to the low base price used when determining the capital gain created by the sale of the property. If it appears that the property was bought for 5, when it was actually 10, when it is sold for 15 the taxable gain is 10. That translates into 50% more taxes. It is not in the interest of the buyer to use a lower sales price. A buyer only stands to lose in this situation.

DESIGNATION OF BENEFICIARY AND SUBSTITUTE BENEFICIARY

Usually the above clauses are followed by a clause to designate the trust's beneficiaries and substitute beneficiaries. Some banks will include this information in one of the first few clauses instead of including it in a clause of its own.

It is important to clearly understand the differences between the two beneficiaries and how they are used in the trust agreement.

The beneficiary of the trust is the person who has the right to use and enjoy the property held in trust and to give instructions to the bank/trustee with regard to the property. There may be one or more beneficiaries. When there is more than one, all of them are treated as co-owners and the legal provisions regarding co-ownership regulate their rights and obligations to the property. For more information on co-ownership see Chapter Thirteen.

Substitute beneficiaries, on the other hand, are not co-owners, at least not immediately. A substitute beneficiary is only intended to take the place of the actual beneficiary upon the beneficiary's death. A substitute beneficiary does not have any rights to the property held in trust until he becomes an actual trust beneficiary due to the death of the beneficiary.

The reason for having substitute beneficiaries is to avoid having to go through probate to have the trust rights assigned to the decedent's heirs. By including a substitute beneficiary, there is no question as to who is the heir to the trust rights.

When there is more than one beneficiary it is essential that the trust agreement clearly indicate that each substitute beneficiary takes the place of the beneficiary for which he was designated upon the death of such beneficiary. Moreover, the agreement should also indicate that the other beneficiaries agree to such substitution and renounce any rights they may have as co-owners of the trust rights. This is to avoid any confusion as to who has the right to the decedent's rights in the trust upon his death.

Many of the trust agreements do not include this distinction and therefore leave open the possibility that one of the other co-owners has the right to the decedent's interests in the trust instead of the substitute beneficiary. This is especially a problem when a spouse is a co-beneficiary in the trust and their children are named as substitute beneficiaries.

Although there are many methods to determine who has the right to the decedent's interest in the trust, the best one is to make the intentions clear from the beginning. If there is any doubt, the final answer is determined by a judge; which then makes the whole point of designating a substitute beneficiary meaningless.

PURPOSES OF THE TRUST

Every trust agreement includes a clause that lists the purposes of the trust. The following list is a typical example of what is included in this type of clause:

➢ The stipulation that the bank/trustee holds title to the property of the real estate in trust.
➢ The specification that the beneficiaries have the rights to use and exercise their rights in the property as it best suits their interests, always subject to the provisions of all applicable laws.
➢ The provision that the bank/trustee can lease the real estate in trust for periods not longer than 10 years. In this case, the beneficiary shall receive the income that such lease creates.
➢ The specification that the bank/trustee transfers the ownership of the real estate held in trust to the beneficiaries themselves or to any individual or corporation that has the power to acquire the real estate according to the law. In all cases, the proceeds from the real estate should transfer to the beneficiaries or their assigns.
➢ The stipulation that, upon beneficiary's request, the bank/trustee shall grant a mortgage security in the real estate in trust to secure the obligations contracted by the beneficiary; in the title granting the security, it should be noted that the bank/trustee does not contract any payment obligation.

➤ The provision that, upon termination of the trust, the bank/trustee transfers the real estate ownership to the individual or legal entity legally empowered to acquire it, delivering to the beneficiaries the proceeds of the real estate transfers.

It should be noted that leasing and mortgaging the property held in trust is possible. The limit of ten years for leases is set by law and is applicable to residential properties.

RIGHT TO MAKE IMPROVEMENTS

The trust agreement should also contain a clause that allows the beneficiary to make improvements on the property. This includes any kind of construction permitted by law.

The agreement normally includes provisions that limit the liabilities related to the improvements to the beneficiary. To do this, provisions similar to the following are included as obligations of the beneficiary:

➤ Negotiate on behalf of the bank/trustee the licenses, permits, appraisals, etc., required, provided that the beneficiary shall assume all liability for possible violations of legislation concerning construction, as well as any other responsibility derived from work, construction or improvements to the existing property.
➤ Give termination notice and any other pertinent information, also on behalf of the bank/trustee.
➤ Notify the bank/trustee periodically regarding improvements made so that the bank/trustee may increase the value of the property held in trust and make the necessary accounting entries.

RIGHTS OF THE BENEFICIARY

The specific rights of the beneficiary are usually contained in a clause and identified as such. However, sometimes these rights are sprinkled throughout the agreement. Either way, as long as they are included in the agreement the effect is the same. The following are the most essential rights and should be included in every trust agreement:

➤ **Right to modify or amend the trust agreement** in whole or in part at any time. Any change to the trust agreement must be with the prior written consent of the bank/trustee and be recorded before a public notary. Such changes must not infringe upon provisions of the Foreign Investment Law or any other applicable law.

➤ **Right to assign or encumber the beneficial trust rights** in any manner. In order that the bank/trustee recognize any assignment or encumbrance of the trust rights, the following shall be required:

1. A notarial notification to the bank/trustee.

2. In the event the beneficiary assigns his rights, such assignment shall be made by a notary public and the bank/trustee shall appear before him in order to accept the assignment.

3. Fulfillment of the provisions set forth in the trust agreement.

➤ **Right to mortgage on the real estate in trust.** Upon the beneficiary's request, the bank/trustee must proceed to grant a mortgage on the real estate in trust in order to secure the obligations contracted by said beneficiary. Within the instrument establishing the security interest, it should be noted that the bank/trustee is not obligated in any manner and simply agrees, upon the beneficiary's request, to encumber the property held in trust.

TAXES AND OTHER OBLIGATIONS

Taxes or any other obligations derived from the real estate held in trust are the responsibility of the beneficiary. As such, the trust agreement will include provisions that require the beneficiary to prove to the bank/trustee 's satisfaction that he has fulfilled all outstanding obligations before assignment or termination of the trust agreement.

The bank/trustee is not obliged to defend the ownership of the property in trust. However, the trust agreement should state that upon receipt of any notice, judicial complaint, or any demand concerning the real estate in trust, the bank/trustee must promptly notify the beneficiary or the attorney designated for that purpose. This is so the defense of the ownership may be assumed by the beneficiary through his lawyers. It is best if this notification is made in writing and allows enough time for the beneficiary to act accordingly.

If the beneficiary is difficult to reach, it is advisable that a Mexican attorney be appointed to receive such notifications. The attorney should be granted a power of attorney for lawsuits and recovery so that he is able to take immediate action if necessary. It is also prudent to include provisions in the trust agreement that indicate that the bank/trustee shall grant powers for administrative acts and/or for process and collections in favor of the person named by the beneficiary.

The beneficiary or his attorney should attend to such notifications quickly because normally the notification terminates any liability of the bank/trustee to act on behalf of the beneficiary. In case of litigation time may be very important and deadlines can be missed if action is not taken immediately.

DURATION OF THE TRUST

The law gives the following causes for the termination of a trust:

The trust is extinguished:

1. By the fulfillment of the purpose for which it was constituted.

2. By such fulfillment being impossible.

3. By the impossibility of fulfilling the suspensive condition on which the trust depends, or for not having used the trust within the term specified for its establishment or, in its default, within a term of twenty years following its establishment. Strictly speaking, in this case the trust is not extinguished but rather it never comes into existence.

4. By having fulfilled the resolutory condition to which the trust had been subject to.

5. By an express agreement between the trustor and the beneficiary of the trust. This would not be applicable in most real estate trusts in the restricted zone because those trusts are irrevocable.

6. By revocation made by trustor, when he has expressly reserved such right at the time the trust was created.

7. When the trust is constituted in favor of the fiduciary.

The trust may be for a term of up to 50 years and may expire for any of the reasons listed above as long as they are consistent with the provisions of the trust agreement. Therefore it is important that the trust agreement clearly indicate that the trustor/seller does not reserve the right to revoke the trust as provided for in # 6 above. In other words, all real estate trusts in the restricted zone should always be irrevocable and this should be clear indicated in the agreement.

The agreement should state that upon termination of the established term, the bank/trustee shall proceed, as instructed by the beneficiary, to sell the real estate to the individual or corporation having legal capacity to acquire the property. The beneficiary or his assigns shall receive the proceeds of such sale. If the beneficiary does not instruct the bank/trustee concerning the disposition of the property in trust, when the established term expires, the bank/trustee shall order a real estate appraisal with an authorized credit institution. The bank/trustee shall then proceed to sell the real estate through a public broker, delivering its proceeds to the beneficiary or its assign.

A beneficiary should read the trust agreement carefully. Very often the bank/trustee will include a 5% commission on the sale of the property upon the termination of the trust's term if the beneficiary has not given any other instructions.

BANK/TRUSTEE FEES

One of the most important sections in the trust agreement is that which deals with the various fees the bank/trustee charges for maintaining the trust. The fees charged by banks can differ greatly--a buyer should take the time to find out what the bank/trustee is charging and compare it to other banks.

The following is a guideline for determining the different concepts and approximate values to be applied to each:

➢ Review and acceptance of trust payable upon the signing of the trust agreement: $350 to $750 US
➢ Annual administration: 0.20 to 1% of the value of the property held in trust per annum, or a minimum of $250 to $3,300 US payable annually. One should expect to pay 1% for properties valued at $25,000 US and below. The rate of .20% is reserved for properties valued at $1,000,000 and above. The fee is reduced at a rate of 0.05% for each $35,000 increase in the value of the property until 0.45% and $350,000 is reached. From this point to one million dollars the rate is reduced 0.05% for each $170,000 increase in the value of the property.
➢ Execution of private titles and contracts different from the trust agreement and of acts not provided for in the trust agreement, $250 to $500 US for each execution.
➢ Up to 3% moratory interest per month, if trust fees are not paid on time and while these remain unpaid.

> Up to 1% of the recorded value of the property or of the sales price, which ever is higher, for the assignment of trust rights. Sometimes this fee is waived; it doesn't hurt to ask!

Most of the banks are beginning to adjust the property values of trusts on a yearly basis. However, the bank/trustee may make these adjustments sooner, especially if the property is being sold. At any rate, the bank trust fees normally are due and payable once a year.

The bank/trustee will normally include provisions in the trust agreement, which guarantee the payment of their fees. The provision usually specifies that the bank discontinue performance of any administrative procedure, or any partial or whole cancellation of this trust, while there is any fee indebtedness or any other fee in favor of the bank/trustee. All fees, together with the corresponding value added taxes, must be paid by the beneficiary before any such actions can take place.

REPORTING REQUIREMENTS TO BANK/TRUSTEE

The amounts charged by the bank are calculated using the bank appraised value of the property, therefore, a beneficiary must know what reporting obligations he has with regard to improvements. Most trust agreements require that the beneficiary notify the bank/trustee of improvements made to the property within 15 days. Some banks will also require notification if any bank appraisal is done on the property, also within the 15-day limit.

ASSIGNMENT OF RIGHTS AGREEMENT

This type of agreement (*cesion de derechos*) is used when the property being purchased is already held in trust. It is an assignment of rights because the buyer is actually purchasing the beneficial rights the seller has in the real estate trust which holds title to the property.

In order for the assignment to be legal it must be carried out before a public notary or a public broker and it must abide by the terms and conditions of the trust agreement. The bank/trustee also needs to notify the Ministry of Foreign Affairs so that the assignment may be authorized and the new beneficiary can agree to the calvo clause.

First, when purchasing a property that is held in trust, the buyer should ask the seller for a copy of the seller's trust agreement. Since the buyer is purchasing the rights contained in this agreement he should review it to see if it meets the standards laid out above in the previous sections on trust agreements. If there are changes to be made this is the time to request them.

The bank/trustee fees should be reasonable. In some cases, the fees were set years ago and are very reasonable. Trusts established in the late 1980's, on the other hand, sometimes set fees much higher because of the government bank monopoly, which existed throughout that decade. A buyer will want to check around to get an idea of what the current fees are then ask to have his adjusted accordingly.

Both the beneficiary and the substitute beneficiary need to be changed. As mentioned earlier, the substitute beneficiary is important and should not be left out. If the substitute beneficiary is left blank there will be an additional fee to add one later.

The parties to the assignment of rights contract are either the seller/beneficiary and the buyer or the bank/trustee and the buyer. Under no circumstances should the buyer accept an assignment of trust rights without the consent of the bank/trustee.

Over the years there have been many assignment contracts executed without the knowledge or consent of the bank/trustee, even some that have been recorded and filed with the Public Registry. But, it should always be remembered that it is the buyer who has to deal with the bank in the future. Once the seller is paid he may disappear. Therefore it is in the buyer's interests to make sure that the bank/trustee is fully aware of and consents to the assignment of trust rights.

There are many arguments regarding the need to inform the bank concerning the assignment of trust rights. Some believe it is not necessary since the assignment concerns personal property rights, rather than real property rights, therefore, the transaction may be executed in a private agreement. These arguments must not persuade a prospective buyer. The main concern is to comply with the conditions set forth in the trust permit and the trust agreement. More importantly, a buyer does not want to fight with the bank/trustee to have his rights recognized nor does he want to discover after the transaction that the seller still owes bank trust fees!

To avoid all of these situations, the buyer must ensure the assignment of rights agreement includes the consent of the bank/trustee and authorization from the Ministry of Foreign Affairs. By doing so he can rest assured that he will be registered as the new beneficiary of the trust and that all trust fees are current.

If the seller has chosen to the have the bank/trustee represent him in the assignment, the bank's trust representative will execute the contract with the buyer before a public notary or a public broker. If the seller is executing the assignment agreement, consent from the bank/trustee is granted through a letter of instruction sent to the notary or the public broker.

The contents of the assignment should be similar to the trust agreement. After all, all of the rights the buyer is purchasing are contained in that agreement--the assignment only recognizes the transfer.

If the trust agreement needs to be changed this would be the time to address such concerns with the bank/trustee. The should keep in mind that he has the right to change the bank/trustee if the conditions of the agreement do not meet his satisfaction. Since there are transaction fees that must be paid to carry out the assignment, if a change of bank/trustee is called for this would be the best time to do so. The buyer could save money in extra fees by having several changes made at the same time.

STEP SEVEN: CLOSING AND TITLE TRANSFER

"Closing" is defined as: "1. The act of transferring ownership of a property form seller to buyer in accordance with a sales contract. 2. The time when a closing takes place." In a Mexican real estate transaction, closing takes place at the moment the transaction is recorded before a public notary or public broker. However, although the sales contract is binding for the buyer and the seller, it is not **perfected** until it is filed with the public registry. *Black's Law Dictionary* defines **perfect instrument**: "An instrument is said to become perfect or perfected when recorded (or registered) or filed for record, because it then becomes good as to all the world."

The public notary files the sales contract, trust agreement, etc. with the public registry shortly after he has recorded it. The buyer will receive a certified copy of the contract just as soon as it has been filed.

Proof of filing is normally on one of the last pages of the recorded contract in the form of a stamp giving the time and date it was filed.

The **closing date**, or the date on which the seller delivers the deed and the buyer pays for the property, is the date the contract is recorded by the notary. As far as the buyer and seller are concerned, the transaction is closed at the moment the contract is executed before the notary, so the sales price is paid at this time. The notarized contract is a public instrument and as such cannot be unilaterally reversed by any of the parties. This is why most transactions are closed at this stage.

In transactions involving trust agreements the bank/trustee usually acts on behalf of the buyer when it comes to closing. For this reason, the buyer's signature is not required and he will not necessarily appear before a public notary. It is best not to release any funds until it is certain that the seller has actually executed the sales contract. Often the seller will execute the agreement in the presence of the notary before the bank does. This is not a problem as long as the bank also executes within the term set by the notary. The buyer should arrange with the bank/trustee and/or the notary to be notified once the seller executes the sale contract. The buyer then can pay the purchase price knowing that the seller cannot back out of the transaction.

TAXES, FEES, AND CLOSING COSTS

There are two taxes that are applied to real estate transactions:

1. The income tax generated from the sale of the property; and,

2. The property acquisition tax.

When the title documents are executed with a public notary, all taxes arising from the transaction must be paid, as well as the notary fees. As a general rule, the seller pays the capital gains tax and the buyer pays the acquisition tax. Although it is possible to negotiate that the seller pay half of any other fee or expense, such as notary fees and the like, if it is a seller's market, the seller inevitably refuses to pay anything more than the capital gains tax.

Closing costs vary widely and are determined by the type of transaction being carried out. The following table is helpful in determining the approximate amount in each case and who is responsible for paying it.

ALL REAL ESTATE TRANSACTIONS:

Concept	Amount	Who Pays
Certificates of no encumbrances and no tax lien	$200 - $300	Negotiable
Notary fees	$750 - $1200	50/50
Filing fee - Public Registry	$100 to $300	Buyer
Appraisal fee	$300 to $500	Negotiable
Acquisition tax	2% of sales price	Buyer
Income tax	34% of the gain or 20% of sales price	Seller
Attorney's fees	Negotiable	Each pays his own attorney

ADDITIONAL FEES FOR REAL ESTATE TRUSTS

CONCEPT	AMOUNT	WHO PAYS
Bank/Trustee acceptance fee	$350 to $750 flat fee or same as annual fee	Buyer
Bank/Trustee annual fee	1% to 0.20% per annum of the value of the property held in trust, or a minimum of $250 - $3,300	Buyer
Trust permit fee	50 years – approx. $600.00	Buyer
Trust assignment	Term last – approx. $300.00	Buyer
Foreign investment registration	$300 - $400	Buyer

STEP EIGHT: FEDERAL CONCESSIONS

THE FEDERAL ZONE

The most common concession is the federal zone concession. A buyer need only concern himself with this concession if purchasing beachfront property. For more information on the federal zone see Chapter Three. A federal concession can only be applied for once the applicant acquires trust rights to the property adjoining the federal zone.

A federal zone concession costs relatively little so acquiring one is advisable once a buyer has completed the steps in the preceding sections. It is not a requirement. The advantage in having the federal zone concession is that it allows the concessionaire to build or make improvements in the federal zone and, maybe more importantly, it eliminates the possibility of someone else getting the concession for that area. It is unlikely that a concession will be granted to someone other than the owners of the property adjoining the federal zone, but it is possible.

If a buyer purchases property already held in trust and the beneficiary has the federal zone concession, the buyer needs to contact SEDESOL to have the concession put in his name. The assignment of concession rights must be approved by SEDESOL in order to be valid. A buyer cannot assume that because he purchases beachfront property he is automatically entitled to the concession held by the former trust beneficiary.

All applications involving foreigners are subject to special procedures and the opinion of the General Direction of the Federal Real Estate (*Dirección General del Patrimonio Inmobiliario Federal*). An application for a federal zone concession is submitted before the local office of the Secretary of Social Development (*Secretaria de desarrollo social*) otherwise known as SEDESOL.

Some or all of the following information is submitted depending on the property and the kind and location of improvements.

APPLICATION

The application is presented in triplicate, in writing, signed by the applicant or by his legal representative, and must contain the following:

1. Applicant's name. In the case of a corporation or legal entity, the trade name or corporate name.

2. Domicile and address at which to receive notifications.

3. Exact location of the area being applied for, indicating state, municipality, colony, town, housing subdivision and name of the place.

4. Indication of the total surface needed for the concession.

5. Description of the area for concession, according to its legal nature as follows: a) Federal Maritime Terrestrial Zone; b) Lands Gained From the Sea; c) Lands Gained From Any Other Maritime Water Tanks.

6. Detailed description of the metes and bounds of the total surface.

7. Description of the use, exploitation and/or improvement of the federal area.

8. For the exploitation of materials, a description of its use and precedence, as well as its characteristics, extraction volume and commercial value (where the material is obtained from, its characteristics, quantity of extraction, calculate the volume of stratum and existing deposits that are intended for the extraction and the commercial value consistent with the local current markets).

9. Applicant's legal capacity with regard to the property adjacent to the federal zone applied for, and a determination of the relationship as follows: Owner; *Ejidatario*; Joint Tenant; Possessor; Usufructuary; Tenant; Others.

10. Explanation that the use claimed for the federal area is congruent with the corresponding Urban Development Plans authorized for that zone. (Federal, State and/or Municipality).

11. Indication of any installations or improvements in the area where applicant is applying for concession; if so, an indication of their characteristics and estimated value.

12. Term requested for the concession.

13. Amount of the total investment.

14. If the adjacent property is intended to be integrated with the federal zone, the application should contain an indication of the following: a) The use, exploitation or improvements of both; b) The type of work/construction projected to be done in both. c) The amount to be invested in both.

15. Description of the installations to be carried out in the federal zone, indicating the different stages to be taken for the execution of the project.

16. Depending upon the magnitude of projects and investments to be executed, SEDESOL will require the applicant to amplify its application, explain, or add more elements to it, to better understand, according to the policy of this agency.

17. For the investments referred to above, or depending on the use or exploitation of the federal land applied for in the concession, the applicant should determine if it causes a negative ecological impact in that area.

18. Declaration stating whether the applicant has had other concessions in the federal maritime terrestrial zone or in lands gained from the sea, and, as the case may be, providing all necessary information to identify such concessions.

The following documents should also be presented in triplicate, together with the concession application:

➤ **To accredit applicant's legal status: a) Individuals:** certified copy of applicant's birth certificate, and, if applicable, a naturalization letter. b) **Legal entity or Corporation:** certified copy of the Articles of Incorporation, if applicable, power of attorney granted to the applicant stating that he has legal capacity to act as a legal representative of said corporation. c) Documents stating legal and financial status of the corporation.

➤ **To accredit applicant's legal status in regard to the adjoining property**: a) Certified copy of the property deed, trust, or like legal document. b) Document stating applicant's legal capacity in relation to the property abutting the federal zone (Tenant, Possessor, Usufructuary, etc.).

> **Technical Requirements**: a) A plot map giving graphical statistics of the delimitation of the federal maritime terrestrial zone or, in its case, delimitation of the lands gained from the sea, which should be approved by SEDESOL and by the federal zone agency that corresponds to the property. b) A survey map of the projects, legally approved by the corresponding authorities, as well as a description of said projects. c) A programmed schedule of the investments and projects execution. d) Eight photographs of the area the applicant is applying for, taken from the ocean to the land, from the most important spots and from the different cardinal points if possible.

> **Additional Documentation**: a) A favorable ecological impact report issued from SEDESOL if applicable. b) Appraisal for revenues on the existing construction, said appraisal shall be issued by the National Real Estate Appraisal Commission. c) Any other technical, administrative and legal documents that the Secretariat may require to fulfill this application.

EXTENSION OF APPLICATIONS

Any concessionaire, who wishes to extend his concession, should apply for an extension at least 30 natural days before the concession's expiration date. If he doesn't comply, the rights he holds will expire.

The Extension Application should contain the following:

> File number and Concession date.
> All the requirements mentioned in number 1, 2, 3 and 12 of the Application section above.
> Verification or rectification, as the case may be, the use, exploitation or improvements made regarding the public property in question, as well as the total surface area requested.
> Any improvements or installation affected by the concession, according to the original concession, should be listed with a description and estimated value. This is necessary because upon the termination of the concession such improvements will become property of the Federal Government.
> An express statement that the concessionaire agrees to cover the fees related to the use, enjoyment and exploitation of the federal zone as well as any other improvements.
> If there is a project for a new construction, as well as any additions, modifications, or demolition, the above information

should be submitted in order to obtain an authorization from SEDESOL.

➤ The amount to be invested and schedule of execution.

➤ Appraisal for revenues on the existing construction issued by the National Real Estate Appraisal Commission (*Commisión de Avalúos de Bienes Nacionales*).

CHAPTER 7

TRANSACTIONS TO AVOID

THIS CHAPTER IDENTIFIES CERTAIN TYPES OF TRANSACTIONS THAT SHOULD BE
AVOIDED SUCH AS THE USE OF AN IRREVOCABLE POWER OF ATTORNEY, STRAW MEN
OR PRESTANOMBRES AND THE POSSIBLE CONSEQUENCES WHEN THEY ARE USED.

IRREVOCABLE POWER OF ATTORNEY

The irrevocable power of attorney is commonly misused and misunderstood in real estate transactions in Mexico. This is often due to erroneous interpretations of the law, but mostly, it results from ignorance and the desire to find the "easy way" to get around the law.

First, one thing is indisputable: to avoid problems with the law, one should not try to get around the law. This sounds obvious to most, but it is not so obvious to others. There are many people whose first inclination, while attempting to carry out a real estate transaction in Mexico, is to immediately look for some way around the use of a real estate trust. There is no way.

Before examining how irrevocable powers of attorney are used in Mexican real estate transactions, it is helpful to define what exactly a power of attorney is under Mexican Law.

The Spanish translation of "power of attorney" is *"poder notarial," "carta poder,"* or simply *"poder."* When referring to a *poder* one must distinguish between the document and the faculties that are granted by the document.

In the first case a *poder* is the document by which a person legally proves that he may represent another person to carry out a legal transaction. This document may take two forms: the *carta poder* or the *poder notarial.*

The *carta poder,* which may also be translated as a "letter of proxy" has very limited usage. Although it is still used for some administrative procedures and for representation in corporations for shareholder's meetings, it has fallen out of use due to limitations imposed by the Civil Code. The Civil Code limits the use of a *carta poder,* signed before two witnesses, to transactions which are more than $200 but less than $5,000 unless otherwise expressly provided for by another law.

The *poder notarial* is the most common form of a power of attorney in Mexico, and the only form that may be used for real estate transactions. As the name implies, this type of power of attorney must be executed before a public notary. Any public notary can draft a power of attorney for you. Usually the public notary will only provide a power of attorney in Spanish, so someone who does not understand Spanish must have a translation done or have an attorney draft the document in English and Spanish.

The faculties, or powers, granted by the grantor of the power of attorney may be general (*poder general*) or special (*poder especial*) in nature. General powers of attorneys are granted when the grantor wishes to give the attorney-in-fact (the person who is granted the power of attorney) the power to represent him in an undetermined number of cases, regardless of the type of power of attorney granted. On the other hand, if the grantor wishes to restrict the attorney-in-fact's ability to represent him to a specific number of cases or transactions, then a special power of attorney is granted.

The Civil Code provides for three types of general powers of attorney:

1. General power of attorney for lawsuits and collections (*poder general de pleitos y cobranzas*). Here the attorney-in-fact may represent the grantor in any case dealing with a lawsuit or the collection of a debt.

2. General power of attorney to administrate property (*poder general para administrar bienes*). This power of attorney allows the attorney-in-fact to administrate or supervise matters relating to the property of the grantor, without having the power to sell, transfer, or dispose of the property.

3. General power of attorney for acts of ownership or domain (*poder general para ejercer actos de dominio*). This type of power of attorney is the most important and should only be granted under very special circumstances. In this case the attorney-in-fact has all the powers which would normally be reserved exclusively to the grantor, including the power to sell, transfer, or dispose of property, without any limitations whatsoever.

The three types of general powers of attorney are arranged hierarchically. The attorney-in-fact having a general power of attorney for acts of ownership would also have all the powers contemplated by the other two types of powers of attorney. The powers to administrate property would also include powers for lawsuits and collections.

The law also provides for what is known as a "limited general power of attorney" (*poder general limitado*). The intention here is to possibly limit a general power of attorney to a specific type of business. For example, a property owner may want to grant a power of attorney for the administration of property to be exercised only in relation to those cases that involve the owner's house in Cabo San Lucas.

The power of attorney is general because the attorney-in-fact's powers are not limited to a specific number of cases or transactions. It is limited because the attorney-in-fact's powers are limited to his ability to represent the owner in matters concerning the property in Cabo San Lucas only, and not, for instance, the property in San Jose.

If a general power of attorney is granted without any specific limitation included in the document, it is understood that the attorney-in-fact may represent the grantor in relation to any matter which falls under the power granted. In other words, using the example above, if the property owner grants a general power of attorney for acts of ownership to empower an attorney-in-fact to sell the house in Cabo San Lucas, he could also sell the house in San Jose regardless of the owner's intentions. Granted, the attorney-in-fact is breaking the law because he is acting without the owner's consent. Nevertheless, he has the legal capacity to execute the sale.

Typically, a power of attorney is used in real estate transactions as a means of gaining control over a property while not transferring title. The seller receives payment and grants the buyer a power of attorney to dispose of the property. These transactions are often carried out in the restricted zone because the foreign buyer does not want to set up a trust, or the buyer does not want to pay taxes. Since the buyer has legal control of the property, as explained above, he believes there is no danger of loosing that control.

These types of transactions are illegal as well as dangerous. By giving the buyer control over the property both parties have conspired to break the law. There is no reason to participate in this kind of transaction. If a property buyer decides to break the law and is caught, he will very likely loose the property and face criminal charges. If he is not caught, the buyer still runs the risk of loosing the property. If the seller dies, the power of attorney is extinguished upon his death.

Straw Men "*Prestanombres*"

A straw man, or *"prestanombre"* in Spanish, is defined as "A person who is set up as a cover or a front for a questionable enterprise." Over the years, the use of *prestanombres* is becoming more common in the restricted zone as a substitute to transferring title. A prospective buyer must never try to use someone else's name to take title to a property regardless of the circumstances. Such transactions usually include the use of a power of attorney, or some other guarantee that the buyer can control title transfer in the future. These transactions are dangerous and totally illegal. A buyer must never be fooled into believing that "no will ever know." Those who buy property illegally may learn a painful and expensive lesson.

Another form of *prestanombres*, which is just as dangerous and illegal, is the use of a Mexican corporation, as a front for a foreigner, to take title of property in the restricted zone in violation of the law. In these cases, the corporate by-laws of the Mexican corporation include a clause that prohibits foreign investors from holding shares in the corporation. This allows the Mexican corporation to take title to property in the restricted zone just as a Mexican individual can. Typically, the foreigner then arranges some kind of control over the shares to supposedly protect his interests in the property held by the corporation.

Since Mexican Law does not allow corporations to issue bearer shares, all shares must be issued in the name of a specific individual. Therefore, there is no real security in having physical possession of the stock certificates without being registered in the share registry of the corporation. The foreigner has no corporate power and, therefore, shares he holds can be canceled and new ones issued to the shareholder registered in the corporation's share registry.

SANCTIONS

The penalty for noncompliance or violations of the real estate provisions of the Foreign Investment Law is a fine of up to the amount of the transaction.

The law states:

> In case of contrivance of acts with the intention of **permitting the possession or disposal of real property in the restricted zone to foreign individuals** or legal persons or to Mexican companies without a foreigners exclusion clause, in contravention to that which is provided by the Second and Third Titles of this law, the offender shall be penalized by a fine up to the amount of the transaction...

CHAPTER 8

THE MEXICAN LEGAL SYSTEM

THIS CHAPTER IS INTENDED TO SERVE AS A GENERAL REFERENCE ON MEXICAN LAW
CONCERNING REAL ESTATE. THIS REFERENCE INFORMATION MAY BE HELPFUL IN
UNDERSTANDING THE RIGHTS AND RESPONSIBILITIES OF A FOREIGNER HOLDING
REAL ESTATE IN MEXICO.

INTRODUCTION

Mexico has a "civil law" legal system, whereas the United States has a "common law" legal system. In a civil law system, the application of the law is based on a codification of the laws and legal principles. These codes reflect very general divisions in law that have developed over the years. Most of Mexico's civil law comes from the French Civil Code, known as the Napoleonic code.

Case law, which is the basis of the common law system, is not used in a civil law system. Although case law is relevant in Mexico, it is not used in the same way as it is in the United States. The differences between the two systems are diminishing, especially since the United States is using a similar system in the form of uniform codes.

The Mexican constitution divides federal power into three branches: legislative, executive, and judicial. The executive branch is more powerful than the other two branches, and has some legislative powers, such as issuing regulations.

Mexico is a republic and has a federal system. The country comprises 31 states, each of which independently regulates its citizens by State Constitution, Civil Codes, Code of Civil Procedures, Penal Code, and Penal Procedures Code. Although some States have made changes to these laws, for the most part they closely follow their federal counterparts that apply to the Federal District.

CIVIL LAW

In the Mexican legal system, civil law regulates the civil relations between individuals, their marital status, the organization of the family, legal capacity, the status of personal and real property, and civil contracts. It is important to understand the difference between civil law and other branches of the law, such as business law, labor law, etc. Civil law can be divided into five categories: persons, goods and property, successions and inheritance, obligations, and contracts.

The Civil Code *(Código Civil)* in Mexico is the backbone of the entire legal system. Most other branches of the law have some link with the civil code in one way or another. A foreigner in Mexico is subject to the provisions of the Civil Code. It is in the best interests of a foreigner wishing to purchase property in Mexico to be aware of the rules that apply to him so it is wise to have a basic knowledge of the general principles contained in the Civil Code.

BASIC LEGAL PRINCIPLES

Men and women are equal in the eyes of the law. This provision is recognized both in the civil code as well as in the Mexican Constitution.

No law or any other governmental order may be applied retroactively if it is damaging or an impairment to someone. In other words, a law cannot be passed and then applied to situations or facts that took place before the law was passed if by doing so someone is negatively affected. If the law is intended to cure or remedy an otherwise unjust situation, without harming anyone, it can be retroactive.

The force of the law does not depend on the will of those to whom it is to be applied. This basic principle may be reduced to a statement: a person is subject to the provisions of the law. Only certain individual rights may be renounced and only when such renunciation is precisely in relation to a specific right, and it does not directly affect the public policy or harm others.

Some provisions of the law are seen as alternatives rather than obligations and are only to the benefit of an individual or group of individuals. These legal provisions are known to be of private interest. On the other hand, when a provision of the law is intended to be to the benefit of everyone or to society as a whole, such provisions are considered to be in the public policy.

A foreigner in Mexico is generally free to do whatever he likes as long as he does not violate the law or public interests. Any acts to the contrary are considered illegal, or, in the case of public interests, null and void. The importance of this provision should not be over looked. Many laws in Mexico state that they are in the public interest, and thus none of their provisions may be renounced.

Ignorance of the law is not an excuse for disobeying it. Disuse or custom is no excuse either: if the law is still on the books, it is still enforceable. Most of the other branches of the law have some link with the civil code. For this reason it is good to have a basic knowledge of the general principles contained in the Civil Code.

The scope of application of Mexican Law is limited to anyone within Mexican territory as well as any events that occur within Mexican territory. The only exceptions to this rule are cases that are subject to foreign law by treaties with Mexico, or cases that expressly stipulate that foreign law would apply.

The Civil Code establishes the following rules for the determination of the applicable law:

➤ All legal acts validly originating in any Mexican state or in any foreign country in accordance with their law shall be recognized in Mexico.
➤ The laws applicable to their domicile determine the status and legal capacity of individuals.
➤ The establishment, regulation, and extinction of real property rights, as well as leasing contracts and temporary use agreements related to real property are regulated by the law applicable in the place in which they are located, even when the person who holds title to the property is a foreigner.
➤ The formalities required for legal acts are regulated by the applicable law of the place where they were executed, with the exception of those acts that fall under federal law. Generally, the

Civil Code from each state mostly regulates civil matters; while federal law regulates business matters.

➢ With the exception of the above, the consequences of legal acts and contracts are regulated by the law of the place where they are executed, unless the parties validly designate the application of another law.

Article 17 of the Civil Code states that when someone acquires excessive profit by taking advantage of the ignorance, inexperience, or distressed state of another person, the disadvantaged person has the right to demand that the contract in question be declared null and void. Or, he can demand that there be an equitable reduction to his obligation, plus the payment of damages. In this provision the law is intended to protect people from being swindled. For it to be applicable, two basic conditions must be met:

1. That which was exchanged in a transaction was totally disproportionate and permitted excessive profit. What constitutes "disproportionate" and "excessive profit" is determined by a judge.

2. That one party took advantage of the other due to his relatively weak position. There must be a direct connection between the excessive profit obtained and the exploitation of the other party. If it cannot be shown that the person intentionally exploited the other person to obtain excessive profit, this provision does not apply.

The damaged party has a term of one year from the time of exploitation to take legal action before his right lapses.

PERSONS

LEGAL CAPACITY AND INDIVIDUAL ATTRIBUTES

This part of the law deals primarily with one's legal capacity and attributes. Basically, it states that all persons have rights and responsibilities and, therefore, have the capacity to act as independent adult individuals within the confines of a society and its laws. Often "legal capacity" is used synonymously with "legal personality" because one's capacity to act as an independent adult within the confines of a society and its laws is directly affected by his individual legal attributes.

Such legal attributes can be divided into categories:

➤ **Marital status** *(el estado civil)*: This is whether a person is single, married, or divorced.

➤ **Legal capacity**: To have full legal capacity a person must be at least 18 years old, he must have complete control of his mental faculties, he must not be a deaf-mute who neither reads nor writes, he must not be addicted to drugs or alcohol.

➤ **Name**: In Mexico this includes first or given name or names, as well as father's surname and mother's surname, in that order. For example, the author's name would be Dennis John Peyton Callan.

➤ **Domicile**: The law recognizes three classes of domiciles: actual, legal, and conventional. A person's **actual domicile** is where he lives on a permanent basis. In the absence of this domicile, the principal business domicile is used, or if neither apply; a person's domicile is wherever he is found. A **legal domicile** is where the law determines a person's residency for the purposes of exercising his rights or for complying with his obligations, regardless if he can actually be found there or not. This is mostly applied to cases of minors, military personal, and convicts. Legal entities, such as corporations, associations, and the like, have their domiciles where their principal or administrative offices are located. A **conventional domicile** is where a person wishes to receive notification for legal matters, or for contractual purposes. Often this will be a lawyer's domicile.

➤ **Patrimony**: This is the total mass of existing or potential rights and liabilities attached to a person for the satisfaction of his economic needs. Simply put, it refers to all rights and obligations that may be given monetary value.

➤ **Nationality**: This is determined by citizenship, and Mexicans may not have dual citizenship.

INDIVIDUALS AND LEGAL ENTITIES

Under Mexican Law there are two types of persons: Individuals *(personas físicas)* and legal entities *(personas morales)*, such as corporations, associations, and institutions formed by individuals.

Individuals enjoy the rights and protection of the provisions of the Civil Code from the moment of conception. This legal capacity *(capacidad de goce)* takes effect even before birth and is lost only upon death.

In Mexico, legal age--the age at which a person may by law assume the rights and responsibilities of an adult--is eighteen. An adult enjoys unlimited legal capacity to buy and sell property and engage in any activity that is not prohibited by law. Minors, on the other hand, have limited legal capacity inasmuch as they are incapable of exercising their rights and fulfilling their obligations alone and therefore require a legal representative to exercise their rights and assume their obligations.

In the case of legal entities, since they are created by law, they must depend on legal representatives for the implementation of all of their rights and obligations. Therefore, the only attributes they have are name, domicile and nationality.

Legal entities are regulated by type of entity. Legal entities have many different forms: partnerships, clubs, unions, corporations, or governmental agencies.

REPRESENTATION OF CHILDREN

Children are normally represented by their parents. Under the provisions of the Civil Code, there is *"patria potestad,"* or **paternal power**. Paternal power is the sum total of rights and obligations which parents initially have with regard to their minor children.

Article 414 of the Civil Code provides for paternal power over children resulting from a marriage to be exercised in a certain order:

1. The father and mother;

2. The father's mother and father;

3. The mother's mother and father.

If a child is born out of wedlock, and if both parents live together, then they both exercise paternal power. If the parents are not living together, then the parent who has custody of the child exercises paternal power.

Only the people who adopt them can exercise paternal power over adopted children. It cannot be extended to include the parents of the adoptive parents (the child's adopted grandparents) from either side of the marriage. In order for any of the grandparents to exercise paternal power, both of the child's biological parents must be unable to do so.

The persons who exercise paternal power over a child have the responsibility to care for and educate the child as any good parent would do.

Paternal power is terminated under certain conditions:

> The death of the person who exercised the right provided that there is no other person who shared that right;
> The emancipation of the minor resulting from marriage (emancipation is the process by which a minor is liberated from either paternal power or a guardianship due to marriage);
> The child reaches adulthood.

The person who exercises paternal power loses this right in certain circumstances:

> When they have been expressly sentenced to such loss, or have been convicted of two or more felonies;
> In the event of divorce paternal power is lost by the parent who is found culpable;
> When the well being of the child is at risk due to mistreatment, abandonment, etc.

GUARDIANSHIP

Guardianship, *"tutela,"* is intended to protect minors who for one reason or another are not subject to paternal power, and to protect adults who do not have legal capacity to act on their own behalf. A guardian acts on behalf of a person who otherwise would have legal capacity to do so on his own. In addition to the guardian, the law also requires that a conservator (*curador*) be assigned to oversee the guardian and to administrate, directly or indirectly, the property of the minor or incapacitated person.

Essentially, the guardian has the same obligations as those provided for under paternal power, i.e., they are responsible for the well being and education of the minor or the incapacitated person under his guardianship.

Persons who fit specific criteria are subject to guardianship:

> Minors not subject to paternal power;

➢ Adults who do not have control of their mental faculties due to insanity, idiocy, or imbecility;
➢ Illiterate deaf-mutes;
➢ Alcoholics and drug addicts.

The law provides for three types of guardianships: testamentary, legitimate, and court-appointed.

TESTAMENTARY GUARDIANSHIP

Testamentary guardianship is established by designating a person as guardian by means of a will left by the person who exercised paternal power over one or more of his descendants. Testamentary guardianship takes precedence over all other normal designations of paternal power. For example, if a widow established testamentary guardianship with regard to her ten-year-old surviving son, such designation is legal even though the law stipulates that the child's father's parents exercise paternal power.

LEGITIMATE GUARDIANSHIP

Legitimate guardianship is established in the absence of someone to exercise paternal power and the absence of a testamentary guardianship. Siblings or other close relatives of the minor or incapacitated person carry out this type of guardianship.

In the case of incapacitated adults, a husband or wife has guardianship over his or her spouse, and adult children have guardianship over their widowed parents.

COURT APPOINTED GUARDIANSHIP

Court appointed guardianship is established in the absence of someone to exercise legitimate guardianship or in the absence of a testamentary guardianship. A court appointed guardianship is also necessary in the event that the guardian becomes incapacitated and no other substitute is available.

All guardianships are extinguished under certain conditions:

➢ By the death of the minor or incapacitated person subject to the guardianship.
➢ By the disappearance of the state of incapacity affecting the person in question.
➢ When a minor reaches adulthood.

> If the person subject to the guardianship becomes subject to paternal power due to adoption, or reuniting the child with someone who can legally exercise paternal power.

FAMILY PATRIMONY

The family patrimony law is intended to assure that food and housing for all family members are protected. To do this the law provides for certain assets to be legally protected from any encumbrance or lien. Family patrimony can consist of two kinds of assets:

> A house to live in.
> Farm land that provides sustenance for the family, in certain cases.

Families differ as to the amount and value they put into a home, therefore the law limits the amount that is considered as family patrimony to the equivalent of 10 times the yearly minimum wage corresponding to the area of residence.

In order for family patrimony to be established, specific requirements must be met:

1. The person must be an adult or be emancipated;

2. The person must live in the place which is to be included in the family patrimony;

3. The person must prove that a family relationship exists that would benefit from the establishment of a family patrimony, and prove the family relationship by submitting certified copies of the appropriate certificates from the Civil Registry.

4. The person must prove that he has clear title to the property to be included in the family patrimony.

5. The person must prove that the value of the property does not exceed 10 years of minimum wage at the time and place in which the property is located.

The title to the property that is included in the family patrimony does not transfer over to the family that benefits from the family patrimony. There is simply a filing made at the public registry (*registro público de la propiedad*) which indicates that the property in question has been designated as such. From the date of the filing, the property becomes inalienable and cannot be encumbered. Once the family patrimony is terminated, the title once again reverts back to normal title in benefit of the owner.

Family patrimony is terminated for 3 reasons:

1. All family members no longer have the right to support

2. The family does not reside in the house for more than one year without just cause.

3. When agricultural property is not cultivated for two consecutive years without just cause.

FAMILY RELATIONSHIPS

The law recognizes three types of family relationships.

1. Consanguinity relations: related by blood.

2. Affinity relations: related by marriage, includes in-laws.

3. Civil relations: related by adoption, applies only to the persons involved in the adoption--does not extend to other family members of the person adopted or to other family members of the person adopting.

MARRIAGE

Under Mexican Law, marriage is a contract between a consenting single man and a consenting single woman to mutually assist each other. Because of the nature of the relationship the contract is considered to be civil.

The law allows marriage between minors, the man being at least sixteen years old and the woman at least fourteen years old. Minors must have the consent of their parents if they are still living. If the parents are not living, the grandparents on their father's side, or in their absence, the grandparents on their mother's side, give consent.

Foreigners may also be married in Mexico, either to another foreigner or to a Mexican national. Foreigners must obtain a permit from the Ministry of the Interior *(Gobernación)*. The marriage contract is valid only if it is executed before a judge or an official of the Civil Registry and subsequently inscribed in the marriage section of the Civil Registry. To initiate this process, a written application is filed in the Civil Registry.

The law establishes specific impediments for the execution of the marriage contract:

➢ One or both of the parties are not old enough to get married.
➢ Lack of consent to be married by one of the parties. This usually only applies to minors who by definition need the consent of a guardian or an adult who has paternal power over the minor in question.
➢ The existence of a blood relationship between the parties.
➢ Adultery: anyone convicted of adultery may not enter into marriage.
➢ Attempting to take the life of a person in order to marry that person's spouse.
➢ The uses of physical or moral force to induce someone to consent to marriage.
➢ Alcoholism or drug addition by either of the parties.
➢ Certain illness.
➢ Either party is already married.
➢ The existence of a guardianship is an impediment to the guardian to marry the person subject to the guardianship.

PROPERTY OWNERSHIP IN MARRIAGE

The law provides for two ways of handling property either party to a marriage contract own at the time they are married: joint ownership of property, which is known as *"sociedad conyugal;"* or separation of property, which is known as *"separación de bienes"*.

Sociedad Conyugal: All property the husband and wife own separately prior to the marriage is jointly owned after the marriage. Any property acquired after the marriage is also jointly owned. Once the marriage contract is signed the husband and the wife become co-owners, and therefore all legal documents that transfer or encumber any of the property of the couple must be executed by both to be valid.

Separación de Bienes: Each person retains ownership of all the property owned before the marriage as well as any property they may acquire individually during the marriage, including wages, salary, etc. It is possible to have partial separation of property, in which case any property that is not expressly designated as forming part of one of the parties property, is considered jointly owned property.

DIVORCE

There are two types of divorce provided for under Mexican Law:

1. Necessary divorce

2. Voluntary divorce

NECESSARY DIVORCE

This type of divorce is based on circumstances that are considered to be dangerous to the married couple themselves or to members of their family. The law's intent is to eliminate such danger by separating the husband and wife.

There are established grounds for a necessary divorce:

➢ Adultery, provided that it is proved beyond a doubt.
➢ One spouse incites the other to acts of violence or to commit a crime.
➢ Immoral acts committed by either spouse that may risk corrupting their children.
➢ Any incurable hereditary or contagious disease, or incurable impotency, which occurs after entering into marriage.
➢ Any incurable mental illness.
➢ One spouse abandons the home for more than six months without just cause.
➢ The formal declaration of abandonment or the presumption of death.
➢ Extreme cruelty, threats or grave injustices caused by one spouse to the other.
➢ Lack of participation by one spouse to comply with his or her marital obligations as provided for in the Civil Code, such as sharing in the household expenses, educating the children, etc.
➢ One spouse is sentenced to prison for a term of more than two years for having committed an infamous crime.
➢ Continual disagreement between the spouses caused by immoderate and habitual drug use, or for drunkenness that threatens to cause the ruin of the family.

The spouse who is affected by any of the above causes must file for divorce within six months following the event or circumstance that typifies such cause for divorce.

VOLUNTARY DIVORCE

This type of divorce is filed for by mutual consent of any adult married couple.

CHAPTER 9

PROPERTY AND PROPERTY RIGHTS
THIS CHAPTER EXAMINES THE LEGAL CLASSIFICATION OF PROPERTY AND THE DISTINCTION BETWEEN PERSONAL AND REAL PROPERTY

INTRODUCTION

Most property law in the United States originates in English common law and is not influenced by Roman law, which plays an important role in the development of the principals of Mexican Law. Mexican Law approaches the division of property in the Roman tradition: it is divided into movable and immovable property. The law recognizes rights and obligations *in rem* (real property) and *in personam* (personal property) over both types of property. Other characteristics of property law in the United States, such as life estates, remainders, reversions, conditional fees, and equitable and legal ownership, are not generally recognized, as such, under Mexican Law.

Mexican Law has a more socialistic approach to property ownership than the United States has. In "Motives of the Civil Code," published by the commission that drafted the current Civil Code, the reasoning is explained:

> In treating the matter of property the Commission eliminated the individualistic tendency prevalent in Roman Law... and our Civil Code... and accepted the progressive theory which considers property rights as a means of accomplishing a truly social function. Therefore, property was not considered as an individual right of the owner, but as a changeable right that should be adapted to social necessities.

To this end, and in accordance with the relative constitutional provisions, certain limitations were imposed upon property in order that the decision to leave one's property unproductive would not be left to the discretion of the owner, and so that he would not use his rights in detriment to others or the general interests. The general criteria in this matter followed by the Commission was to guarantee the owner the enjoyment of his property under the condition that when exercising his right he bring about social benefit.

Various provisions of the Civil Code reflect this socialist tendency:

"Article 16. The inhabitants of the Federal District are under the obligation to carry out their activities and to use and dispose of their property in a way that does nothing to harm the community, under the sanctions established in this Code and in the respective laws."

"Article 830. The owner of a thing may enjoy and dispose of it within the limits and in the manner designated by law."

"Article 840. It is not lawful to exercise the right of property in such manner that its exercise would give no result other than to cause damage to a third party, without benefit for the owner."

The following relates to the preceding article:

"Article 1912. When in the exercise of a right, damage is caused to another, there is an obligation to indemnify such damage, if it is proved that the right was exercised merely for the purpose of causing the damage, without profit to the owner of the right."

The following relates to the use of property:

"Article 837. The owner or lessor of realty has the right to exercise the proper actions to prevent the security, peace and the health of those who inhabit the property from being impaired by the misuse of the property of a neighbor."

"Article 838. The owner of land is not the owner of the minerals or substances mentioned in the fourth paragraph of Article 27 of the Political Constitution of the United Mexican States, nor of the waters which the fifth paragraph of the same Article provides shall belong to the nation."

"Article 839. Excavations or constructions cannot be made in a parcel of land which would cause the soil of the neighboring property to lose the necessary support, unless the indispensable props be erected so as to avoid all damage to such neighboring property."

The Civil Code does not define the concept of property. Article 830 of the Civil Code states that "The owner of property may enjoy and dispose of it within the limits and in the manner designated by law." Article 831 of the Civil Code goes on to say "One's property cannot be occupied against his will, except for reason of public utility and with indemnification."

A person may have title to property or rights. All legal relationships have either property or rights as their cause. The subject matter here is property as it pertains to all property or goods having economic value, and property which forms part of a person's assets, or what is known as *"patrimonio"* in Mexican Law.

Patrimonio is defined as the totality of a person's assets and liabilities capable of being evaluated. Article 2964 of the Civil Code gives an indirect definition of *patrimonio:* "A debtor is liable for the fulfillment of his obligations with all his property, except for property which is inalienable or not subject to attachment in accordance with law." In other words, he must respond with all of his assets or *patrimonio.*

Within the group of all the material objects that exist there are some that may be acquired. This is to say that they may be acquired by someone or by the State. In Spanish, such material objects are known as *"bienes"* or goods.

There are other material objects that either by law or by their nature cannot be acquired. Such cases are considered as being excluded from commerce. An object is considered excluded from commerce by its nature when an individual cannot possess it exclusively, and by provision of law, when the law declares it cannot be reduced to private ownership.

CLASSIFICATION OF PROPERTY

Mexican Law divides property in the Roman tradition. The basic classifications of property are real or immovable property *(bienes inmuebles)* and personal or movable property *(bienes muebles*

PERSONAL/MOVABLE PROPERTY

Personal/moveable property is divided into two groups: personal/moveable property by nature, and personal by law. Personal/moveable property by nature refers to material objects that may be moved from one place to another without being destroyed. Personal/moveable property by law refers to any property that the law specifically defines as personal/moveable property, or all other property not considered by the law as real property. Obligations, rights or actions that have personal/moveable property as their cause, or amounts demandable by virtue of a personal action, are also deemed personal/moveable property by law. There are other examples of personal/moveable property by determination of law:

➤ Share certificates in associations or companies.
➤ Vessels of all kinds.
➤ Building materials resulting from demolition, for repair, or for new construction, provided that they are no longer included in the construction.
➤ An author's rights.

REAL/IMMOVABLE PROPERTY

Article 750 c.c. defines real/immovable property:

➤ The soil and constructions attached thereto;
➤ Plants and trees while united to the ground and pending fruits of such trees and plants while not separated therefrom by harvests or regular cuttings;
➤ Everything which is united to real/immovable property in a permanent manner, so that it cannot be separated without deterioration of the real/immovable property or of the object attached thereto;
➤ Statues, relieves, paintings, and other objects of ornamentation, placed on buildings or estates by the owner of the real/immovable property in such manner as to reveal the intention to unite them permanently to the realty;
➤ Dovecotes, beehives, fishponds, or analogous breeding places, when the owner preserves them with the intention of maintaining them united to the realty and forming part thereof in a permanent manner;

> Machines, receptacles, instruments or utensils, intended by the owner of the real/immovable property directly and exclusively for the industry or exploitation of the same;

> Fertilizers intended for the cultivation of an estate, which are on the lands where they are to be utilized, and the seeds necessary for the cultivation of the estate;

> Electrical apparatus and accessories attached to the soil or buildings by the owner of such soil or buildings, unless otherwise agreed

> Springs, ponds, cisterns, and water currents, as well as aqueducts and pipe lines of any kind which serve to conduct liquids or gases to a property or to extract them therefrom;

> Animals which constitute the breeding stock in rural estates devoted totally or partially to cattle raising; as well as working animals indispensable for the cultivation of the estate, while they are devoted to that purpose;

> Dikes and constructions which, although floating, are intended by reason of their object and conditions to remain at a fixed point of a river, lake or coast;

> Rights *in rem* on real/immovable property;

> Rolling stock of railroads, telephone and telegraph lines, and fixed radio-telegraph stations.

PUBLIC AND PRIVATE PROPERTY

Property may also be classified as public or private.

Public Property

Public property is property that belongs to the Federation, the states, or the municipalities. This includes territorial waters, national air space, all underground minerals, rivers, lakes, highways, public parks, public buildings, and schools, etc.

The Civil Code divides public property ownership into three categories:

1. Common use property,

2. Property destined for a public service,

3. Government property.

Common use property is inalienable--it cannot be bought or sold--and it is not subject to prescription--it cannot be acquired through adverse possession (see Property Acquisition section). Anyone can use this property as long as they are not breaking the law.

A concession is required from the government to obtain exclusive use or enjoyment of public or common use property. If a concession is not obtained and the enjoyment of common property is obstructed, the guilty party is subject to penalties, the payment of damages and losses caused by such obstruction.

The Federation and states or municipalities own properties destined for public service and government properties. Such property is inalienable and not subject to prescription as long as it is used for that purpose.

When a public roadway is sold in accordance with the law, the owners of the abutting properties are to be notified that they have the preferential right to acquire that part pertaining to them. This right of first refusal must be exercised within eight days following the notice. If such notice is not given, the abutting property owners have the right to sue for the recision of the sales contract within six months from the date the sale was executed.

Private Property

Private property refers to everything owned by individuals or legal entities. Only those with the consent of the owner may enjoy these properties.

Foreigners are limited in their capacity to acquire real/immovable property by the provisions of Article 27 of the Mexican constitution and its regulations.

TANGIBLE AND INTANGIBLE PROPERTY

Property may also be classified as tangible and intangible, or corporeal or incorporeal. Tangible property refers to something palpable or concrete or discernible by the touch; such as material assets or property which has a physical existence. Intangible property is property that has no physical existence, such as easements, patents, etc.

PERSONAL PROPERTY WITHOUT AN OWNER

This type of property, *"BIENES MOSTRENCOS,"* refers to personal/moveable property that is abandoned, or to lost chattels that's owner is unknown.

Lost or abandoned property must be delivered to the nearest local municipal authority within three days from the time it is found. The local authority then has the property appraised and issues the finder a detailed receipt. The local authority then posts public notifications for one month, at intervals of ten days, stating that at the end of the thirty-day period the property will be sold at auction if no one claims it.

If someone appears to claim the property, the municipal authority sends all the relevant information to a judge (according to the value of the article), so that the claimant may prove his ownership.

If the claimant is declared owner by the judge, the property in question is delivered to him after deducting expenses. In the event that the claimant is not declared owner or if no one claims the property within the term allotted, the property is sold at public auction. In that case, twenty five percent of the price is given to the finder, and the other seventy five percent is given to a charitable institution designated by the Government.

VACANT PROPERTY

Vacant property *(BIENES VACANTES)*, is defined as real/immovable property that has no certain and known owner.

The law requires that whoever has information of the existence of vacant property, and wants to receive the legal percentage of the value of the property as the discoverer, must notify the district attorney's office of the locality where the property is located. The district attorney's office may then begin proceedings before a competent judge to declare the property vacant and assign it to the Federal Treasury. The discoverer is entitled to twenty five percent of the property's *cadastral* value.

PERSONAL VS. REAL PROPERTY RIGHTS

Personal property rights are those which are based on relationships between two people, both having rights and obligations. Such obligations may consist of the right to demand that the other party relinquish his rights to property, or do or not do something regarding the property.

Real property rights deal with relations that exist between people but also include some relationship to immovable property. One person is in possession of the property while everyone else is obligated to respect his or her right of possession over the property.

CHAPTER 10

CLASSIFICATION OF REAL PROPERTY RIGHTS
THIS CHAPTER EXAMINES THE DIFFERENT RIGHTS OF POSSESSION SUCH AS
USUFRUCT, HABITATION AND EASEMENTS, AND THE RIGHTS INVOLVED IN A
MORTGAGE GUARANTEE

REAL PROPERTY RIGHTS OF POSSESSION

USUFRUCT

Usufruct is "the right to utilize and enjoy the profits and advantages of something belonging to another so long as the property is not damaged or altered in any way." Usufruct is established when the owner of property temporarily assigns the right to the use and enjoyment of the property, while maintaining the right to dispose of the property. The right of usufruct means, "to use the fruits," either cost-free (gratuitously) or for payment (onerously), of property one does not own.

The person who receives the property (the usufructuary) should make an inventory of the property received. If a property is given freely, the usufructuary is responsible for the conservation and maintenance of the property.

HABITATION

Habitation is "the right to occupy free of charge a property belonging to someone else that which is necessary for himself and his family." Habitation rights are applicable when a person works in agriculture or a ranch where independent lodging is not available. Therefore, habitation rights in a building may not be assigned, encumbered or leased to a third party. The provisions for usufruct regulate the rights of habitation.

EASEMENTS

An easement is "A right, such as a right of way, afforded a person to make limited use of another's real/immovable property." An easement is established when two parcels of real estate, owned by distinct owners, and the owner of one is given the right to some benefit involving the property of the other owner. The property that receives the benefit is called the **dominant property**, and the property that supports such benefit is called the **servient property**. Easements may be divided into **voluntary easements** and **legal easements**.

Voluntary and Legal Easements

Voluntary easements are established by agreement between the owners of the properties involved. **Legal easements** are established by law. The law establishes a Legal easement taking into account the location of the property and the public and private benefits of the property. Legal easements may be for **public or communal benefit**, or simply **statutory easements**. When easements are for public or communal benefit, they are regulated by special laws and regulations and, in their absence, by the general provisions of the Civil Code. Statutory easements are governed by the rules applicable to the three easements established by law: drainage, aqueduct, and passage; and the provisions provided for voluntary easements.

An easement consists of the owner of a servient property not doing or tolerating something. However, in order for the owner of the servient property to be required to allow or carry out an easement, the conditions of the easement must be expressly determined by law or by contract.

Types of Easements

There are continuous or discontinuous, and apparent or non-apparent easements. **Continuous easements** are those that the use of which may exist indefinitely without anybody being required to do anything to maintain their existence. **Discontinuous easements** are those which depend on some act of man for their existence. **Apparent easements** are those which are visibly marked for use by external works or signs. **Non-apparent easements** are those which are not visibly marked to indicate their existence.

Until they are extinguished, easements are inseparable from the property on which they are imposed, and are transferred with the conveyance of ownership. Easements are also indivisible. This means that if the servient property is subdivided among various owners, the easement is not affected and each owner must proportionally honor the easement. Likewise, if the dominant property is subdivided, each owner may use the entire easement without any limitation. However, if the easement is established in benefit of only one section of the subdivided dominant property, only the owner of that section may continue to use the easement.

Legal Easement of Drainage

Lower lands are subject to receive the waters, as well as stones or earth carried by them, which naturally, or in consequence of agricultural or industrial improvements, flow onto them from higher lands; when received on account of such improvements, the owners of the servient property are entitled to compensation. When a rural or urban property is enclosed between others, the owners of surrounding properties must permit the drainage of the central property. If the owners cannot agree as to the dimensions and direction of the drainage conduit, a judge decides the issue. In doing so the judge applies the legal provisions applicable to easements of access or right of way whenever possible.

The owner of property on which any kind of water restraint construction exists or is needed, must either make the necessary repairs or construction on their property, or permit the owners of property exposed to possible damage to make them. This applies to cases where it is necessary to remove materials that are impeding the course of the water that causes damage to property or danger to third persons. All owners benefiting from such works must contribute to their cost in proportion to the benefit received. Experts (*peritos*) determine the amount paid by each property owner.

If the water flowing onto the servient property becomes unhealthy for domestic or industrial uses, it must be restored to a proper condition at the cost of the owner of the dominant tenement.

Legal Easement of Aqueduct

Anyone wishing to dispose of water he has used, has the right to conduct it through intermediate properties, except through buildings and their yards, gardens and other dependencies, upon compensating the owners and those of lower lands through which the water percolates or falls. The person making use of this right of easement must construct the necessary channel through the intermediate properties, even if there are already canals for other waters, unless the owner of the intermediate property offers their use without disadvantage to the person using the right of easement. The passage of waters must also be permitted across the canals and aqueducts in the readiest way, provided that the course and volume of the water in the latter are not altered or the waters of the two are not mingled.

Where it is necessary to carry the aqueduct through a public road or stream, permission is first attained from the corresponding public authority, which is granted subject to the condition that the water be carried across without obstructing or damaging the road or stream.

Before making use of the above right, the party claiming it must:

➤ Prove that he has the right to dispose of the waters he seeks to conduct;
➤ Show that the passage which he requests is the most convenient one for the purposes for which he wants to use the water;
➤ Show that it is the least burdensome for the properties through which it is to pass;
➤ Pay the value of the land which the canal is to occupy, as estimated by experts, and ten per cent more;
➤ Indemnify the immediate damages including those resulting from dividing the servient property into two or more parts, and any other depreciation.

Where the servient owner of property offers the use of existing canals, the party conducting the water must pay, in proportion to its volume, the value of the canal and the costs of its maintenance, and other costs caused by the passage of the water. The amount of water carried through a canal on another's land is only limited by the capacity of the canal. The capacity of the canal may be enlarged once the owner of the dominant property pays the costs of the enlargement. He must also pay the value of the extra land used and for any damages caused. These provisions also apply to the drainage of swamplands.

The easement of waters includes the right of passage for persons and materials for the use and repair of the aqueduct and the care of the water conducted, under the terms provided for legal easements of passage. Water concessions granted by the government are made without prejudice to or interference with rights previously acquired by other persons. Everyone making use of an aqueduct on his own or another's land must construct and maintain all the necessary works to prevent injury to others. This includes cleaning and preventing stoppage. If there are several parties making use of an aqueduct, they all contribute to the expenses in proportion to their use, unless otherwise prescribed or agreed.

The owner of the servient property may enclose or fence it, or build upon the aqueduct in such manner as not to injure it or hinder repairs and cleaning. If the owner of the servient property needs to construct a dam in order to make better use of the water to which he has a right, and he does not own the land needed to support the dam, the owner of the land needed is required to establish the necessary easement after receiving compensation.

Legal Easement of Passage

The owner of a property shut off from public access by other properties has the right to require passage to a public road. This right is exercised upon payment of compensation for any damage caused by the easement. The parties involved agree to the amount of compensation, or, if that is not possible, an expert determines the amount. The action to enforce the compensation is subject to **prescription** but the passage obtained is not affected in any way.

The owner of the servient property has the right to indicate the place where the passageway is established; however, if the judge declares it to be unreasonably difficult or inconvenient for the dominant property, the landowner must designate another way. If all else fails, a judge designates a more convenient passageway, seeking to reconcile the interests of the parties. As a general rule, the landowner designates the shortest way through several estates, if the passage is not too inconvenient or costly. If all choices are equal in distance, a judge designates the passageway. The width of the passageway should serve the needs of the dominant property. If a passageway between a property and the highway already exists, only the property through which the existing passageway runs is required to permit passage.

The owner of a rural property may, upon proper indemnification, require permission for the passage of his livestock through neighboring properties to conduct them to watering-places.

Miscellaneous Legal Easements

The owner of a tree or bush near the property of another may require the latter to permit him to gather the fruits that he cannot reach from his side. The owner of the tree or bush is liable for any damage he causes in gathering such fruits.

If, in constructing or repairing a building, it is necessary to pass materials through the property of another, or to place upon it the scaffolding or other objects for the work, the owner of the property through which the materials must pass must consent to it once he is compensated for any damages caused to him.

At times, it is necessary to set posts or string wires on the property of another for the purpose of establishing private telephonic communication between two or more estates, or for the purpose of conducting electric power to a property. The owner of the property needed must permit such posts or string wires once he is properly compensated. This easement carries with it the right of passage of the persons and the transport of the materials necessary for the construction and maintenance of the line.

Voluntary Easements

General Rules: The owner of a property may establish whatever easements upon it and in such manner as he sees fit, as long as they do not violate the law or injure third persons. Only those having full and complete rights of alienation create easements. The right of alienation means that they can legally sell the property without the consent of another person. If there are several owners, an easement cannot be established on their property without the consent of all of them. An easement on property in favor of the common property (property owned by several persons), may be taken advantage of by all of the co-owners of the dominant property, subject to the conditions on which the easement was acquired.

Acquisition of Voluntary Easements

Continuous and apparent easements may be acquired in any lawful manner, including prescription; but non-apparent continuous easements, and discontinuous easements of any kind, cannot be acquired by prescription.

The person claiming an easement must prove his right even though he has possession of the easement. The existence of a sign of an apparent easement between two properties, established or maintained by the owners of both properties, is considered a title for the continuance of the easement when the property is sold, unless, at the time of division, the contrary appears in the deed of conveyance of either. The establishment of an easement carries with it the right to all necessary means of using it, and that right ceases with discontinuance of the easement.

Voluntary Easements: Rights-Obligations.

Rights and Obligations of the Parties: The use and extension of voluntary easements is governed by the terms of the instrument establishing them, or, in absence of such provisions, by definite rules:

➢ The owner of the dominant property, at his cost, makes all works necessary for its use and maintenance, and must likewise make all necessary improvements to protect the owner of the servient property from unnecessary burdens. The owner of the dominant property is liable for damages caused by his failure or lack of care.

➢ Surrendering the property on which the easement exists to the dominant owner discharges any obligation assumed by the servient owner to make or pay for any work. If the place originally designated for the easement becomes seriously inconvenient, the servient owner may offer the dominant owner a more convenient one, and the latter cannot refuse it if it is not disadvantageous.

➢ The servient owner may also make such works as may render the easement less burdensome to him if it does not damage the dominant owner. If damage is caused, he must restore the former conditions and pay any damages incurred by the dominant owner.

➢ Any doubt regarding the use or extension of an easement is decided in the way least burdensome to the servient owner but not so as to impair the use of the easement.

Extinction of Easements

Voluntary Easements

A voluntary easement is considered extinct under established conditions:

➢ When there is a merger of both properties, servient and dominant, in the same person, and the easements are not revived by a subsequent separation of the properties, except in cases of apparent signs, as provided above. However, if the act of merger was in its nature severable *(resoluble)*, the easements revive when the severance takes place.

➤ If the easement is continuous and apparent, and it is not used for **three years** from the time the apparent sign of easement disappeared, it is considered extinct; if the easement is discontinuous and non-apparent, and has not been used for **five years** due to the act of the servient owner it is considered extinct; however, if the servient owner did not act to prevent its use, or the use continued notwithstanding, there is no prescription.

➤ When the properties become, through no fault of the servient owner, in such condition that the easement cannot be used. However, the easement is revived if the properties afterward become serviceable, unless the period of prescription has lapsed in the meantime.

➤ By remission made gratuitously or for a consideration by the dominant owner;

➤ Upon the expiration of any time limit under which the easement was established, or upon the performance of any condition subject to which the easement was established. The manner of use of an easement may prescribe in the same way as the easement. Use of the easement by any one of several joint owners keeps the easement from prescription; and if, for any reason, prescription does not run against any one of joint owners, it will not run against the others.

Legal Easements

Legal easements established for public or communal uses are lost if not used for ten years. There must be proof that during such time the persons who used them have acquired another easement of the same kind at another place. If the dominant and servient properties come into the possession of the same owner, the easement is terminated. The easement revives if the properties are again separated even if no apparent sign is preserved.

The owner of a property subject to a legal easement may release himself from it under certain conditions:

➤ If the legal easement was created in favor of a whole town or community and that community is not affected as a whole by the release of the easement. If there is an affect on the community, the property owner must have the consent of the town council (*ayuntamiento*) to be released from the easement.

➤ A property owner cannot release himself from easements of public use.

➤ For release from an easement of passage and drainage, the property owner must have approval of the owners of the surrounding properties, or at least of the owner of that through which the new easement is established.

➤ The renouncement of the legal easement of drainage is only valid when in conformity with the corresponding regulations.

REAL PROPERTY RIGHTS IN GUARANTEE: MORTGAGE

NATURE OF A MORTGAGE

Normally a mortgage is a voluntary lien over real estate in which a person willingly gives a lender the right to take real property if he fails to repay a loan. The **mortgagor**, or borrower, gives the mortgage to a lender, or **mortgagee**, to secure repayment.   In most cases two documents are involved: a **promissory note** and the mortgage itself.

The promissory note serves as the buyer's promise to make repayments. The note is not recorded since it is not an interest in real property. However, it still has an important function: in the case of foreclosure against the property and the amount received from the sale of the property is not enough to cover the outstanding debt and accrued interest, the promissory note serves as the basis for a deficiency judgment against the borrower for the balance.

The mortgage contract itself is the document by which the lender has the right to make a claim against the mortgaged property for repayment of a loan. The mortgage is the document that allows the foreclosure, not the promissory note. Moreover, since the mortgage gives the mortgagee an interest in the property mortgaged, it also allows the transaction to be recorded in the public registry.

PROPERTY SUBJECT TO MORTGAGE

Under Mexican law a mortgage *(hipoteca)* is a real guaranty imposed upon property that is not delivered to the creditor. This guaranty gives the creditor the right, in case of non-performance of the obligation secured, to be paid from the value of the property, in the grade of preference established by law. A mortgaged property remains subject to the mortgage even when it is transferred to another person.

A mortgage can only be imposed upon property that can be clearly and legally identified. For example, a portion of a parcel of real estate cannot be mortgaged unless the property is first divided. This is due to the fact that the mortgaged portion of the property cannot be legally identified until it is parceled out and registered as such.

In general terms, the following principals regulate a mortgage:

➢ The mortgage establishes real property rights in favor of the creditor since the lender has the right to force the sale of the property for repayment.
➢ The mortgage rights based on a credit relationship.
➢ A mortgage is given on real property that can be legally identified and sold.
➢ A mortgage must be done before a notary and with regard to specific property rather than referring to all the property one owns.
➢ Possession of the mortgage property is not lost; and
➢ The mortgagee has foreclosure rights and preference of payment.

Additionally a mortgage is indivisible with regard to the credit guarantee and divisible with regard to the property mortgaged. In other words, if several properties are used to secure one debt, the exact amount that each property will be encumbered must be determined, so that each can be redeemed from the encumbrance upon payment of the amount it secures.

A mortgage, although not specifically stated, extends to other portions of the property:

➢ The natural accessions of the mortgaged property;
➢ The improvements to the property made by the owner;
➢ Movable objects permanently incorporated by the owner into the property and which cannot be removed without injury to the property or to such objects;
➢ New buildings constructed by the owner on the mortgaged property, and to new floors added to the mortgaged buildings.

PROPERTY NOT INCLUDED IN A MORTGAGE

Unless otherwise agreed, a mortgage does not include certain encumbrances:

> The industrial fruits of the mortgaged property if produced before the creditor demands payment;
> The rents due and unpaid at the time payment is demanded.

PROPERTY WHICH CANNOT BE MORTGAGED

There are specific encumbrances which cannot be mortgaged:

> The pending fruits and rents separate from the property producing them;
> Movable objects placed permanently on the buildings for ornament or convenience, or for the service of some industry, unless they are mortgaged together with the buildings;
> Easements, unless mortgaged together with the dominant estate;
> The right to receive the fruits in usufruct as granted in accordance with the Civil Code to ascendants upon the property of their descendants;
> Use and habitation;
> Property in litigation, unless the demand on which the suit is founded is preventatively registered in the Public Registry as notice of *(lis pendens)*--the suit is registered as pending, or if the mortgage instrument states that the creditor had knowledge of the litigation. In either case, the mortgage remains subject to the outcome of the litigation.

The mortgage of a building erected on the land of another person does not include the surface area of the property on which the building stands. **Bare ownership** *(nuda propiedad)* means the property is owned but not the use of the property, such as a property that is leased or is a usufructuary. Bare ownership may be mortgaged; in which case, if the usufruct becomes the owner, the mortgage extends to include such usufruct if so provided. Property already mortgaged may also be mortgaged subject to the **rights of preference** *(prelacion)* established in the Civil Code.

A **co-owned property** cannot be mortgaged without consent of all the owners. However, a co-owner may mortgage his undivided interest, and when the property is divided, the mortgage will cover his corresponding part. In such cases, the creditor has the right to intervene in the subdivision of the property to prevent his debtor from being allotted a part of less value than he is entitled to.

A mortgage on real/immovable property rights continues only so long as the rights continue to exist. If the rights should be terminated through the fault of the mortgagor, he must establish another mortgage to the satisfaction of the creditor or pay all losses and damages. If the mortgage is on usufruct and the usufruct is terminated by the usufructuary, the mortgage continues to exist until the time when the usufruct would otherwise have terminated.

A mortgage is established by the debtor or by another person in his favor. If the owner's right or title in the property to be mortgaged is conditional or limited in any way, he must declare this fact in the contract and identify the nature of his ownership. Only the person who has the right to alienate (sell) the property can mortgage it and only property that can be alienated can be mortgaged.

IMPAIRMENT OF SECURITY AND CHANGE OF FORM

If the property mortgaged becomes insufficient to secure the debt, regardless if the debtor is at fault, the creditor may require that the mortgage be increased until it is sufficient, in the judgment of experts, to secure the principal obligation. In such case, the circumstance of the decrease of value of the property would be subject to the opinion of experts *(peritos)*. If the value of the property is shown to be insufficient, and the debtor does not increase the mortgage within eight days after the corresponding judicial declaration, the mortgage is taken as due and the mortgage credit is collected.

If the mortgaged property is insured and a fire or an accident destroys it, the mortgage continues to exist on the ruins of the property, and the insurance money is subject for the payment. If the mortgage debt is due, the creditor may demand the retention of the insurance money. If the mortgage debt is not yet due, the creditor may require that it be held to pay the debt when it becomes due. The same rules apply to the proceeds where the mortgaged property is seized for public uses or sold at judicial sale.

A mortgage continues to exist for the entire property mortgaged even though the obligation secured is reduced. Likewise, a mortgage also affects any part of the property remaining when the rest has disappeared. In such cases certain provisions apply:

> Where several properties are mortgaged to secure one credit, it is determined what portion of it affects each property, and each is redeemed upon payment of the corresponding part of the debt;

> When a property is divided, the mortgage charge is equitably apportioned among the several parts. If the parties do not agree to the mortgage charge, the distribution of the lien is made by judicial decision.

Without consent of the creditor, the owner cannot lease a mortgaged property, nor agree to receive payment of the rents in advance for a term exceeding the duration of the mortgage.

All mortgages are executed by public instrument *(escritura publica)*. This means that the contract is recorded before a public notary and subsequently filed with the public registry.

A mortgage is never tacit (understood), nor general: it must always be registered to be effective against third persons. The law divides mortgages into two categories: those contracted voluntarily by agreement; or those of necessity when the law requires anyone to give a mortgage on determined property.

VOLUNTARY MORTGAGES

Voluntary mortgages are those agreed on between parties or placed by the owner on his property. Where a mortgage is made to secure a future obligation, or one subject to suspensive conditions that are duly registered, it is effective in respect to third persons from the time of its filing in the public registry. If the condition is resolutory, the mortgage is effective against third persons until the fulfillment of the condition is noted in the register. In all the foregoing instances, the interested parties must require that the corresponding conditions be noted in the margin of the mortgage inscription in the public registry. Without the marginal note, the mortgage can neither benefit nor prejudice third persons.

Any act or agreement between the parties which modifies the mortgage obligation is not binding against third parties unless it is recorded in the public register under a new filing.

The secured credit may be assigned in whole or part, provided that the assignment is made in the same form required for the mortgage, the assignment is registered, and provided that the debtor is notified.

Duration Of Voluntary Mortgages

A mortgage generally continues for the entire time that the obligation secured continues to exist. When the obligation secured has no fixed due date, the mortgage cannot be for more than ten years. When the term of the secured obligation is extended, the mortgage is also extended for the same amount of time, unless it is expressly agreed otherwise.

At times, the term of a mortgage is extended before its due date. The first time it is extended, the mortgage retains its original filing priority during the extension and the term of prescription. If the mortgage is extended a second or more times, it retains the preference derived from its registration only for the term of the extension and the term of prescription mentioned above. For the second or subsequent extension, it would only have the priority of preference corresponding to the date of its last registration. The same rule applies when the creditor grants an extension for the payment of his credit.

NECESSARY MORTGAGES

These mortgages refer to the special and express mortgages which certain persons are required by law to give to secure property administered by them, or to secure the credits of certain creditors. Necessary mortgages may be required at any time even though the cause requiring it has ceased to exist, provided that the obligation of certain persons or creditors to be secured by the mortgage remains unfulfilled.

If several properties are offered for mortgage, and the parties do not agree on the portion of the charge to be imposed on each of the properties, or the parties do not agree on the adequacy of the property offered for the necessary mortgage, the issue must be settled by a judge. A necessary mortgage continues to exist as long as the obligation secured by it exists.

When Necessary Mortgages are Required

The following circumstances may demand a necessary mortgage to secure their credits in the absence of other adequate guarantees.

1. A co-heir or co-distributee *(participe)* may demand a necessary mortgage upon the real or immovable property distributed, to the

extent of their respective warranties *(saneamientos)* or on the excess of property they may have received;

2. Descendants, whose property is administrated by their ascendants, may need a mortgage on the property of the ascendants, in order to guarantee the preservation and return of the property of the descendants;

3. Minors and other incompetents may demand a necessary mortgage upon the property of their guardians, to secure the guardian's administration of the property of the minor or incompetent;

4. Legatees, for the amount of their legacies, if no special mortgage was required by the testator;

5. State, municipalities and public institutions, may require a mortgage on the property of those persons who are the public body's administrators or tax collectors, to secure the revenues of those persons' respective offices.

In the cases of numbers 2 and 3 above, certain persons may require the mortgage:

➢ Legitimate heirs of the minor, where the minor's parents are mere administrators of his property;
➢ The legitimate heirs and by the curator of the **incompetent**, where the guardians administer the incompetent's property, or by the Local Council of *Tutelas*, who oversee such guardianships;
➢ The *Ministerio Público* (District Attorney), in cases where those above mentioned do not demand it.

Those having the right to require a necessary mortgage may also object to the sufficiency of that which is offered for mortgage, and to ask its amplification whenever the mortgaged property becomes insufficient to secure the credit.

TERMINATION OF MORTGAGES

A mortgage is effective against third persons until its inscription in the public registry is canceled. The cancellation of the mortgage may be requested and must be ordered:

➢ When the property mortgaged is extinguished or ceases to exist;
➢ When the obligation secured is terminated;

➢ When the right of the debtor with respect to the mortgaged property is resolved or terminated;
➢ When the mortgaged property is seized or appropriated for public benefit;
➢ When the mortgaged property is sold at judicial sale
➢ By express remission of the creditor;
➢ By declaration that the mortgage action is prescribed.

A mortgage terminated by delivery of payment *(dacion en pago)*, revives if such payment is ineffective, either because the thing given in payment is lost through the fault of the debtor while it is yet in his possession, or because the creditor loses it by eviction. In such cases, if the registry has already been canceled, the mortgage is revived only from the date of a new inscription in the registry; but in all cases the debtor must compensate the creditor for all losses and damages suffered.

CHAPTER 11

PROPERTY OWNERSHIP AND POSSESSION
THIS CHAPTER EXAMINES PROPERTY OWNERSHIP AND THE RIGHTS OF POSSESSION,
POSSESSION BY GOOD AND BAD FAITH, AND THE LOSS OF POSSESSION

PROPERTY OWNERSHIP

Mexican property law does not define ownership. It defines, instead, the basic rights to which an owner is entitled regarding his property. The law simply states that a property owner has the right to use, enjoy, and dispose of (sell, donate, etc.) his property within the limits of and in the manner designated by the law.

A property owner may assign the use or enjoyment of property ownership without losing the right to dispose of the property. For example, leasing the property gives use of the property to someone else, leaving the owner with the right to sell the property as long as the new owner respects the lease.

The following provisions of the Civil Code apply to limitation on property:

Article 839. Excavations or constructions cannot be made in a parcel of land that would cause the soil of the neighboring property to lose the necessary support, unless indispensable props are erected so as to avoid all damage to such neighboring property.

Article 840. It is not lawful to exercise the right of property in such manner that its exercise would give no result other than to cause damage to a third party, with no benefit for the owner.

Article 843. No one may build or establish plantations near fortified places, forts, and public buildings, except in accordance with the conditions required in the special regulations on the subject.

Article 845. No one may build near the wall of another or near a party wall, pits, sewers, aqueducts, ovens, forges, chimneys or stables. No one may install deposits of corrosive matters, steam engines, or factories devoted to uses that may be dangerous or noxious. They may, however, if they observe the distances prescribed by the regulations, or if they construct the necessary protective works in accordance with the provisions of such regulations. In the absence of regulations, they must seek and comply with expert opinion.

Article 846. No one may plant trees near the property of another, except at a distance of two meters from the division line if large trees are planted, or of one meter if bushes or small trees are planted.

Article 849. The owner of a wall, not a party wall, adjoining the property of another, may open windows or openings in the wall to receive light. The window must be at such height that the lower part of the window is at least three meters from the floor of the dwelling house to which it gives light. The window or opening must have iron bars and gratings built into the wall and with wire netting, the meshes of which shall be three centimeters at most.

Article 851. Projecting windows, or balconies or other similar projections are not permitted over the property of a neighbor beyond the dividing line separating the estates. Also, views from the side or oblique views over such property are not permitted unless there is a distance of one meter.

Article 853. The owner of a building is obliged to construct his roofs and roof terraces in such manner that the rain waters will not fall on the neighboring ground or building.

POSSESSION

There is an old saying in property law that possession is nine-tenths of the law, which indicates the importance of possession. There is confusion in determining the difference between possession and ownership. Most property rights violations are actually violations of peaceful possession rather than violations of the right of ownership. Ownership serves as evidence of the right to the possession of property, but possession does not always serve as evidence of ownership.

The meaning of possession varies depending on its use, but it generally means that a person has control of a physical object. According to law that deals with real and personal/moveable property, when a person buys property he also acquires ownership "subject to the rights of the party in possession." It is usually assumed that the possessor has some property rights in the property that he possesses.

RIGHT OF POSSESSION

Possession may be exercised over physical objects, such as personal or real/immovable property, or rights.

The possessor of an object is the person who, in fact, **exercises power over it**. If a person possesses an object due to his dependence on the owner of the object and possesses it for the owner under orders and instructions from the owner, that person is not considered the possessor.

It is generally accepted that one exercises power over personal/moveable property by using it and over real/immovable property by inhabiting it, provided that it is done in accordance with the law. In other words, possession rights are only exercised over property and rights that can be acquired. If the property or right is excluded from commerce by its very nature or by law, then it cannot be private property or subject to possession.

By law, public property, as defined earlier, is not and cannot be subject to possession. For this reason, it is excluded from commerce so it cannot be subject to adverse possession, prescription, or *usucapion*.

The possessor of a right is he who enjoys it. In other words, a person possesses a right by receiving the benefits it affords.

When something is given to another person, granting him the right to retain it temporarily in his possession as usufructuary, lessee, pledgee, depositary, or under some analogous title, both the giver and receiver are considered possessors of the article. The original owner has original possession, and the other has derived possession.

The distinction between original and derived possession is important in various situations.

Derived possession results from a legal act in two cases:

1. Resulting from the exploitation of an object, and therefore involving real/immovable property rights; and,

2. Resulting from collaboration between various persons, which involves personal/moveable property rights.

Without some kind of legal connection to the property, a person possessing it has neither original nor derived possession; his relationship to the property is merely coincidental.

In the case of despoilment or dispossession of the derived possessor, the original possessor has the right to request that the derived possessor be restored possession. In the event that the derived possessor cannot or does not wish to recover such possession, the original possessor can request that possession be returned to him.

In any event, in order for the possessor, derived or original, to have the right to an injunction or writ of possession (*despojo*) to regain possession of the property in question, no more than one year must have passed from the time that despoilment or dispossession occurred.

WHO HAS THE RIGHT OF POSSESSION?

Article 803 of the Civil Code states that "every possessor must be maintained in or restored to possession as against those who have not a better right to possess." In other words, anyone who has possession of an object is protected so as to maintain that possession. If he has been deprived of possession, he should be restored to such possession unless someone else has a superior right to possession.

Who has the better right to possession? The law states that possession based on title has the better right to possession. In the case of real/immovable property, the title must also be filed with the Public Registry of Property to maintain the better right to possession.

Title is understood to be the cause giving rise (*causa generadora*) to the possession. This normally refers to the contract or fact, which caused or enabled the possessor to take possession of the object. In this sense, especially in the case of real/immovable property, a contract is normally the cause giving rise to the right of possession. The contract is the title by virtue of which one has the right of possession, which, in the case of real/immovable property, must be filed with the Public Registry of Property to be binding before third parties.

Preference in possession is ranked:

1. That based on title.

2. In the case of real/immovable property, the title which is recorded.

3. In the absence of title, or if the titles are equal, the older possession is given preference.

Acquisition of possession may be exercised by the person directly, by his legal representative, by his agent, or by a third person without agency.

In the case of possession by a third person without any agency, possession is not obtained until the person in whose name the act of possession was executed ratifies the act of possession.

In the event that several people possess an undivided object, each one may exercise possessory acts with regard to the common object, provided he does not inhibit the possessory acts of the other co-possessors. Additionally, in the event that the property is divided, each co-possessor is considered the sole possessor of his portion of the divided property for the whole time the property is held jointly.

If someone has possession of an object, it is assumed that he also has ownership of all legal effects.

This is a very important principle in Mexican Law. It is intended to protect one's possessions. Normally, the person who possesses an object is its owner. The protection is not founded in possession itself, but rather in the principle that, when there is a doubt as to who really is the owner, the person who is in possession of the property is given the benefit of the doubt.

There are many reasons why this type of protection is maintained. Generally, it is intended to prevent people from taking the law into their own hands by trying to regain possession of property they believe is rightfully theirs.

The person who exercises power over a property is presumed to own it. In the event that the possessor had possession by some other means, such as a lease or other personal or real/immovable property rights, it is not assumed that he is the owner of the property because his contract/title to the property clearly indicate that he is not. In this case, he is a possessor in good faith, and it is presumed that he obtained possession from the owner.

POSSESSION BY GOOD AND BAD FAITH

In the event that one's possession of property is challenged, the first thing to be determined is whether the property was acquired in good or bad faith.

By law, good faith is always presumed, and the burden of proving a possessor's bad faith is the obligation of the accuser. Possession acquired in good faith is not reversed unless it can be proved that the possessor knows that he possesses property unduly.

Good Faith Possession

The Civil Code defines **good faith possession**:

➢ Possession acquired by a title sufficient to give the right to possess.
➢ Possession with defects of title that prevent the possessor from rightfully possessing when the possessor is unaware of such defects.

Bad Faith Possession

On the other hand, **bad faith possession** is defined as:

➢ Possession acquired without any title to possess, and
➢ Possession where the possessor knows the defects of his title that prevent him from possessing the property rightfully.

The Civil Code identifies four situations that deal with good and bad faith possession and the rights and obligations of the parties involved.

Possessors in Good Faith With Title

A person who, in good faith, acquired possession of property by a title conveying ownership, has the following rights:

➢ The right to keep any of the crops, yields, harvests or any other fruits that the property might produce while his possession in good faith is not interrupted;
➢ The right to retain the property possessed until payment for necessary expenses and useful expenses is made;

> The right to remove voluntary improvements, provided that no damage is caused to the property improved, or if there is damage, that the property is restored to its proper condition or functioning;
> The right to be paid for expenses, plus interest, from the day they were incurred, and to be paid for the natural and industrial production left to the benefit of the property because they had not reached full growth or development at the time when the possession was interrupted. In this case, the possessor is not liable for deterioration or loss of the property possessed, even though it occurred due to his actions; however, he is liable for any benefit that he may have obtained from such loss or deterioration.

In other words, since the possessor held the property in good faith as if he were the owner, he should not be responsible for any detriment or damage to the property. His inactivity to prevent such detriment could be attributed to the fact he believed he owned the property, and therefore, in his mind, the cost of preventing such loss or deterioration was not warranted. If, however, the possessor received any profit due to the loss or deterioration of the property, such profit should be returned to the rightful owner as compensation.

Bad Faith Possession With Title for More Than One Year.

In this case the person has to have quietly, continuously, and publicly possessed the property with the intent to claim property rights for more than a year, even though in bad faith, provided no crime was committed. In such a case, the possessor has the following rights:

> The right to two-thirds of the cultivated fruits or emblements that he causes the property to produce. The other third is given to the owner of the property provided that he makes claim for the recovery of the property before the end of the period of prescription. He does not have any right to natural or civil fruits.
> The right to be paid the necessary expenses and to withdraw useful improvements without detriment to the property. His only liability is for loss or deterioration he caused to the property.

Cultivated fruits or emblements are the crops or products of the land legally belonging to a tenant, which are a result of his work. Natural fruits are the spontaneous products of the soil and the offspring or other products of animals. Civil fruits are the rents of buildings, the price for the lease of lands, etc.

Bad Faith Possession With Title for Less Than One Year.

In this case the possessor is not entitled to natural, civil, or cultivated fruits, and is obligated to restore any fruits received. However, he has the right to be reimbursed for "necessary expenses." Necessary expenses are those that are ordered by law, and those without which the property would deteriorate or be lost.

He is also responsible for loss or deterioration he caused to the property or loss caused by a fortuitous event or force *majeure*; unless he can prove that the fortuitous event or force *majeure* would have occurred if its owner had possessed the property. He is not liable for losses that result naturally by the passing of time.

Possession Acquired by Committing a Crime

A possessor who acquired possession of property by any criminal act is obligated to restore all fruits produced by the property, as well as those that it failed to produce due to culpable omission.

The possessor is also responsible for loss or deterioration he caused to the property or loss caused by a fortuitous event or force *majeure*, unless he can prove that the fortuitous event or force *majeure* would have occurred if the property had been possessed by its owner. He is not liable for losses that resulted naturally from the passing of time.

LOSS OF POSSESSION

Possession of property is lost for any of the following reasons:

➢ Abandonment
➢ Sale *(a titulo oneroso)* or gratuitous assignment
➢ Destruction, loss or exclusion from commerce
➢ Judicial decision
➢ Despoilment, if despoiler possesses for more than one year
➢ Recovery of possession by the owner
➢ Expropriation for reason of public benefit.

The possession of rights is lost when it is impossible to exercise them or when they are not exercised within the time allowed by the statute of limitations pertaining to that right.

CHAPTER 12

PROPERTY ACQUISITION
THIS CHAPTER EXAMINES THE DIVISION OF PROPERTY ACQUISITION AND THE
LEGALLY RECOGNIZED FORMS OF ACQUIRING PROPERTY

CLASSIFICATION OF PROPERTY ACQUISITION

The acquisition of property refers to the legal event or act by which a person acquires the domain or ownership *(dominio)* over real or personal/moveable property.

The acquisition of property is classified in the following manner.

TRANSFER OF GENERAL OR SPECIFIC TITLE

Transference by general title occurs when all the assets and liabilities of a person are transferred without specifically mentioning them, such as in the case of inheritance. Specific title transfers occur when the transfers involve property that is explicitly set forth or defined, as in the case of testamentary gift, devise or bequest *(legado)*, or acquisitions by contract.

ORIGINAL OR DERIVED ACQUISITION

Original acquisition refers to a property acquired that did not belong to anyone before the acquisition such as in the cases of occupation and accession. Derived acquisition refers to a property acquired that had belonged to someone and was legally conveyed to another by contract, inheritance, etc.

GRATUITOUS TRANSFER OR CONSIDERATION FOR TITLE

Transference of title for consideration refers to situations in which payment of some kind is received for the property being transferred.

The payment may consist of money, property, or services, which are exchanged for the title to the property. Transference by gratuitous title refers to transactions in which title is transferred to the acquirer without consideration.

TRANSFERENCE *INTER VIVOS* AND BY CAUSE OF DEATH

Transference *"inter vivos"* refers to those that occur between living persons. Transference by cause of death refers to transfer due to the death of the owner of the property.

LEGALLY RECOGNIZED FORMS OF ACQUISITION

The law recognizes the following specific forms to acquire property ownership.

OCCUPANCY

Occupancy is the act of taking possession of previously un-owned property with the intent of obtaining the right to own it.

Only property that does not have an owner may be subject to occupancy. Therefore, only personal/moveable property may be acquired through occupancy because real/immovable property is either private or the municipality, state, or federal government owns it. Common examples of property that may be acquired through occupancy are animals acquired by legal hunting or fishing or treasures discovered where the legitimate owner is unknown.

OCCUPATION OF WATER

Article 27 of the Mexican constitution states that the water rights within the territorial limits of Mexico correspond originally to the nation. The same article establishes which waters are property of the nation and which may be acquired by private parties. Section (1) states:

> "Only Mexicans by birth or naturalization and Mexican companies have the right to acquire ownership of lands, waters and their easements, or to obtain concession for the exploitation of mines or waters.

The State may grant the same right to foreigners, provided they agree before the Ministry of Foreign Affairs to consider themselves as nationals and not to invoke the protection of their governments in matters relating thereto; under penalty, in case of noncompliance with this agreement, forfeiture of the property they had acquired to the benefit of the nation. Under no circumstances may foreigners acquire direct ownership of lands or waters within a zone of one hundred kilometers along the borders and fifty kilometers along the beaches of the country."

Articles 933 through 937 regulate the occupation of waters by private parties that, by definition, are not considered property of the nation in the terms of article 27 of the constitution. All other waters are regulated by the corresponding federal water laws and regulations.

The owner of property which contains flowing water, springs, wells, constructed cisterns or dams has the right to dispose of any water obtained, provided that the rights of other property owners downstream or below the property are not impaired. However, in the event that the water flows from one property to another, its use is considered a public benefit and therefore regulated federally.

Finally, Article 937 of the Civil Code makes provisions to assure that every property owner has adequate water to exploit his land, and is another example of the socialistic tendency adopted by legislators of the Civil Code. Article 937 of the Civil Code states that the owner of real/immovable property who cannot provide himself with the water required to make suitable use of such property except through very costly work, may require the owners of neighboring properties who have surplus water to furnish him the necessary water in exchange for payment as determined by experts.

ACCESSION

Accession is the right of an owner to increase the value of a property by improvements or natural growth.

Literally, "accession" means that something has been added, and as applied to property, it means that new value has been added to existing property by labor or by the addition of another property or by a combination of both. As a general rule, the owner of the property improved becomes the owner of the improvements.

Article 886 defines the right of accession as follows: the ownership of property includes the right to everything that the property produces or which is naturally or artificially united or incorporated to it. The same principle applies to whatever is built, planted and sowed by another person, as well as the repairs or improvements made by another person on the property.

Moreover, legally, it is always presumed that the owner of the property made such improvements at his cost. In determining the right of accession, the concepts of good and bad faith play an important role. In the case of a person who makes improvements to someone else's property, he is considered as acting in bad faith in the following situations:

> If the improvements are made on property that he knows does not belong to him and without prior written consent from the owner.
> If a third party makes the improvements using materials he owns on property he knows does not belong to him and without prior written consent from the owner.

On the other hand, the law considers the owner of the property to be acting in bad faith in cases where improvements are done within his view and with his full knowledge, and he does nothing to stop such improvements from being completed.

ARTIFICIAL AND NATURAL ACCESSION

Under Mexican Law, **accession** falls into two categories, artificial or natural. **Natural accession** is that which results from nature, such as, when a portion of a land is united with another parcel due to water currents, earthquakes or other natural phenomenon.

Artificial Accession

Artificial accession is man-made, and is associated with either real or personal/moveable property. In cases of accession, two basic principles apply:

1. An accession is governed by the same rules that apply to its principal.
2. No one may, at the cost of another, become enriched without cause.

In cases involving real/immovable property, the accession may take the form of construction, planting, or sowing, and it may involve any of the following situations:

> **The owner of the property constructs, plants, or sows with someone else's materials.** If the owner made the improvements in good faith, then he is entitled to the improvements by paying for the materials used. If the improvements were made in bad faith, then he must pay for the materials used and cover any damages or losses incurred. The owner of the seeds, plants, or materials does not have the right to destroy the work done in order to recover his property, but he does have the right to recover plants that have not taken root.

> **The owner of the materials who constructs, plants, or sows on someone else's property.** If the improvements were made in good faith, and the owner of the property also acted in good faith, he would have the following alternatives:
> > To take over the improvements and reimburse the person who made the improvements for the value of the materials.
> > To demand that the person who contracted or planted pay the price of the real/immovable property.
> > To demand that the person who sowed pay rent.

If the improvements were made in good faith, and the owner of the property acted in bad faith, the owner of the property is only able to demand the price of the property or the rent as indicated above. Since the owner of the property acted in bad faith, he is not entitled to the right to make the improvements his property. In other words, the owner either has to pay for the improvements or sell the property to the person who constructed or planted.

> **Someone constructs, plants, or sows on someone else's property, with a third party's materials.** In this case, the intent of the law is to protect both the owner of the property and the owner of the materials used to make the improvement. If the owner of the property benefits from the improvements made, he also has the obligation to pay for them, whether the improvements were made in good faith or not. However, this obligation is only enforced if the person who made the improvements in bad faith was unable to pay for them. If the property owner does not benefit from improvements made in bad faith, he has the right to demand that the work be demolished and that his property be restored to its original condition at the cost of the person who made the improvements.

In cases where someone in bad faith builds, plants or sows on someone else's property, he loses what he built, planted or sowed, and has no right to claim any indemnity from the owner of the property or to recover any materials used.

CONVEYANCE AND SALE

Conveyance and Sale are the two general classifications for the acquisition of property due to the transfer of title from one person to another by the following contracts: Assignment, Sale, Barter (*permuta*), and Donation.

ADVERSE POSSESSION (*PRESCRIPCION POSITIVA*)

Adverse possession (*Prescripcion Positiva*) is a way of acquiring property by possessing it under certain conditions for a specified period of time. The law requires that such possession be with the intent of ownership, and that it be passive, continual, public and for a certain amount of time.

INHERITANCE (*SUCCESION*)

Inheritance *(succesion)* is the act or process of becoming entitled as a legal beneficiary to the property of a deceased person as well as to the rights and obligations that are not extinguished upon death. An inheritance is determined by testamentary execution in the form of a will *(testamentaria)*, or by provisions of the law *(legitima)*.

CHAPTER 13

CO-OWNERSHIP

THIS CHAPTER EXPLAINS HOW CO-OWNERSHIP IS CLASSIFIED, ITS BASIC PRINCIPLES, AND THE RIGHTS AND OBLIGATIONS OF CO-OWNERS

DEFINITION

Article 938 of the Civil Code defines co-ownership as a situation in which various people share an undivided interest in real or personal/moveable property. The provisions for co-ownership are very similar to what is known as "tenancy in common" in the United States. Mexican Law contains no provisions similar to joint tenancy with the right of survivorship or tenancy by the entirety as they are used in the U.S.

CLASSIFICATION OF CO-OWNERSHIP

Co-ownership is classified as follows:

➤ **Voluntary** co-ownership is created by agreement, while **obligatory** co-ownership refers to relationships that exist because it is impossible, due to the nature of the property, to divide or sell it.

➤ **Temporary** co-ownership refers to situations where the parties agree to maintain their ownership relationship for any specific amount of time; **permanent** co-ownership, though, refers to those situations in which the law does not allow termination because the property cannot be divided.

➤ **Regulated** co-ownership refers to those types of co-ownership that are subject to specific legislation which deals with the joint ownership of inherited property, condominiums, and *"medianeria,"* property with a jointly-owned partition or dividing wall. **Unregulated** co-ownership refers to any other situations involving co-ownership, and therefore is regulated by the general provisions for co-ownership of the Civil Code.

➤ *Inter-vivos* are those situations that are created during one's life, and that **by cause of death** refer to co-ownership created by inheritance.

Basic Principles Of Co-Ownership

➤ All acts which involve the disposal of the property are valid only by unanimous consent of the co-owners;

➤ The majority of the co-owners as well as the majority of ownership interests determine the administration of the property. In other words, if there are three co-owners, and one holds an undivided interest of 80%, the decisions made with regard to the administration of the property require his vote; however, such decisions also require at least two votes to meet the majority of co-owners' prerequisite. Therefore, it is impossible for any one co-owner to unilaterally administrate the co-owned property. If a majority vote is impossible to obtain, a judge decides the matter.

Rights And Obligations Of Co-Owners

The essential rights and obligations of a co-owner are as follows:

Rights

➤ To use and enjoy all of the common property;

➤ To request the division of the common property provided that such a division is possible. The law states that the common property may be divided unless "...either because of the nature of the property or by rule of law, the ownership is indivisible."

➤ To full and complete ownership of his undivided share of the property including the fruits of the property such as rent or crops, and the right to sell, assign or mortgage his rights in the property as provided for by law. However, the sold, assigned, or encumbered rights are limited to those divided rights adjudicated when the co-ownership is terminated, and do not affect the property of the other owners if the property is divided.

➤ To exercise the right of first refusal in the event that one of the other co-owners wants to sell his undivided share of the property.

The law requires that the co-owners notify the other co-owners of sales, through a notary or the courts, in order to allow them to exercise their right of first refusal, which becomes forfeit if not used within eight days of being notified. Any sale made without such notification is null and void, having no legal effect whatsoever. If several co-owners are interested in exercising their right of first refusal, the co-owner with the greater share in the property is given preference, and if they have equal shares, the co-owner is designated by lot, unless agreed otherwise.

OBLIGATIONS

Co-owners have the right to participate in the profits or benefits created by the use of the property, and are obligated to participate in any expenses created in proportion to their respective share of ownership, or in equal proportions if there is no proof to the contrary. Every co-owner has the right to demand that the other co-owners contribute to the expenses and preservation of the common property. The only way a co-owner is exempt from this obligation is by renouncing his participation in the ownership of the common property.

CHAPTER 14

CONDOMINIUM OWNERSHIP

THIS CHAPTER EXAMINES THE DIFFERENT TYPES OF CONDOMINIUM OWNERSHIP, COMMON PROPERTY, OWNERS' RIGHTS AND OBLIGATIONS, PROCEDURES TO ESTABLISH CONDOMINIUM OWNERSHIP, AND MANAGEMENT OF CONDOMINIUM PROPERTIES.

INTRODUCTION

Co-ownership by condominium is an obligatory, permanent and regulated form of co-ownership. Condominium ownership involves any real estate where there is a combination of individual and co-ownership of property. Condominium ownership should not be confused with the co-ownership, even though they are similar, they are not legally treated the same. In co-ownership all the owners have title to all the property held in co-ownership.

In condominium ownership, each person has an exclusive right to his department or unit of property and, at the same time, is also co-owner of the common areas. Moreover, it is possible that several persons be co-owners of a condominium unit, and also be, as a group, co-owners of the common areas of the condominium property. Condominium ownership, therefore, refers to real/immovable property that belongs to several owners, each of which has exclusive rights on each unit and joint ownership rights on the assets and common areas.

Condominium ownership is defined as real/immovable property with vertical, horizontal, or mixed construction, susceptible to individual ownership by various owners, and common areas which are co-owned and undivided.

Article 951 of the Civil Code for the Federal District states that:

When different apartments, housing units, houses or premises of a property, belonging to different owners, constructed in vertical form, horizontal or mixed, susceptible to independent use by having their own exit to a common area of the property or to a thoroughfare, each owner has an exclusive and singular right to the property on his apartments, housing units, house or premises. Additionally, he shall have joint ownership rights to the common areas necessary for his adequate use and enjoyment.

The rights and obligations of the condominium owners are regulated by the condominium's title documents and its regulations, the Civil Code, and the corresponding Condominium Law. Each condominium owner or occupant may use his unit in a quiet and orderly manner, provided that he does not affect the tranquillity of the other owners and occupants. He must not compromise the stability, safety, healthiness or comfort of the condominium, nor incur by omission that which produces the same results.

An owner may not use his condominium for purposes other than those specifically agreed, or in such a way as to be immoral or contrary to good customs. In the event of doubt as to the use of the condominium, the permissible uses are those that are presumed as correct due to the nature of the condominium and its location.

With regard to the services, common areas, and general facilities, all the owners are obligated not to carry out any activity that hinders or makes less effective its operation. The owners must not hinder the enjoyment of common property, or put at risk the safety and tranquillity of the joint owners, even when such activity is carried out in the interior of his property. The common assets of the condominium are limited exclusively to real/immovable property, but also include all the personal/moveable property used for ornament, safety, operation and service, such as gardening and cleaning equipment, as well as furniture used in common areas and in the foyers, etc.

The infringer of these dispositions is responsible for the payment of the expenses that are necessary to recoup or reinstate the services and facilities in question. He is also responsible for the payment of damages that are caused; independently of the fact that violation of this provision is cause for the rescission of the contract in question. In addition to being accountable for the damages caused, the guilty party may also be sued and forced to sell his rights in public auction under the terms of Article 38 of the Condominium Law.

TYPES OF CONDOMINIUM OWNERSHIP

Article One of the Condominium Law states the following:

> When different apartments, dwellings, houses or premises of a property, constructed in a vertical, horizontal or mixed form, susceptible to independent use due to having their own exit to a common area (of the property) or public street, which are owned by different owners, each one of them will have the singular and exclusive property right to his apartment, dwelling, house or premise, and, additionally, the right of co-ownership to the common areas of the property, necessary for adequate use and enjoyment.

In accordance with Article Two of the Condominium Law, there are three types of condominium ownership:

1. When a building which consists of various apartments, dwellings, houses or premises, has common and undivided ownership areas and is owned by various owners.

2. When various apartments, dwellings, houses or premises, with common and undivided ownership areas, are constructed on a piece of real/immovable property with the intention of selling them to various individuals.

3. When the owners of a piece of real/immovable property divide that property into various apartments, dwellings, houses or premises, with common and undivided ownership areas, with the intention of selling them to various individuals.

CONDOMINIUM OWNERS

The law defines "condominium owner" *(condómino)* as the individual or legal entity which, in the capacity of owner, has possession of one or more apartments, dwellings, houses or premises. For the effects of the condominium law, the owner of a condominium is the person who, having executed and complied with an agreement to acquire the condominium property, is considered as owner.

Every owner is entitled to the exclusive ownership right to his apartment, dwelling, house or premises and the co-ownership to common areas in proportion to the value of his apartment, dwelling, house or premises as determined in the condominium's title documents.

Therefore, a condominium owner is defined as:

> A legal entity or individual that it is in possession of one or more units in the capacity of owner.
> The person that, having executed a contract by virtue of which, upon compliance, becomes the owner.

In the first hypothesis, it is assumed that a legal entity or individual is a joint owner due to the fact that he is in possession of units. As such, the other joint owners are not obligated to request that such an owner produce property in order to demand compliance of all the obligations that correspond to a joint owner.

In the second hypothesis, condominium ownership is attributed to anyone who has signed a contract to acquire the property in the future, as in the case of a promissory agreement or a reserve title agreement. In these two cases, the buyer does not yet have title to the condominium property; however, even when the acquisition of the property is deferred, the law considers such a buyer to be an owner from the date of the contract.

A possible problem arises when the buyer does not comply with the terms of the promissory agreement or the reserve title agreement, and, therefore, does not gain title to the property. In such cases, who is responsible for condominium dues?

The other condominium owners are not parties to the promissory agreement or to the reserve title agreement, therefore, they are not affected by the noncompliance of the contract. The rights and obligations involved in condominium ownership are not personal; rather, such rights are dependent on the provisions inherent to the objective character of being a condominium owner.

Therefore, the rights of the buyer are those which are specified in the promissory agreement or the reserve title agreement, however, such rights cannot surpass or violate the rights legally provided for under condominium ownership. The obligations of the buyer, in addition to those that are normally included in such agreements, also include those legal provisions that concern condominium ownership. The obligations also include those established in the condominium regulations, and in the agreements of the condominium owner's meetings. In the event of noncompliance of the buyer, any future possessor or owner is liable before the other owners for any outstanding obligation created by such noncompliance.

COMMON PROPERTY

The law defines common property as follows:

> The land, cellars, entrances, foyers, galleries, passageways, staircases, courtyards, gardens, parks, paths, interior streets, meeting facilities, sports and recreation facilities, spaces dedicated by the construction licenses as sufficient for vehicles parking; as long as such areas are of general use;
> The premises intended for the administration, and the housing of the janitor and security guards; as well as those intended for the general facilities and common services;
> Constructions, facilities, appliances and other objects that serve as use of common satisfaction, such as wells, cisterns, elevators, hoists, incinerators, cooking stoves, ovens, pumps and motors; sewage and water ducts; distribution channels for drainage, heating, electricity and gas; safety construction, ornamentation and similar fixtures, with the exception of those which are exclusively for each individual unit;
> The foundations, structures, retaining walls and the ceilings of general use,
> Any other part of the property facilities that is designated as such by the unanimity of the joint owners, to use or to enjoy in common or that is established as such in the Regulation of the Condominium or in the title deed.

Within the common property it is important to distinguish between property which belongs to all the joint owners, and the property which is common only to contiguous owners, such walls and divisions that separate units.

Only the contiguous joint owners own common walls and floors and other divisions that separate the individual units. Owners of condominium units all have the same rights regardless of their physical location. In other words, owners of more desirable units, such as those on the ground floor and the penthouse do not have more rights than the remaining joint owners. Unless the Regulations of the Condominium establishes otherwise, the owners of a ground floor unit may not occupy or make exclusive or preferential use of the foyers, cellars, gardens, courtyards which surround his unit. Likewise, the owners of the penthouse or top floor may not occupy the attics or ceiling, or add new floors, or other constructions. The same restrictions are germane to the other joint owners of the condominium property.

When certain areas of a condominium's common property are leased, or are used for commerce, a percentage of the obtained profits must be applied to the administration, maintenance and operation expense funds as determined annually by the condominium owners' meeting.

RIGHTS AND OBLIGATIONS OF CONDOMINIUM OWNERS

Each condominium owner has an exclusive right to his apartment, housing unit, house or premises, and a right to the joint ownership of common assets of the property in proportion to the value of his property, as set forth in the title deed of the condominium.

The value of the units does not vary, and the fact that they were not acquired on the same date, or at the same price for equal units, does not, in any way, affect the value used for determining one's proportional share of the common property. This is because the values used are all determined in the condominium's title deed, and such proportions are calculated on those original values and do not change. Therefore, even if the sale value of any unit should change, due to changes in the market, the proportions that correspond to each unit in the common assets of the condominium stay the same.

However, when additions or improvements are made to a unit, the common property proportion that corresponds to each joint owner can vary. In such cases, a new calculation of the property's value must be carried out, based on a legally authorized appraisal. It must be approved by the condominium owners' meeting and filed with the Public Registry of Property. The common property proportion that corresponds to a unit should always be included in any sales agreement and be the same as what is filed with the Public Registry of Property.

The common property proportion used in the law only refers to rights of ownership and not to use rights, which are equal for all. In other words, if one unit is worth more than another unit, this fact does not entitle the owner of the first unit to use the common assets more than the other owners.

Condominium owners are allowed to make all kinds of repairs and additions to the interior of their units provided that it does not affect the structure, the principal walls or other essential elements of the building, or lead to damage to the condominium's stability, safety, healthiness, or comfort. Similarly, no one may cut clear spaces or windows, or paint or decorate exterior walls in a form that is inharmonious with the rest of the condominium structures or that may damage the general aesthetics of the property.

Each co-owner has the right to make use of the common assets and enjoy the services and general facilities pursuant to its nature and ordinary fate, provided that he does so without restricting the rights of the other co-owners. However, if a co-owner abandons or waives his right to use any of the common assets, he is still subject to the obligations imposed by the law, the title deed, the Regulation of the Condominium and the other relevant legal dispositions.

Every co-owner can use, enjoy and dispose of his property within the limitations and prohibitions of the law, and of the provisions of the title deed and of the Regulation of the Condominium. However, a co-owner may not sell or lease part of his property, such as a flat or bedroom, service rooms or a private site for parking.

In the terms of article 38 of the Condominium Law, violation of these provisions is cause for the rescission of the contract in question, or the violator may also be sued and forced to sell his rights in public auction. He is also accountable for the damages caused. To exercise this action, a resolution by a special owners meeting is required. Those who represent a minimum of 75% of the value of the condominium property must agree upon this resolution.

If the condominium is destroyed in whole or in a proportion that represents at least three-fourths of its value as determined by a legal appraisal, the condominium owners may agree to the reconstruction, or to the division of the property and the common assets that remain, or to its outright sale. The majority must represent at least 51% of the total value of the condominium. If the destruction does not reach three-fourths, owners who represent at least 75% of the total value of the condominium is needed to adopt any of the above alternatives.

In either case, if the condominium owners meeting agrees to reconstruction, the owners who voted against reconstruction or the minority, are obligated to contribute to the reconstruction in proportion to the value of their respective units, or they may sell their rights. Such a sale may be in favor of the majority, if the minority agrees;

however, in any event, after six months the sale becomes compulsory at the appraisal price determined by a public broker or by a trust institution.

Every condominium owner has the right to attend and participate in condominium meetings. Each owner's voting rights is determined to be in direct relation to the percentage of his ownership as set forth in the condominium's title documents. An owner and his tenant, or any other assignee may decide who has to perform determined obligations before the other co-owners, and in such cases, the assignee may represent the owner in condominium meetings. The owner is ultimately responsible for compliance to the obligations that are assumed by the assignee.

All owners must pay their proportion of the administration, maintenance and operation expense funds that are approved by the condominium owners meeting in accordance with the condominium's regulations or in accordance with a resolution adopted by the condominium owners meeting. When certain areas of a condominium's common property are leased, or are used for commerce, a percentage of the obtained profits must be applied to the administration, maintenance and operation expense funds as determined annually by the condominium owners meeting.

A Condominium property may be encumbered, without the consent of the other owners, but only when privately owned property is encumbered along with the corresponding share of the co-owned property. Likewise, it is impossible to sell only the privately owned property without including its share of the co-owned property.

Although the Condominium Law does not specifically mention that a condominium owner has the right to lease his property, such a possibility is implicitly granted in various provisions of the law. The same holds true for bailments given the similarities of the two agreements and the fact that they do not violate any of the general provisions for condominium ownership.

The law is not clear regarding the treatment of third parties that have possession of condominium property by lease or bailment. The condominium regulations should contain clauses that allow interested parties the right to sue for the rescission or cancellation of such contracts if a third party possessor violates the title documents of the condominium by using the unit in question for purposes other than those allowed. By doing so, the condominium's administrator can sue to have the occupant evicted, and can demand the payment of damages.

The law states that if a tenant does not comply with condominium obligations, the administrator may sue for eviction with the consent of the owner of the unit in question. If the owner opposes such action, then the administrator may take legal action against both the owner and the occupant under the terms of article 38 of the Condominium Law as stated above.

The condominium law gives a tenant of a condominium the right of first refusal to purchase the unit he is leasing should the owner decide to sell it. The law states that in the event that a condominium owner with a tenant occupying his property desires to sell his property, he must first notify the tenant through the condominium's administrator, through a Public Notary, or through the court. The notification must include the price offered, the terms, and other conditions of the proposed sale. The tenant then has ten days following the notification to exercise his right of first refusal.

The law does not provide the right of first refusal to other condominium owners. Until the condominium law changed on June 23, 1993, it was possible to include such a right in the condominium's regulations. However, it is doubtful that such provisions are binding given that each condominium unit is owned separately and not subject to the provisions of co-ownership.

Every co-owner is responsible for the expense of maintaining his common floors, pavements, walls or other divisions among contiguous premises. On the other hand, in vertical construction condominiums, all the co-owners pay for repairs and construction required for the roof, the exterior, and the cellars.

The following rules apply to work done to the common assets and general facilities of the condominium:

➢ Work necessary to maintain the condominium in good, safe, stable, and conserved state, so that the services operate normally and effectively, are carried out by the Administrator. The Administrator carries out such work under license, if necessary, of the competent authorities, and with the authorization of the Surveillance Committee. Authorization from the condominium meeting is not required. All expenses are paid from the condominium's maintenance fund. In the event that no funds are available, or unforeseen work needs to be done, the Administrator must summon a condominium meeting so that action may be taken in accordance with the Regulations of the Condominium;

➤ The seller is accountable for construction defects of the condominium. The remainder of the joint owners may repair such defects in the proportion to what each one owns in the total value of the condominium. In such case, they may demand payment from the seller, or cash the performance bond for the contraction and defects. The government determines the amount and the term of the bond upon issuing the building permit.

➤ In order to have work done to improve the appearance or comfort of the condominium, which may or may not increase its value, authorization of the condominium owners meeting is required. The authorization must be approved by a favorable vote of owners who represent 75% of the total value of the condominium.

➤ The joint owners carry out urgent repairs or replacements in the common assets and general facilities if the Administrator is not available.

➤ The expenses incurred for the operation, repair, conservation and maintenance of the general facilities and services, as well as the common areas and assets, are covered by the joint owners in the proportion to what each one owns in the total value of the condominium.

The law prohibits any work which jeopardizes the safety, stability, and conservation of the condominium or which affects the comfort of the owners. The same is true of any improvements or modifications, which permanently hinder the use of a common service or area, or those which somehow reduce the value of an individual condominium unit, even if one single owner is affected. However, in the latter two cases, the improvements or modifications may be carried out with the unanimous agreement among the joint owners and, if the value of an individual condominium unit is reduced, provided that the affected owner is compensated to his complete satisfaction.

ADMINISTRATIVE PROCEDURES TO ESTABLISH CONDOMINIUM OWNERSHIP

Before construction may begin on property to be used for a condominium project, certain procedures must be carried out:

1. The interested property owner or owners must obtain a declaration from the government which indicates that the project is feasible and complies with urban planning, development regulations, and which grants a building permit for up to 120 condominium apartments, dwellings, houses or premises.

2. In order to change the property from individual ownership to condominium ownership, the property owner or owners must make a condominium ownership statement before a public notary (*escrtitura publica*) indicating the following:

   ➤ The layout, dimensions and property lines of the condominium property which clearly indicate individual ownership areas from co-owned areas.

   ➤ Written proof that the declaration from the government mentioned above was obtained as well as all of the necessary building permits.

   ➤ A general description of the construction and quality of building materials.

   ➤ Descriptions of each apartment, dwelling, house or premise including parking areas.

   ➤ The value of each apartment, dwelling, house or premise and the percentage that each represents in the total value of the whole condominium project.

   ➤ The general use of the condominium as a whole and the particular use of each apartment, dwelling, house or premise.

   ➤ The use and characteristics of common areas.

   ➤ The terms and conditions of the performance bond for the contraction and defects. The government determines the amount and the term of the bond upon issuing the building permit.

   ➤ The conditions under which any of the above may be modified.

   ➤ In addition to the above information, as an exhibit to the notarized document, certified copies of a general survey and plans for each apartment, dwelling, house or premise, and common areas; as well as the regulations of the condominium must also be included. This and any other necessary documents are delivered to the administrator of the condominium project who is legally responsible for carrying out its provisions.

3. Once the condominium ownership documents above are completed and notarized, they are then filed with the Public Registry of

Property (*Registro Publico de la Propiedad*). This document serves as title to the property and allows the individual condominium units to be sold separately and registered as such in the Public Registry of Property.

4. Finally, the condominium ownership documents are also filed at the municipal land register in order that each condominium unit is assigned a property tax identification number.

Any contract used for the acquisition of ownership of condominium property must include the above information and state that the interested buyer was given a copy of the condominium regulations certified by a public notary.

Condominium ownership is voluntarily dissolved by agreement of a minimum of 75% of the owners unless the condominium's title documents require a higher percentage. The condominium's title documents are modified in accordance with the provisions of the condominium's regulations, but the above percentage may not be lower than the 75% required by the law. The corresponding Public Notary or, as the case may be, the Director of the Public Registry of Property is responsible for assuring that all urban planning and development provisions are complied with.

ADMINISTRATIVE ORGANIZATION OF CONDOMINIUMS

Administratively, condominium ownership is organized much like a Mexican corporation. There is a condominium owners' meeting, a surveillance committee, and an administrator. The administration of the condominium is carried out in many different ways and by one or more people. Some condominiums like to hire a management company, or create a condominium owners association, while others prefer to appoint a sole administrator or a managing board nominated from owners. This section examines administration without a condominium owner's association, though the book goes on to discuss administration under Home Owners Associations later.

The formation of an association *(asociación civil)* is not necessary for all condominium properties. Associations have advantages but they also require greater expenses: public notary fees for its creation, revision and extinction; notarial powers of attorney granted to the association's legal representative when he is appointed, etc. They also require more formalities and tax obligations, which, if not attended to, cause more headaches than anything else does.

It is possible to administrate a condominium project with an informal association without establishing a formal association. The size and type of condominium complex is often the determining factor when deciding if a formal association is necessary. Smaller condominium complexes with a minimal amount of facilities are less likely to require an association. Their legal relationship with third parties is less than large complexes with many employees.

In cases of informal associations, the only obligation the condominium owners have is to keep an authorized minutes book *(libro de actas)*, and to pay any taxes or social security payments for employees which the condominium may hire. Other taxes likely to need paying are property taxes on common assets, and income tax on any income generated from the exploitation of the common assets.

Because of the nature of condominium ownership, the law provides for representation of the condominium and its owners through a common representative who is granted sufficient powers. A sole administrator and the surveillance committee, consisting of one or more condominium owners can carry out the administration.

This form of administration has both advantages and disadvantages. When one of the owners is the administrator, he is more likely to give greater attention to the matters of the condominium, and generally, he charges for his services. However, often most owners are not willing to accept the responsibilities of administration. They may not have the time, or they do not want the hassle of confronting the other owners for collection or to insist that they respect the rights of others.

CONDOMINIUM OWNERS' MEETING

The ultimate power and control reside in the condominium owners through the condominium owners meeting *(asamblea de condómino)*, which may be either general meetings or group meetings. General meetings are those in which all the owners attend, and group meetings are those which are limited to a specific number of owners.

The law makes reference to group meetings in article 36 of the Condominium Law which states that when a condominium property consists of different parts, such as several staircases, courtyards, gardens, and facilities intended to serve one segment of owners, the related expenses are charged to the group of benefited owners, in accordance with the condominium's regulations. The same holds true for staircases, elevators, hoist and other elements, appliances or facilities that are used by only a segment of the owners.

All of the condominium owners have the right to attend these meeting which are regulated by the following guidelines:

➢ General meetings must be held at least once a year and as many times as they are legally convened.
➢ Each owner has the right to the number of votes equal to the percentage of the value his unit represents in the total value of the entire project, which appears in the corresponding property title.
➢ In the election or removal of the administrator or of the surveillance committee, each condominium unit is limited to one vote.
➢ In cases where an owner's property is affected by a mortgage, or the property was sold under a reserve title contract, or any other contract which makes a person the owner upon compliance of its terms; the owner or future owner's voting percentage is limited to the amount that he has paid, provided that it represents at least half of the sales price. His creditor or the person who has reserved title rights exercises the remaining voting rights. If the person has paid less than half of the sales price, he is not entitled to vote. This provision only governs if the creditor or titleholder attends the assembly. To do so, they must first be registered in the condominium's creditors register and possess written proof of the registration issued by the administrator prior to attending. This is explained later in this chapter in the section regarding the administrator.
➢ Voting is exercised personally unless the condominium's regulations provide for representation.
➢ The resolutions of the meetings are passed by majority vote unless the law or the condominium's regulations require otherwise.
➢ In the event that one owner represents 50% of the votes, 50% of the remaining votes are required to pass resolutions. If a resolution cannot be passed, either the 50% owner or the minority group may, if the condominium's regulations allow, submit the

matter in question to arbitration or to a judge so the matter can be resolved.

➢ The meetings are presided over by the person and in the form indicated in the condominium's regulations. The administrator of the condominium acts as the secretary, or, if the administration is carried out by a company, the person the company designates acts as secretary.

➢ The secretary must keep a minutes book and the secretary, or a public notary, as well as the chairman of the meeting and the surveillance committee must authorize the meeting's minutes. It is recommendable that an attendance list signed by those who attend the meeting be kept to avoid situations where people say they did not attend when in fact they really did.

➢ The secretary must always keep the minutes book available to the owners and registered creditors. The secretary must notify them in writing as to each of the resolutions adopted by the meetings.

Meetings are called by the administrator, or by owners or by creditors who represent at least 25% of the value of the condominium when this value is accredited by a competent judge, as well as by the surveillance committee.

Notification of the condominium meeting must be made at least 10 days prior to the date of the meeting. The notification must indicate where within the condominium complex the meeting will be held, the month, day, and hour the meeting will be held, and it must include a copy of the meeting's order of the day or agenda.

When the meeting is held after the first summons, at least 90% of the voters must be present to have a quorum. If there is no quorum, another meeting must be held. After this second summons only 51% of the voters are required for a quorum. If there is still not enough persons in attendance, a third meeting must be called. After the third summons, resolutions are passed by a majority vote of those who attend. All resolutions legally adopted by the condominium owner's meeting are binding for all owners including those who were not present or those who voted against whatever was adopted.

Condominium meetings have the following powers:

➢ To appoint and remove the administrator and the surveillance committee, in accordance with the provisions of the condominium's regulations. They also have the power to determine how much the administrator will be paid for his services. The administrator does not have to be one of the condominium owners. Up to three people are appointed to the surveillance committee.

➤ Determine which activities the administrator is personally responsible for and in which activities he acts as the representative of the owners.

➤ Determine the amount and type of guarantee the administrator pays to assure that he carries out his duties faithfully and manages the maintenance and administration funds correctly.

➤ Approve the annual balance submitted by the administrator and the yearly budget.

➤ Establish the fees paid by the owners for the funds for maintenance and administration of the property. These funds should have enough to cover three months' expenses. The meeting must also establish the fees paid by the owners for the reserve fund. The payments are determined in proportion with the value of each apartment, dwelling, house or premise. The payments are divided into monthly payments and are paid in advance. The initial amounts required for both the reserve fund and the maintenance and administration fund must be stated in the condominium's regulations. The funds' money not immediately used may be invested but only in fixed and immediate return investments.

➤ Take legal action against the administrator for violations of the law, the condominium's regulations, or the condominium's title documents *(escritura constitutiva)*.

➤ Instruct the administrator in his activities and duties.

➤ Make changes to the condominium's regulations and title documents as provided for by law.

➤ Carry out all other activities and powers granted by law, the condominium's regulations or title documents.

THE ADMINISTRATOR

Condominium properties are managed by an administrator appointed by the condominium owners meeting in accordance with the law and the condominium's regulations. The administrator is the legal representative of the condominium and is responsible for his actions. In basic terms the administrator executes the decisions of the condominium owners meetings, and oversees the everyday care and organization of the condominium property. An individual or a company can hold the administrator's position.

The law establishes the following powers and obligations of the administrator of a condominium property:

1. To maintain an authorized register of creditors. The register reflects those creditors who choose to attend condominium meetings by notifying the administrator within a month from the date the credit was established, or in the month of January of each year. The register is also used to keep the balances due to creditors for each owner and the consent of both with regard to the correctness of such balance. These calculations are important because they also determine how many votes both the creditor and the owner have in condominium meetings. In the event that there are discrepancies in these balances or there is an unwillingness of the debtor to consent, the balance due is determined by the surveillance committee.

2. To take care of and watch over the condominium property and the common services required, and to promote the integration, organization, and development of the community.

3. To maintain the books and documents related to the condominium and to make them available to the condominium owners.

4. To attend to the operation and up-keep of the utility services and the installations required for the condominium.

5. To carry out all acts required for the administration and conservation of the property.

6. To have any necessary construction work done which is required for the general maintenance, security, and conservation of the property, as well as that necessary to maintain functioning public utilities.

7. To execute the decisions of the condominium meeting unless they are delegated to another person.

8. To collect the money owed by the condominium owners for the maintenance, administration and reserve funds.

9. To pay the condominium's maintenance and administration expenses in accordance with the condominium's regulations.

10. To issue receipts to each of the condominium owners for payments made to maintenance, administration and reserve funds.

11. To deliver a monthly report to every condominium owner with the following information:

    ➢ The expenses of the preceding month paid from the maintenance and administration funds.

    ➢ A list of the fees paid by the owners and the amounts still owed to the maintenance, administration and reserve funds.

    ➢ The current balance of the maintenance, administration funds and an explanation of what the funds will be used for in the following month.

    ➢ The condominium owners should sign a receipt indicating that they received this report. The condominium owners have a term of five days from the date they receive the report to present observations or objections. After this term, it is assumed that they agree with the report's contents.

12. To summon the condominium owners meeting at least 10 days prior to the date of the meeting. The summons must indicate the place within the property or the place agreed to in the condominium's regulations; the month, day, and hour it will be held; and the agenda or order of the day for the meeting. In addition to the written notification delivered to the condominium owners, the administrator must also post a copy of the summons for the meeting in a location on the property that is visible to all of the owners.

13. To demand that an owner pay for damages created by that owner due to violations of provisions of the Condominium Law.

14. To see that the provisions of the law, the condominium's regulations, and the condominium's title documents are duly observed.

15. To carry out any other activities and comply with the obligations, which are established for his position by the law, the condominium's regulations, and the condominium's title, documents.

The administrator, while being the legal representative of the condominium, does not have complete and total powers over the condominium's property. The law states that the administrator has the power to represent the condominium in matters related to the administration of property and for lawsuits and collections. Any additional powers, such as the power to sell condominium property, or any other powers that require specific mention by law, require authorization from the condominium owners' meeting by majority vote representing 51% of the owners.

The actions and demands made by the administrator, within the scope of his powers in accordance with the law or the condominium's regulations, are binding for all the co-owners. The condominium owners' meeting may limit or revoke the administrator's powers at any time. The majority vote required to carry out such limitations is indicated in the condominium's regulations.

THE SURVEILLANCE COMMITTEE

The surveillance committee is made up of up to three people who are co-owners. Its principal obligation is to oversee the administrator to ensure that he fulfills his obligations in accordance with the law, the condominium's regulations and title documents. The committee must also ensure that the resolutions adopted by the owners' meeting are carried out.

The surveillance committee has the following rights and obligations:

➢ Make sure that the administrator complies with the resolutions adopted by the owners' meeting.
➢ Determine outstanding balances due, for the creditors' register, in the event that there are discrepancies or an unwillingness of an owner/debtor to consent to the balances determined by the administrator.
➢ Authorize necessary construction and repairs.
➢ Verify the balance statements submitted by the administrator to the owners' meeting.
➢ Verify investments in the acquisition of implements and machinery from the reserve fund.
➢ Report to the owners' meeting with regard to the administration of the condominium.
➢ Verify any reports of noncompliance by the owners received from the administrator and report to the owners' meeting.
➢ Collaborate with the administrator in the observation of the owners to ensure their compliance with their obligations.

➢ Summon the owners' meeting when the administrator has failed to do so within three days; or when it judges it necessary in order to notify the owners of irregularities of the administrator. In the latter case, it should also notify the administrator to appear.
➢ Carry out any other activities and comply with any other obligations which are established by law, the condominium's regulations, and the condominium's title documents.

THE CONDOMINIUM REGULATIONS

The Regulations of a Condominium must contain at least the following:

➢ The rights and obligations of the joint owners with regard to the assets of common use, specifying such assets; any limitations on exercising such rights;
➢ The policies regarding the administration, maintenance and operation of the condominium;
➢ The policies necessary to sponsor the integration, setup and development of the community;
➢ The manner by which the condominium owners' meetings is summoned and the person that will preside over it;
➢ How the Administrator and the Surveillance Committee are appointed and the powers they have;
➢ Requirements needed to hold the post of Administrator and participate in the Surveillance Committee ;
➢ Remuneration of the Administrator and the Surveillance Committee;
➢ Cases for the removal of the Administrator and/or the Surveillance Committee.

EXPENSES, TAXES AND CONTROVERSIES

As mentioned above, all owners must pay their proportion of the administration, maintenance and operation expenses, and contribute to any reserve funds. The condominium owners meeting approves these expenses and funds in accordance with the condominium's regulations or a resolution adopted by the condominium owners meeting. Likewise, when certain areas of the condominium's common property are leased, or are used for commerce, a percentage of the obtained profits are applied to the common funds, as determined annually by the condominium owners meeting.

When a condominium consists of different parts, such as several staircases, courtyards, gardens, and facilities intended to serve a segment of the owners, any special expenses generated by those parts are charged to the segment of owners that benefit. The same holds true for staircases, elevators, hoists and other elements, appliances or facilities. The condominium's regulations should establish special procedures for the distribution of such expenses.

If an owner does not pay his monthly contribution to the condominium's common funds, an interest payment is added to the amount owed. The percentage used for the interest is fixed by condominium regulations, or, if the regulations do not mention anything in this regard, the percentage is set by law.

If an owner is behind in three payments, legal action is taken in summary executory proceedings *(aparejada ejecución en al vía ejecutiva civil)* for the total amount plus interest and penalties in accordance with the condominium's regulations.

The regulations of the condominium also establishes that when an owner is overdue in his payments, the Administrator splits the amount owed among the remaining owners, in proportion to the value of their properties, until the outstanding amount is recovered. When the owner who is overdue pays what is owed, the Administrator then reimburses the other owners the amounts that they paid plus interest.

Violation of these provisions is cause for the rescission of the contract of the owner in violation, or, the guilty party is sued and forced to sell his rights in public auction. He is also accountable for the damages caused. To exercise this action, a resolution of a special owners meeting is required and owners who represent a minimum of 75% of the value of the condominium property must agree. The infringing or delinquent owner is summoned to the meeting to defend himself. In cases of noncompliance involving people who occupy a condominium unit but do not own it, the administrator sues for eviction with the previous consent of the owner. If the owner does not consent, the administrator then proceeds against the owner and the occupant.

Regarding tax payments, the law states that owners are liable for the payment of property tax which corresponds to their unit. They are each liable for taxes on the parts of the co-owned assets which correspond to each of them and for any other taxes which are generated by the condominium.

Any controversies regarding the application of the Condominium Law, the regulations of the condominium, the title deed, and the transference of ownership, as well as any other applicable legal provisions, are submitted to arbitration if the regulations of the condominium so provide, or to the competent courts. Any written agreements executed in the arbitration, as well as those mutually executed by the owners or with its administration, with prior acknowledgment of the parties' signatures, is binding for all concerned.

ENCUMBRANCES

Generally, encumbrances are limited to each individual condominium unit. Each of the owners is only held responsible for encumbrances levied against his property. The law states that any contract or provision that establishes the joint liability of the condominium owners for encumbrances related to condominium property is not binding. Debts that originate in obligations contained in the title deed, or that are due to a transfer of title, provisions of law, or condominium regulations, enjoy security with a security interest in real/immovable property on the condominium unit in question, even though the unit is transmitted to third parties.

CONDOMINIUMS IN THE RESTRICTED ZONE

Condominium property in the restricted zone is held in trust if it is sold to a foreigner. Therefore, it is imperative that the bank/trustee grant a power of attorney to the beneficiary/condo owner to exercise his rights in all matters related to the condominium property.

This is not a detail to overlook. If a foreigner does not have a power of attorney from the bank/trustee, legally he cannot vote or act as an owner in condominium meetings. More importantly, if a foreigner acted in the capacity of owner without a power of attorney from the bank/trustee, any agreement made in condominium meetings is void.

APPENDIX A

ESCROW IN MEXICO: DOES IT EXIST?

By Christopher M. Leo, Esq.

When an American, Canadian or other foreign citizen attempts to buy property in Mexico, he or she is confronted with a huge task: how to insure that property rights transfer when money is given to the seller. In a real estate transaction in the United States, most people use escrow to protect the money and title transfer.

Escrow means:

Any transaction wherein one person, for the purpose of effecting the sale, transfer, encumbrance or lease of real or personal property to another person, delivers any written instrument, money, or title to real or personal property, to a third person to be held until some specified event occurs. Upon that event's occurrence, the item to be delivered by the third party is delivered to the beneficiary, grantee or obligee (California Code of Finance Section 17003).

In the eastern half of the United States an attorney handles this transaction. On the West Coast, an escrow company, title insurance company, or an attorney handles escrow. These companies are licensed and regulated by the state. The main problem here is that the property transaction to be effected is in Mexico.

The word "escrow" is not easily translated into Spanish. One term that is often used is *arras*. *Arras* is roughly translated as follows: a sum of money or property that one party to a contract deposits with the second party to a contract upon the execution of a contract for a specific purpose. Normally, *arras* is used to assure performance and fulfillment of the terms and conditions of an existing contract. As one can see, the major difference between "escrow" and *arras* is that escrow always involves an independent third party, while *arras* does not.

One other Spanish term that is used in place of escrow is *depósito*, which means exactly what it sounds like. It is a deposit where one person gives another person something to hold and then that item is returned. There are all types of *depósitos*, but none of them carry the protection and guarantees that an escrow agreement does. There is also no involvement of an independent third party.

The participation of third parties in escrow services in Mexico presents some very serious problems. First of all, when an individual or company offers escrow, one has to assume the service being offered is for the public at large. This company is holding money in the company account until certain conditions are met. At the time those conditions are met, the funds are released. But Mexican law strictly prohibits any individual or company from receiving funds from the public to comply with an unsettled obligation, i.e. a real estate transaction. The penalty for violating this law is 2 to 10 years in jail and a fine of 5 to 500 times the minimum wage in effect in Mexico City. Also, these "escrow" or "closing" companies in Mexico are not licensed or regulated by the Mexican government, as are their US counterparts. Since escrow as Americans know it does not exist under Mexican law, many foreigners have been misled into thinking that the people they were hiring were as qualified as the escrow companies in the United States.

An additional point to make concerning the Mexican real estate industry is that real estate brokers in Mexico who sometimes act as "escrow agents," are not licensed or bonded to sell real estate in Mexico like their counterparts in the US. Even if they have a license in the US, that license does not cross the border and become valid in Mexico. Also, if the brokers are not Mexican citizens, they could be conducting business illegally. To conduct business in Mexico one needs either an FM-3 visa for a non-resident business and pleasure or an FM-2 visa which is for permanent residency. These concerns may be alleviated in Mexico with real estate leaders like Century 21 Mexico and ReMax, but at this time, no license is required to sell real estate in Mexico. Therefore, the legal expression "*caveat emptor*" or "buyer beware" is a fact of life when conducting a real estate transaction in Mexico.

In addition to these concerns, there are fundamental components of a Mexican real estate transaction that a foreigner buying property in Mexico should consider. For example, in the US, the escrow officer takes care of the title report, the conveyance of deeds of trust, and the documents to clear all existing liens on the property. The escrow officer also prorates the taxes, makes sure all documents are executed properly, records all necessary documents and disburses documents, funds and a closing statement. Also included in those duties is usually the obligation to pay real estate broker fees after the transaction is official and complete. Many times in Mexico, the funds are placed into an account, (not a trust account), where the broker is already paid and the real estate transaction is nowhere near complete. The title is not clear and free, the trust documents for the property have not been checked, the notary has not been consulted nor has he looked over the trust documents, and the bank has not been notified as trustee of the *fideicomiso* (trust) which holds title to the property.

Foreign investors are left with the problems of how to insure that the title to the property actually passes and how to insure that their money stays safe until the transaction is completed. One way is to get the bank involved and have it handle the finances. The bank can set up a trust account and hold the money until the transaction is complete. The bank charges a set up fee and it charges a percentage of the money held as their commission.

Another way to ensure that the transaction goes smoothly is to place the money with an American attorney in a trust account the attorney has set up specifically for this particular transaction. The attorney has a license to practice law and has a fiduciary duty (the highest possible duty/obligation by law) to protect and keep safe property received from clients or third persons (Rule 1.15 of the ABA Model Rules for Professional Responsibility*)*. An American attorney that serves as an escrow agent is governed by the applicable law of fiduciaries even though he provides no legal services in the transaction.

A problem with the preceding solution is that an attorney in the States can handle funds, but he may not read Spanish and he cannot practice law in Mexico. The answer is to find a good Mexican attorney who has substantial real estate experience and who has the ability to communicate with the attorney in the United States and explain that the transaction is complete and recorded. Upon clearance from the Mexican attorney, the American attorney can sign off on the transaction and release the funds.

By executing the real estate transaction in this manner, the funds do not leave the United States, the broker is paid after the transaction is completed and peace of mind is obtained until the title to the piece of Mexican property is transferred. So to re-emphasize, when considering buying property in Mexico, it is important to remember that escrow, as it exists in the United States, does not exist in Mexico.

APPENDIX B

US Tax Consequences Of Mexican Property Acquisitions

Taxes! Taxes! Taxes! The word makes people nauseous. Tax regulations in the US are difficult to understand. Add a foreign country's (such as Mexico) tax laws on top of the US regulations, it is that much more complex.

This section attempts to solve the network of complex tax requirements and tax regulations surrounding the buying, selling and ownership of Mexican property as it applies to a US citizen. Also included are certain tax strategies that help reduce the tax burden in the US.

REAL PROPERTY TAXES AND INTEREST

FEDERAL TAXES

Under Internal Revenue Code Section 164(a), the person upon whom they are imposed can deduct local, state, and foreign real property taxes. These taxes must be imposed in the year in which they are paid or accrued. Thus, any US citizen who pays taxes in Mexico on property can deduct those taxes from their US taxes.

Under Internal Revenue Code Section 163(a), a US taxpayer may generally deduct interest paid or accrued within the tax year of indebtedness. This interest must be on a debt secured by one's principal residence or second residence. Therefore, any interest paid on a Mexican residence is deductible if it is one's main home or second home.

However, there are problems concerning interest deductions. First, there are almost no programs that provide mortgages for Americans who own homes in Mexico. Kidder Peabody and an Investment Group in Denver are working on a program, but it is not yet available. The majority of real estate transactions performed in Mexico are accomplished through the use of a promissory note for payments or through the use of an installment contract. The second problem is that there is not a revenue ruling nor a tax case which provides a definitive answer on whether foreign interest paid is deductible on one's US taxes.

Finally, a bank fee paid yearly to the Mexican bank that administrates the *fideicomiso* (trust) may be deductible. It depends on whether the personal property rights are held individually or through some corporate form. If it is held individually, the fee paid is deductible under certain restrictions for services rendered.

If a corporation holds the property rights there are two possible scenarios. If it is a Mexican corporation, then the fee is not deductible. If the beneficiary of the *fideicomiso* is a US corporation, the fee is deductible just as it is for an individual under the same service restrictions.

STATE TAXES

The rule varies from state to state. Generally, however, the state does not impose a tax upon the ownership of Mexican property since the property is located outside of the state.

CAPITAL GAINS TAXES

Under Internal Revenue Code Section 1001(c), gains from the sale or exchange of property are recognized for tax purposes unless otherwise provided for by law. The gain from the sale or exchange of property is the excess of the amount realized from that sale or exchange over the property's adjusted basis (Internal Revenue Code 1001(a)). The adjusted basis of this property is generally the original cost plus the cost of any improvements to the property less any depreciation (Internal Revenue Code 1011, 1012, and 1016). The amount realized on the sale or the exchange is the total of all money received plus the fair market value of all other property or services received (Internal Revenue Code 1001(b)).

Once the computation of the capital gain is finished, one should look to reinvest that money. Some or all of the tax on the gain from the sale of a **principal** residence can be postponed or rolled over if a **new principal** residence is bought or built within two years after the sale of the old residence.

In such a case, the gain on the sale is recognized only to the extent that the adjusted sales price of the old residence exceeds the cost of the new residence. For example, one has decided to sell one's home and move to Mexico for part of the year. The home in the US sells for an adjusted sales price of $210,000 with a basis of $80,000. The new home in Cabo San Lucas costs $240,000. The $130,000 gain is not recognized for tax purposes if the house in Cabo is bought within two years. But there are still two hurdles to overcome.

One, the house in Cabo must be the principal residence. If a person owns one home and lives in it, then it is his principal residence. One must look at the residence requirements before the postponement of capital gains taxes can be used. Residency in Mexico is acquired once a US citizen obtains an FM3 visa from the Immigration Service Office of Mexico.

Two, there is a requirement that the new home be held in the same name as the home sold in the US. Since a foreigner does not technically own the house in Mexico because the Mexican bank holds the land in trust, the Internal Revenue Code requirement is not met, so the gain probably cannot be rolled over. But, one can ask for a private ruling to determine if the gain can be legally rolled over into the Mexican residence.

If a person is over 55 years of age, he is eligible to exclude $125,000 for a once in a lifetime elective exclusion for gain on the sale or exchange of the principal residence (Internal Revenue Code 121). In addition to the age requirement, the person must have owned the home for 3 of the previous five years. Temporary or other seasonal residences do not qualify. This exclusion is available under both federal and California law.

Under the recent US/Mexico Income Tax Treaty, Article 13, Capital gains received in Mexico are taxable in Mexico. The capital gains rate in Mexico is either 34% of the gain or a flat 20% of the sales price. This can be rolled over as well into another piece of Mexican property. However, for US tax requirements, it must be the principal residence and not a vacation home.

Estate, Gift And Generation Skipping Taxes

Estate Taxes

The US estate and gift tax applies to the transfer of property at or near death. This includes property transferred by will, revocable *inter vivos* trusts (IRC 2038) and certain transfers within three years of death (IRC 2035). For US citizens and resident aliens, all property, wherever located, is included in the gross estate and subject to US taxes. This includes the personal property right one has as a beneficiary of a *fideicomiso*.

Residency for estate tax purposes is not the same as that for income tax purposes. A resident for estate tax purposes is a person who acquires a domicile in a place by living there for even a brief period of time, without an intent to stay indefinitely. For income tax purposes, a resident is one who is lawfully in the country, meets the substantial presence test or takes a first year election to be treated as a resident.

Once residency is determined, one can attempt to find out how much US estate tax is owed. The rates range from 18% on the first $10,000 to 55% on a taxable estate of $3 million. This is a substantial amount to pay. But if one executes a second will or trust as a resident of Mexico with respect to the Mexican property, there is a good possibility that US estate taxes will not apply to the property.

GIFT TAXES

This US tax applies to all transfers of property made during the transferor's lifetime. It is the donor and not the recipient that is usually liable for the taxes. This applies to gifts made all over the world. For US citizens or residents, there is no gift tax deduction for gifts to a spouse who is a Mexican. But, the donor may exclude up to $100,000 worth of gifts per year to a Mexican spouse. This is an effective way to reduce one's tax liability if subject to US taxes.

GENERATION SKIPPING TAXES

This tax is designed to control a taxpayer's attempt to transfer property to grandchildren to avoid the estate and gift taxes. Normally, the donor sets up a trust where the child of the donor receives the income from the trust and, upon the death of the child, the corpus (the Mexican property rights) passes to the grandchildren. Since the child did not own the Mexican property rights, it cannot be included in the child's estate to be taxed.

The IRS developed the generation skipping tax rule to stop that process. The rule imposes a tax on the passage of the enjoyment of taxes from one generation to the next. It is imposed where estate and gift taxes are not applicable. This is a problem which setting up an offshore corporation can help.

Reporting Requirements

A US citizen who sells real estate is required by the IRS to report the sale of a house. The sale is reported on **Form 1099-S**. The person responsible for the closing of the transaction files the form. If no such person exists, then the form is filed by, in order of priority; the mortgage lender, the transferor's broker, the transferee's broker and finally the transferee. Also included on this form is the real property taxes imposed on the purchaser as a result of the sale or exchange.

By law, any transaction of monetary instruments involving more than $10,000 that crosses the US border into Mexico must be reported to US Customs. The form used is #4790. A monetary instrument includes coin and currency, traveler's checks, and bearer instruments. The information that must be included on the form is the name of the person filing the report, the origin of the monetary instruments, as well as other general information.

There are several types of transactions that do not have to be filed. If money is exchanged in the US between two US banks then the transaction is not filed with Customs. Also, a check, which must be endorsed, is not considered a bearer instrument and is not reported even if it exceeds the $10,000 limit. The bank that receives the check must file the report.

Tax Saving Strategies

For many Americans, carrying out transactions in another country is nerve racking. A suggestion that setting up an offshore corporation is advisable is even more difficult to comprehend. However, once it is thoroughly understood, the benefits of using an offshore corporation for a Mexican real estate transaction are obvious. This section answers some of the basic questions and explains away some misconceptions that people have concerning protective strategies for their assets including property.

Why Not A Foreign Trust?

A prospective buyer may believe that setting up a foreign trust to purchase property in Mexico will shelter them against having to pay US taxes. Under current US tax law, an entity (such as a foreign trust) is subject to US taxes as a foreign trust (1) if the entity is classified as a trust and (2) if the entity's contacts with the foreign situs are sufficient after looking at the country under which the entity was created, the situs of the trust's corpus (the Mexican property rights), the residency of the trustees, the nationality of the grantor and the situs of the trust's administration.

Once these requirements are met, the next hurdle is the Grantor trust rule. Under Internal Revenue Code Sections 678(b) and 679, any US resident transferring property to a foreign trust that has a US beneficiary is treated as the owner of that portion of the trust attributed to the transfer of the property. The transferor must file an information report. Thus, the Mexican property transaction is filed and the taxes must be paid since it is viewed as income to the US transferor. This defeats the purpose of using a foreign trust.

WHY NOT A MEXICAN CORPORATION?

Under US tax laws, setting up a Mexican corporation to purchase and own property in Mexico may protect a US citizen from some of the tax burden, but if the corporation passes the Controlled Foreign Corporation (CFC) rules, it may not. A CFC is defined in Section 957(a) as a foreign corporation (in this case, a Mexican corporation) of which 50% or more of its value or voting stock is owned by US shareholders. Under Section 951(b), a US shareholder is defined as a US citizen who owns or is considered as owning (by applying the rules of ownership of Section 958(b)) 10% or more of the voting power of all classes of stock entitled to vote in the Mexican corporation.

Since the US resident usually holds more than 50% of the shares of the Mexican corporation, it is defined as a CFC. If the Mexican corporation is classified as a CFC, then the US shareholders are taxed on their shares of the CFC's current income even if it is not paid out in dividends.

The US shareholders are taxed upon their net income in accordance with US tax laws. This includes capital gains, foreign exchange gains and rent. Once again, the person is paying too much in taxes.

One way to reduce the tax burden is by using 11 shareholders in the Mexican corporation. But finding 11 unrelated individuals to hold a piece of Mexican property is not easy and time is usually a factor in purchasing property.

WHY AN OFFSHORE CORPORATION?

The better choice when considering options to shelter property from taxes is an offshore corporation (neither Mexican nor US). There may still be some concern about CFC rules. An international financial center provides the answer to this problem. They provide secrecy and confidentiality, security, no taxes and flexibility.

Most offshore financial centers provide for next day incorporation. This is useful for the person executing a real estate transaction in Mexico. A Mexican corporation formation takes anywhere from 45 to 90 days.

Once the offshore corporation is set up, it issues "bearer shares" which means that the shares are not registered in anyone's name. However, there is still reason to have concern over the CFC rules.

The offshore corporation issuing the bearer shares can create a trust to hold its shares. The corporation is viewed as a nonresident alien, which creates an irrevocable foreign trust, not a grantor trust. The trust holds the shares. The beneficiaries of this trust are the US residents who benefit from the land in Mexico.

The US beneficiaries do not pay taxes on the income derived from this corporation since they do not directly or indirectly control the offshore corporation. It is not considered a CFC since there are no US shareholders in the company who own more than 50% of the shares. The US beneficiaries are not required to report the income since the offshore corporation has control of the trust under Revenue Ruling 69-70 and Internal Revenue Code Section 674(a).

The Mexican bank now has an offshore corporation as a beneficiary of its *fideicomiso*. The offshore corporation has its shares in an offshore trust. It has as its beneficiaries US residents. These persons are not required to report their income from the trust since the trust is a non-resident alien trust. No US taxes are paid until there is repatriation of income into the US by the US beneficiaries.

CONCLUSION

The tax relationship between the US and Mexico is less than clear when discussing real estate transactions. With the implementation of NAFTA and the recent US/Mexico Income Tax Treaty, many of these issues will be clarified. For now, one must have a "wait and see" attitude or go offshore on many of the Mexican real estate tax issues.

Christopher M. Leo, is a licensed California attorney and has a masters in International and Comparative Law from Georgetown. He specializes in the areas of international trade law, international tax planning and is an expert on NAFTA issues.

APPENDIX C

SUMMARY OF THE 1989 TIMESHARE REGULATIONS

(Author's Note: The federal timeshare NOM cites theses regulations as a
biographical reference and it is possible that they may be used as a prototype
for local legislation. For that reason I have included them here as an example of
what should be expected at the state level.)

Timeshare properties and transactions involving timeshare properties are regulated by the Timeshare Regulations published on August 21, 1989. The regulations define "timeshare system" *(sistema de tiempo compartido)* and timeshare establishment *(establecimiento)* as follows:

Timeshare system (regardless of the name given to the contract): any contract *(acto jurídico)* by which an individual is granted the use, enjoyment and other rights to a property or part of a property. The property may be a certain unit or a variable unit of a determined class. The use and enjoyment, etc., is granted during a specific period, with previously established determined or determinable intervals.

Timeshare Property: The goods in which the tourist service of the time-share system is rendered.

The above definition is very broad and may be applied to many different circumstances. As a general rule, if a buyer is paying for the right to use any part of real property that is limited to a specific amount of time, he is buying a timeshare.

A timeshare is different from a lease because a lease gives the exclusive right to use and enjoy a specific property. A timeshare differs from a real estate sale because title to the property is not exchanged; the buyer of a timeshare only has the right to use the property for a limited and specific amount of time.

The people involved in a timeshare are the following:

➢ **User/tourist** *(Usuario/turista)*: the person who acquires the rights described in the preceding paragraphs, as well as any other individual who is entitled to use the same.

> **The timeshare operator (*Prestador*):** The person or company in charge of and/or responsible for the administration of the system, and the maintenance and operation of the timeshare establishment.

The timeshare operator is required by law to have a legal domicile within Mexico, and is always subject to Mexican law. Some timeshare companies have contracts which state that, in the event of litigation with regard to the timeshare contract, the dispute will be resolved in accordance with laws of some other jurisdiction, very often the Cayman Islands or some other tax haven. Such provisions are not binding, even when the contract is executed outside of Mexico.

Every timeshare operator is required to register with the National Tourism Registry and is responsible for any violations of the timeshare regulations, the timeshare contract, or any other laws in Mexico. This is true even when the timeshare operator contracts a third party to provide services to the users and the timeshare establishment.

By law, every timeshare establishment must have an operator. If, for any reason, the operator no longer exists, any third party with legitimate interest can solicit the institution of a new operator in accordance with the internal regulation of the establishment and the Timeshare Regulations. The new operator must be registered within three months from the absence of the previous operator.

INSCRIPTION IN THE NATIONAL TOURISM REGISTRY

To register the timeshare establishment and its operator, an application is submitted accompanied with the following documents:

> The operator's certificate of registration before the Federal Registry of Taxpayers;

> If the timeshare provider is a corporation, the public deed by which it was incorporated, and any reforms to the same, all of which must be inscribed in the respective Public Registry of Property and Commerce;

> If the operator is a foreigner he must prove that he is in the country legally and that his visa entitles him to perform such activities;

> In every case, the operator must accredit his legal capacity and the powers he is entitled to;

> An authentic copy of the document by which the operator assumes such character;

> Proof showing that the property has been recorded as a timeshare property. The compliance with this requirement is determined by local ordinance. If there is no ordinance, a unilateral voluntary declaration must be executed before a Notary Public, or be included in a trust contract, and, in both cases, filed as a preventive notice with the Public Property Registry;

> A declaration under oath stating the permits, authorizations and licenses required by federal, state and municipal authorities have been obtained;

> A general description of the timeshare establishment, of the units destined for use, and the services available in them, as well as photographs of the same;

> The timeshare's internal regulations;

> A copy of the application of approval and registration of the timeshare service contract to be celebrated with the users/tourists, stamped by the official clerk of the Federal Consumer Protection Office;

> An insurance policy against total or partial damage of the establishment, to cover the reconstruction or reparation, as well as a policy for personal liability;

> A bond policy for the equivalent of twenty times the individual yearly maintenance fee, as stated in the internal regulations of the establishment, to guarantee the fulfillment of the conditions in which the services are rendered. If the regulations have several maintenance fees, the highest is used;

> Declaration stating whether the establishment is or isn't affiliated to a timeshare exchange organization. If it does have such an affiliation, authentic copies of the respective contract and regulations must be submitted, and

> The documents submitted by the operator to the Ministry of Tourism for timeshare category classifications.

Once the above documentation is submitted, within the next twenty working days, the Ministry of Tourism must carry out a visit of verification at the timeshare establishment. This is done to verify the information submitted and to obtain the information necessary to grant the corresponding timeshare category classification certificate.

The Ministry of Tourism then registers the establishment and the operator in the National Tourism Registry, and, within ten working days, issues the corresponding Tourism Certificate.

The Ministry of Tourism must make a decision regarding any application of inscription within thirty working days from the date of presentation. After thirty days the inscription in the Registry of Tourism is considered as granted.

The Tourism Certificate issued by the Ministry of Tourism must be displayed in a visible place within the principal entrance of the establishment.

If the timeshare establishment is not completely built, it cannot be registered in the National Tourism Registry. However, if the development is being constructed in stages, it is possible to obtain the inscription and the respective Tourism Certificate for the finished stage.

The timeshare operator is obligated to give notice to the Ministry of Tourism if there is any change or modification of the information or of the documents submitted for registration within fifteen working days of such changes or modifications.

CLASSIFICATION OF TIMESHARE PROPERTIES

Timeshare properties are rated into categories of one to five "stars" and "grand tourism" by the government.

In order to grant each establishment its corresponding category, the Secretary takes into consideration many elements:

➢ Amount of Investment;

➢ Number of employees;

➢ Specific location;

➢ Constructions;

➢ Open areas;

➢ Commercial areas;

➢ Parking spaces;

➢ Characteristics of the reception and registration areas;

➢ Number and characteristics of the elevators;

➢ Number of rooms;

➢ Dimensions of the rooms;

➢ Goods and services in the rooms;

➢ Sanitary installations in the rooms;

➢ Services, complementary and recreational installations;

➢ Number and characteristics of food, drinks and show establishments;

➢ Maintenance and conservation services;

➢ Hygiene and security conditions;

➢ Antiquity and state of conservation of the constructions, especially when it concerns constructions with historic or architectural value;

➢ The affiliation or no affiliation with an exchange system of time share;

➢ Hotel service, if available, and

➢ The characteristics of other services in their case.

If a timeshare operator is not satisfied with the government's classification of the establishment, he may request, through a written petition, that the Ministry of Tourism change it. A representative of the government then visits the timeshare establishment and determines if reclassification is warranted within thirty days. This term may be extended for an additional fifteen days if the Ministry decides to obtain the opinion of the Timeshare Advisory Commission.

Any user/tourist may file a complaint against a timeshare operator so that the government carries out a verification visit. If it is determined that the quality of the timeshare's installations or services have diminished, affecting the category conferred to the establishment, the Ministry must grant the operator a term to fix whatever is wrong. The Ministry then orders the operator to notify the user/tourist of the determination within a maximum term of ten working days. This is done to allow the user/tourist the opportunity to exercise his or her rights in the terms of the law and the internal regulations of the timeshare establishment.

If the operator fails to make the required repairs, he may be fined or closed down.

Any promotion or advertising relative to the timeshare establishment must include the Tourism Certificate number and the category granted by the Ministry to the timeshare. It must also state if hotel service is available and list any other services offered.

OPERATING REGULATIONS

Chapter 4 of the Timeshare Regulations establishes the general rules that apply to the operation of a timeshare property. The regulations divide the services related to a timeshare establishment into principal and complementary services.

The principal service of timeshare establishments is to give a person, in exchange for a certain and determined price, the use and enjoyment of some property. It may consist of a certain unit or a variable unit under a determined class, during a specific period, with previously established determined or determinable intervals.

Complementary services are all those which the operator is obligated to offer the user/tourist which are not principal services.

The user/tourist has the right to use the timeshare property according to what is agreed to and the provisions of the timeshare's internal regulations. If there are no provisions in the internal regulations that apply to a given situation, any questions are resolved in accordance with the applicable legislation.

The timeshare operator is required by law to file a copy of the timeshare's internal regulations with the Ministry of Tourism, and to have them inscribed in the National Tourism Registry. The operator is also required to give a copy of the regulations to each user/tourist.

The internal regulations must contain the following information:

➢ It must state the number of daily, weekly, monthly or yearly terms in which use of the timeshare is divided;

➢ It must mention if the terms are set or variable, and list the requirements to vary the dates of use;

➢ It must explain the reservation system;

➢ It must explain the maintenance fees, as well as their origin, application, periods, amounts and how they are changed;

➢ It must describe any extraordinary fees, as well as their origin, application, and how they are determined;

➢ It must illustrate the cases in which the user/tourist has the right to vote on the decision making of the establishment, and explain the voting system and quorum;

➢ It must spell out the system for the designation of representatives of the users/tourists, the powers they have, and discuss the proceedings and causes for the substitution or removal of such representatives;

➢ It must explain the form and periods in which maintenance is performed for the habitants, the services, the installations and the common areas;

➢ It must provide a description of furniture and movable goods;

➢ It must define the occupancy limits of users/tourists per unit;

➢ It must specify the days and hours of the beginning and end of the user periods;

➢ It must clarify the conditions for the use of common areas;

➢ It must illustrate what internal sanctions are applied to a user/tourist who violates the internal regulations, and the proceedings for application of the sanctions;

➢ It must explain how the timeshare operator is designated, the procedure for naming and substituting, and it should spell out the powers, responsibilities and guarantees which the operator must satisfy;

➢ It must clarify the characteristics of the insurance taken out for the timeshare property;

➢ It must list complementary services provided to the user/tourist;

➢ It must explain the type of use applicable to the units--whether individual, or variable within a certain class of units;

➢ It must define the manner in which the timeshare operator fulfills his obligations;

➢ It must illustrate how the users/tourists are notified.

As a general rule, the user/tourist has the right to demand that his rights to use and enjoy the timeshare property be respected at all times. However, the timeshare operator has the right to deny use to any user/tourist who is behind in his timeshare fees.

Most often the internal regulations are able to resolve any conflicts which may arise regarding the use of the timeshare property. The internal regulations are intended to set the general rules that the user/tourist must obey. They must be read carefully. If the regulations do not cover a certain problem, the general laws are applied.

The timeshare operator must acquire civil liability insurance to cover damages against third parties including a detailed coverage for disasters suffered by the users/tourists. The characteristics of this insurance are contained in the internal regulations and kept in force at all times.

Timeshare operators must honor all written reservations they accept from a user/tourist. If the operator is unable to keep the reservation, he must cover the stay of the user/tourist for the time agreed upon in an establishment of similar category.

In the event that there is nothing available in a similar establishment, the operator must immediately pay the user/tourist for expenses incurred traveling to the timeshare property as well as return expenses for transportation by the same means in which the user/tourist arrived. Also, the operator must give the user/tourist another vacation period within the term agreed to by both parties.

When the timeshare establishment participates in exchange programs with other timeshare systems, the operator must send a written notice to the user/tourist containing the capacities, rights and obligations to which they will be subject in the exchange.

The timeshare operator must keep a book of complaints and suggestions, authorized by the Ministry of Tourism, available to the user/tourist within the timeshare establishment. Additionally, the book must have numbered pages and an instruction booklet indicating its use. The representatives of the Ministry of Tourism reads this book during visits of verification in order to pursue existing complaints.

PROTECTION OF THE USER/TOURIST

The Ministry of Tourism receives and pursues any written complaint submitted by users/tourists regarding timeshare operations. This also includes complaints found in the complaint and suggestion books the timeshare operators are required to keep.

The written complaint must be accompanied by an account of the probatory elements of the events stipulated in the complaint. The

Ministry will determine whether or not to proceed to the next step which is a visit of verification to the timeshare establishment in question.

If the complaint is substantiated, the complainant and the operator are summoned by a personal notification before the Ministry of Tourism for a conciliatory hearing. They are given ten working days notice of this hearing which has several purposes:

➢ To urge the parties to settle their interests;

➢ To admit the probatory elements offered;

➢ To value the probatory elements and propose a conciliatory solution to both parties.

The results of the hearing are recorded and a copy is given to each of the parties.

The conciliatory hearing is held before three possible authorities:

➢ The Ministry of Tourism;

➢ A competent public servant from the closest Federal Tourism Delegation to the domicile of the user/tourist;

➢ In the event that the user/tourist has a foreign domicile, the conciliation hearing is held before a representative of the Ministry of Tourism of that country, or before the diplomatic or consular representative of Mexico that is closest to the domicile of the user/tourist.

In the event that the complaint filed does not fall within the scope of the Ministry of Tourism, the Ministry informs the user/tourist where and to whom the complaint is remitted for further attention.

The timeshare operator has the right to have the hearing take place by telephone, but the operator must pay for the long distance charges incurred. If the operator or his representative does not attend the hearing, or make arrangements for a telephone conference, he is fined a maximum of the monthly minimum salary in effect in the Federal District.

The Ministry then summons another hearing to be held within eight working days. If the operator or his representative fails to appear at this hearing, he is fined up to double the amount of the first fine.

Alternatively, if the user/tourist fails to attend the hearing without just cause, the complaint is dropped. If the user/tourist can justify his absence from the hearing, another hearing is scheduled to be held within eight days.

Although the hearing is conciliatory, the Ministry is not bound by the agreements reached by the parties in the hearing. The Ministry may initiate proceedings to impose fines or closure. The decision to do so depends on the seriousness of the infraction committed and the intentions of the guilty party. However, if the parties are able to reach an agreement, this is taken into consideration in determining the type and amount of sanction.

If the user/tourist and the timeshare operator fail to reach an agreement at the hearing, or if the operator does not attend the second hearing, the Ministry will analyze the facts of the complaint to determine if there is a violation and will issue a resolution. In such cases, the user/tourist retains the right to pursue other legal actions against the timeshare operator.

APPENDIX D

FOREIGN INVESTMENT LAW

Signed on December 15, 1993

Published in *Diario Oficial* of December 27, 1993

Amended by reforms of May 12, 1995, June 7, 1995 and December 18, 1996 (published December 24, 1996)

INVESTMENT FIRST TITLE. GENERAL PROVISIONS

CHAPTER I. THE OBJECT OF THE LAW

ART. 1.

This Law is of public order and shall be generally observed in all the Republic. Its object is the determination of rules for channeling foreign investment made in the country and to moderate it to contribute to the national development.

ART. 2.

For the purposes of this Law, the following shall be understood:

I.   Commission: the National Foreign Investment Commission

II.   Foreign investment:

    a)   The participation of foreign investors, in any proportion, in the capital stock of Mexican companies;

    b)   That which is made by Mexican companies with a foreign capital majority; and

    c)   The participation of foreign investors in the activities and acts regarded in this Law.

III.   Foreign Investor: an individual or legal person of a nationality other than Mexican and foreign entities without juridical personality;

IV.   Register: The National Register of Foreign Investments;

V.   Ministry: The Ministry of Commerce and Industrial Development;

VI.   Restricted Zone: The strip of national territory of 100 kilometers along the length of the frontiers and of 50 kilometers along the length of the beaches, to which item I of Article 27 of the Political Constitution of the United Mexican States refers; and

VII.   Foreigners Exclusion Clause: The convention or express agreement which forms an integral part of the by-laws of a company, by which the companies in question shall neither directly nor indirectly admit foreign investors as partners or shareholders, nor admit companies which do admit foreigners as shareholders to participate.

ART. 3.

For the purposes of this Law, investment which foreigners effect in the country as immigrants shall be equivalent to Mexican investment, except in the cases of activities mentioned in the First and Second Titles of this Law.

ART. 4.

(Amended by Decree of December 18, 1996, effective December 25, 1996) Foreign investment may participate in any proportion in the capital stock of Mexican companies, acquire fixed assets, enter new fields of economic activity or manufacture new lines of products, open and operate establishments, and increase or relocate those already existing, except as provided in this Law.

The rules on the participation of foreign investment in the activities of the financial sector considered in this Law shall be applied without prejudice to that which the specific laws on such activities establish.

For purposes of determining the percentage of foreign investment in the economic activities subject to maximum limits of participation, the foreign investment realized in said activities in an indirect manner through Mexican companies with a majority of Mexican capital shall not be computed, provided that those companies are not controlled by the foreign investment.

CHAPTER II. RESERVED ACTIVITIES

ART. 5.

The functions which the laws determine in the following strategic areas are reserved exclusively by the State:

I.   Petroleum and other hydrocarbons;

II.   Basic petrochemicals;

III.   Electricity;

IV.   Generation of nuclear energy;

V.   Radioactive minerals;

VI.   Repealed.

VII.   Telegraphs;

VIII. Radiotelegraphy;

IX.   Mail service;

X.   Repealed.

XI.   Issue of bills;

XII.   Mintage of currency;

XIII. Control, supervision and inspection of ports, airports and heliports; and

XIV.   Others expressly stipulated in applicable legal provisions.

ART. 6.

The following economic activities are reserved exclusively to Mexicans or to Mexican companies with a foreigners' exclusion clause:

I.   Domestic land transportation of passengers, tourists and cargo, not including the messenger and express package services;

II.   Retail trade of gasoline and distribution of liquid petroleum gas;

III.   Radio broadcasting services and others of radio and television, other than cable television;

IV.   Credit unions;

V.   Developmental banking institutions, in the terms of the law on the matter; and

VI.   Rendering of professional and technical services which are expressly set forth in applicable legal provisions.

Foreign investment may not participate in the activities mentioned in this article directly nor through trusts, conventions, business or statutory agreements, pyramid schemes, or any other mechanism which authorizes any control or participation, except as provided in the Fifth Title of this Law.

CHAPTER III. ACTIVITIES AND ACQUISITIONS WITH SPECIFIC REGULATION

ART. 7.

In the economic activities and companies, which are mentioned below, foreign investment may participate up to the following percentages:

I.   Up to 10% in:

Cooperative companies of production;

II.   Up to 25% in:

    a)   Domestic air transportation;

    b)   Air-taxi transport; and

    c)   Specialized air transportation;

III.   **(Amended by Decree of December 18, 1996, effective December 25, 1996) Up to 49% in:**

    a)   Controlling companies of financial groups;

    b)   Multiple banking institutions;

    c)   Securities exchange houses;

    d)   Stock exchange specialists;

    e)   Insurance institutions;

    f)   Bond institutions;

    g)   Foreign exchange houses;

    h)   General deposit warehouses;

    i)   Financial lessors;

    j)   Financial factoring enterprises;

    k)   Financial companies with a limited objective;

    l)   Companies to which article 12 bis of the Securities Market Law refers;

    m)   Stocks representative of the fixed capital of investment companies;

    n)   Companies operating investment companies;

o) Administrators of retirement funds;

p) Manufacture and marketing of explosives, firearms, cartridges, munitions and artificial fire, without including the acquisition and utilization of explosives for industrial and extractive activities, nor the manufacture of mixed explosives for consumption of said activities;

q) Printing and publication of periodicals for exclusive circulation in national territory;

r) Series "T" stocks of companies that hold agricultural, stock-raising and forestry lands in their assets;

s) Freshwater and coastal fishing and fishing in the exclusive economic zone, without including aquaculture;

t) Full port administration;

u) Port services of pilotage to ships in order to carry out domestic navigation operations, in the terms of the Law on the matter;

v) Shipping companies engaged in the commercial operation of ships for interior and coastal navigation, with the exception of tourist cruises and the operation of dredges and naval devices for the construction, conservation and operation of a port;

w) The supply of fuel and lubricants for ships and airplanes and railway equipment, and

x) Companies holding concessions in the terms of articles 11 and 12 of the Federal Telecommunications Law.

IV. Repealed by Decree of December 18, 1996, effective December 25, 1996

The limits stipulated in this article for foreign investment participation may neither be directly exceeded, nor exceeded through trusts, conventions, business or statutory agreements, pyramid schemes or any other mechanism which grants a greater control or participation than that which is established, except as provided in the Fifth Title of this Law.

ART. 8.

A favorable decision of the Commission shall be required for foreign investment participation at a percentage greater than 49% in the economic activities and companies mentioned below:

I.   Port services to ships to carry out domestic navigation operations, such as the towing, mooring of ropes and launching;

II.   Shipping companies engaged in the operation of ships exclusively on the high seas;

III.   **(Amended by Decree of December 18, 1996, effective December 25, 1996) Companies holding concessions or permits for public service aerodromes;**

IV.   Private pre-school, primary, secondary, junior college, college and combined education services;

V.   Legal services;

VI.   Credit information companies;

VII.   Appraisal institutions; and

VIII.   Insurance agents.

IX.   Cellular telephone;

X.   Construction of ducts for the transportation of petroleum and its derivatives;

XI.   Drilling of petroleum and gas wells, and

XII.   **(Added by Decree of December 18, 1996, effective December 25, 1996) Construction, operation and exploitation of railroads as a general means of communication, and furnishing railroad transportation as a public service.**

ART. 9.

Where foreign investment tries to participate, directly or indirectly, in a proportion higher than 49% of a Mexican Company's capital stock, a favorable resolution of the Commission shall be required only when the total value of the assets of the companies in question, at the time of submitting of the petition of acquisition, exceeds the amount determined annually by the same Commission.

SECOND TITLE. ACQUISITION OF REAL PROPERTY, EXPLOITATION OF MINES AND WATERS AND TRUSTS

(Amended by Decree of December 18, 1996, effective December 25, 1996)

CHAPTER I. ACQUISITION OF REAL PROPERTY AND EXPLOITATION OF MINES AND WATERS

ART. 10.

In accordance with that which is provided by item I of article 27 of the Political Constitution of the United Mexican States, Mexican companies with a foreigners exclusion clause or which have executed a convention to which said precept refers, may acquire ownership of real property in the national territory.

In the case of companies whose by-laws include the convention provided in item I of Constitutional Article 27, the following shall apply:

I.   **(Amended by Decree of December 18, 1996, effective December 25, 1996) They may acquire ownership of real property located in the restricted zone, intended for the carrying out of non-residential activities, duly registering said acquisition with the Ministry of Foreign Relations within 60 working days following the date on which the acquisition is made; and**

II. They may acquire real property in the restricted zone, intended for residential purposes, in accordance with the provisions of the following chapter.

ART. 10A.

(Added by Decree of December 18, 1996, effective 30 working days after December 24, 1996) Foreigners who try to acquire real estate outside the restricted zone, or who obtain concessions for the exploration or exploitation of mines and waters in national territory, must previously present a writ to the Department of Foreign Relations in which they agree to what is provided in item I of article 27 of the Political Constitution of the United Mexican States and obtain the corresponding permit from that Department.

When the real estate that they are trying to acquire is in a municipality located totally outside the restricted zone or when

they are trying to obtain a concession for the exploitation of mines and waters in national territory, the permit shall be granted automatically if the refusal of the Department of Foreign Relations is not published in the *Diario Oficial* of the Federation within the five working days following the date of the filing of the application.

When the real estate that they are trying to acquire is in a municipality partially located within the restricted zone, the Department of Foreign Relations shall decide upon the petition within the 30 working days following the date of its presentation.

The National Institute of Statistics, Geography and Informatics shall publish in the *Diario Oficial* of the Federation a list of the municipalities mentioned above, as well as those that are totally located in the restricted zone, and the said Institute shall keep the list up to date.

The Department of Foreign Relations may determine cases, by means of general resolutions that shall be published in the *Diario Oficial* of the Federation, in which foreigners must only file a document in which they agree to what is provided in item I of article 27 of the Constitution in order to have the right to which this article refers, without requiring the corresponding permit of that Department.

CHAPTER II. TRUSTS ON REAL PROPERTY IN THE RESTRICTED ZONE

ART. 11.

A permit from the Ministry of Foreign Relations is required for credit institutions to acquire rights on real property located within the restricted zone as trustees, when the purpose of the trust is to permit the utilization and the improvement of such property without constituting real rights thereon, and the beneficiaries of the trust (*fideicomisarios*) are:

I.   Mexican companies without a foreigners exclusion clause, in the case provided in item II of article 10 of this Law; and

II.   Foreign individuals or legal persons.

ART. 12.

By utilization and improvement of real property located in the restricted zone shall be understood the rights to the use or possession thereof, including, as the case may be, the obtainment of the fruits, products or, in general, any revenue which results from the lucrative operation and exploitation through third -parties or from the trustee institution.

ART. 13.

(Amended by Decree of December 18, 1996, effective December 25, 1996) The duration of the trusts to which this chapter refers shall be for a maximum period of 50 years, which may be extended upon petition of the interested party.

The Ministry of Foreign Relations may verify at any time the fulfillment of the conditions under which the permits provided in this Title are granted, as well as verify the filing and veracity of the contents of the notices provided herein.

ART. 14.

(Amended by Decree of December 18, 1996, effective December 25, 1996) The Ministry of Foreign Relations shall decide on the permits to which this chapter refers, considering the economic and social benefit which the realization of such operations imply for the Nation.

Any petition for a permit must be decided by the Ministry of Foreign Relations within the 5 working days following the date of its presentation before the competent central administrative unit, or within the following 30 working days, if it was presented in the state delegations of the office of the Ministry. Once those periods expire without a decision being issued, the respective petition shall be considered as approved.

THIRD TITLE. COMPANIES

The Formation and Amendment of Companies

ART. 15.

A permit from the Secretary of Foreign Relations is required for the formation of companies. In the by-laws of companies which are formed there shall be inserted the foreigners exclusion clause or the convention provided in item I of Constitutional article 27.

ART. 16.

(Amended by Decree of December 18, 1996, effective December 25, 1996) **A permit from the Ministry of Foreign Relations shall be**

required for companies constituted to change their trade or firm name.

Companies that amend their foreigners exclusion clause in order to admit foreigners must notify the Ministry of Foreign Relations within the 30 working days following that amendment.

If those companies are owners of real estate located in the restricted zone intended for non-residential purposes, they must give the notice to which item I of article 10 of this Law refers within the period provided in the preceding paragraph.

ART. 16A.

(Added by Decree of December 18, 1996, effective December 25, 1996) Every application for a permit to which articles 15 and 16 of this Law refer must be decided by the Ministry of Foreign Relations within the five working days following the date of its presentation. Once that period expires without a decision being issued, the respective application shall be considered to be approved.

FOURTH TITLE. INVESTMENT OF FOREIGN LEGAL PERSONS

ART. 17.

(Amended by Decree of December 18, 1996, effective December 25, 1996) Without prejudice to that which is established in international treaties and conventions to which Mexico is a party, the following must obtain authorization from the Ministry:

I.   Foreign legal persons who are trying to carry out acts of commerce in the Republic on a regular basis, and

II.   The persons to which article 2,736 of the Civil Code for the Federal District in common matters and for all the Republic in federal matters, who are trying to become established in the Republic and who are not regulated laws other than that Code.

ART. 17A.

(Added by Decree of December 18, 1996, effective December 25, 1996) The authorization to which the preceding article refers shall be granted when the following requirements are fulfilled:

a)   That said persons verify that they are constituted in accordance with the laws of their country;

b)   That the partnership contract and other formation documents of said persons are not contrary to the precepts of public order established in the Mexican laws, and

c)   In the case of the persons to whom item I of the preceding article refers, that they shall be established in the Republic or have a branch office or agency therein; or in the case of the persons to whom item II of the preceding article refers, that they have a representative domiciled in the place where they are going to operate, who shall be authorized to be liable for the obligations that they contract.

Every application that complies with the above-mentioned requirements must be authorized within the 15 working days following the date of its presentation. Once this period expires without a decision being issued, the application shall be considered as automatically approved.

The Ministry must remit a copy of the applications and authorizations that it grants on the basis of this article to the Ministry of Foreign Relations.

FIFTH TITLE. NEUTRAL INVESTMENT

CHAPTER I. THE CONCEPT OF NEUTRAL INVESTMENT

ART. 18.

Neutral investment is that which is realized in Mexican companies or in trusts authorized in accordance with this Title and it shall not be computed for determining the percentage of foreign investment in the capital stock of Mexican companies.

CHAPTER II. NEUTRAL INVESTMENT REPRESENTED BY INSTRUMENTS ISSUED BY TRUSTEE INSTITUTIONS

ART. 19.

(Amended by Decree of December 18, 1996, effective December 25, 1996) The Ministry may authorize trustee institutions to issue instruments of neutral investment which they only grant pecuniary rights, in respect to companies, to their holders and, if applicable, limited corporate rights, provided that they do not grant the right to vote in Ordinary General Meetings to their holders.

The Ministry shall have a maximum period of 35 working days as from the day following that on which the application was presented to grant or refuse the requested authorization. Once this period expires without a decision being issued, the respective application shall be considered automatically approved.

CHAPTER III. NEUTRAL INVESTMENT REPRESENTED BY SPECIAL SERIES OF STOCKS

ART. 20.

(Amended by Decree of December 18, 1996, effective December 25, 1996) The investment in stocks without voting rights or with limited corporate rights shall be considered neutral investment, provided that the prior authorization of the Ministry is obtained, as well as that of the National Banking and Securities Commission, when applicable.

The Ministry shall have a maximum period of 35 working days as from the day following that of the filing of the application, to grant or refuse the requested authorization. Once this period expires without a decision being issued, the respective application shall be considered as automatically approved.

CHAPTER IV. NEUTRAL INVESTMENT IN CONTROLLING COMPANIES OF FINANCIAL GROUPS, MULTIPLE BANKING INSTITUTIONS AND SECURITIES EXCHANGE HOUSES

ART. 21.

Repealed by Decree of December 18, 1996, effective December 25, 1996.

CHAPTER V. NEUTRAL INVESTMENT MADE BY INTERNATIONAL DEVELOPMENT FINANCE COMPANIES

ART. 22.

The Commission may decide on the neutral investment which international development finance companies seek to make in the capital stock of companies, in accordance with the terms and conditions which are for that purpose established in the regulation of this Law.

SIXTH TITLE. THE NATIONAL FOREIGN INVESTMENT COMMISSION

CHAPTER I. THE STRUCTURE OF THE COMMISSION

ART. 23.

(Amended by Decree of December 18, 1996, effective December 25, 1996) The Commission shall be composed of the Secretaries of State, of Foreign Relations, of Finance and Public Credit of Social Development, of the Environment, Natural Resources and Fishing; of Energy; of Commerce and Industrial Development, of Communications and Transportation, of Labor and Social Welfare, and of Tourism, who may appoint an Undersecretary as a deputy. Likewise, those authorities and representatives of the private and social sectors who have a relationship with the matters in question may be invited to participate in the sessions of the Commission, having a voice but no vote therein.

The Commission shall meet once every six months, at least, and shall decide on the matters for which it is competent by a majority of votes, with its president having the deciding vote in case of a tie.

ART. 24.

The Commission shall be presided over by the Secretary of Commerce and Industrial Development and shall include an Executive Secretary and a Committee of Representatives for its functioning.

ART. 25.

(Amended by Decree of December 18, 1996, effective December 25, 1996) The Committee of Representatives shall be composed of the public servant appointed by each of the State Ministries represented on the Commission, shall meet at least every four months, and shall have the faculties delegated by the Commission itself.

CHAPTER II. DUTIES OF THE COMMISSION

ART. 26.

The Commission shall have the following duties:

I.   To hand down policy lines in the matter of foreign investment and to design mechanisms to promote investment in Mexico;

II. To resolve through the Ministry, on the procedure and as the case may be, the terms and conditions of the participation of foreign investment in the activities or acquisitions which are specifically regulated, in accordance with articles 8 and 9 of this Law;

III. To be an organ of obligatory consultation in matters of foreign investment for the departments and organizations in the Public Federal Administration;

IV. To establish the criteria for the application of the legal and regulatory provisions on foreign investment, through the issue of general resolutions; and

V. Others which shall correspond to it in accordance with this ordinance.

ART. 27.

The following are duties of the Executive Secretary of the Commission:

I. To represent the Commission;

II. To notify the Resolutions of the Commission, through the Ministry;

III. To carry out the studies which the Commission entrusts thereto;

IV. **(Amended by Decree of December 18, 1996, effective December 25, 1996) To present a trimestral statistical report on the significance of foreign investment in the country to the Congress of the Union, which shall include the economic sectors and regions in which such investment is located; and**

V. Others which shall correspond to him in accordance with this Law.

CHAPTER III. THE OPERATION OF THE COMMISSION

ART. 28.

The Commission must resolve the petitions submitted for its consideration within a period which shall not exceed 45 working days as from the date of filing of the respective petition, in the terms established in the Regulation of this Law.

If the Commission does not decide within the period stipulated, the petition shall be considered approved in the terms presented. Upon the express petition of the interested party, the Ministry must issue the corresponding authorization.

ART. 29.

In order to evaluate the petitions which shall be submitted for its consideration, the Commission shall attend to the following criteria:

I.   The impact on employment and training of workers;

II.   The technological contribution;

III. Fulfillment of environmental provisions contained in the ecological ordinances governing the matter; and

IV.   In general, their contribution to increase the competency of the productive plant of the country.

The Commission, in determining the procedure of a petition, may only impose requirements which do not distort international commerce.

ART. 30.

For reasons of national security the Commission may impede acquisitions of foreign investment.

SEVENTH TITLE. NATIONAL REGISTER OF FOREIGN INVESTMENTS

ART. 31.

The Register shall not be public, and shall be divided into the sections which its Regulation shall establish, as well as determine its organization and the information which must be furnished to the Register.

ART. 32.

The following must be inscribed in the Register:

I.   **(Amended by Decree of December 18, 1996, effective December 25, 1996) Mexican companies in which foreign investment participates, including those in which foreign investment participates through a trust, and neutral investment.**

II.   Foreign individuals or legal persons which carry out commercial acts in the Mexican Republic and branches of foreign investors established in the country;

III.   Trusts of stocks or shares, of real property or of neutral investment, by virtue of which rights in favor of the foreign investment shall be derived.

The obligation of registration shall be incurred by the individuals or legal persons to which items I and II refer, and, in the case of item III, by the corresponding fiduciary institutions. The registration must be carried out within the 40 working days as from the date of the formation of the company or of the foreign investment participation, the notarization or legalization of the documents relative to the foreign company, or formation of the respective trust or authorization of rights of trusteeship in favor of the foreign investment.

Art. 33.

The Register shall issue registration vouchers when the following data are contained in the petition:

I.   In the cases of items I and II:

     a)   Name, trade or firm name, domicile, date of formation, if applicable, and principal economic activity to be carried out;

     b)   Name and domicile of the legal representative;

     c)   Name and domicile of the persons authorized to hear and receive notifications;

     d)   Name, trade or firm name, nationality and immigration status, if applicable, domicile of the foreign investors inside or outside the country and their percentage of participation;

     e)   Amount of capital stock subscribed and paid in or subscribed and payable; and

     f)   Estimated date of beginning of operations and approximate amount of total investment with its forecast.

II.   In the case of item III:

     a)   Trade name of the fiduciary institution;

b) Name, trade or firm name, domicile and nationality of the foreign investment or of the foreign investors who are the founders of the trust;

c) Name, trade or firm name, domicile and nationality of the foreign investment or of the foreign investors designated as beneficiaries of the trust;

d) Date of formation, purposes and duration of the trust; and

e) Description, value, destination and, as the case may be, location of the net wealth of the trust.

Once the registration voucher or its renewal is issued, the Register shall reserve the faculty of requesting declarations with respect to the information presented.

Any modification to the information presented in the terms of this article must be notified to the Register in accordance with that which is established in its Regulation.

ART. 34.

In the formation, modification, transformation, merger, spin-off, dissolution and liquidation of mercantile companies, of civil partnerships and associations and, in general, in all the legal acts or deeds in which the persons obligated to be registered in the Register in the terms of article 32 of this Law, intervene on their own behalf or as representatives, the notaries public shall demand said persons or their representatives to prove their registration on the aforementioned Register, or if the registration is in process, they shall prove that they filed the corresponding petition. If it cannot be proved, the notary may authorize the public deed in question, and report that omission to the Register within the 10 working days following the date of authorization of the deed.

ART. 35.

The subjects obligated to be registered in the Register must annually renew their registration voucher, for which it is sufficient to present an economic-financial questionnaire in the terms which the respective Regulation shall establish.

ART. 36.

The federal, state and municipal authorities shall be obligated to furnish the Ministry with the reports and certifications necessary for the fulfillment of his functions in accordance with this Law and its regulatory provisions.

EIGHTH TITLE. SANCTIONS

ART. 37.

In the case of acts performed in contravention to the provisions of this Law, the Ministry may revoke the authorizations granted.

The acts, conventions or business and statutory agreements declared null and void by the Ministry due to their being contrary to that which is established in this Law, shall not furnish legal effects between the parties nor may they be made valid before third parties.

ART. 38.

Infractions committed against that which is established in this Law and in its regulatory provisions shall be penalized in accordance with the following:

I. If the foreign investment carried out activities, acquisitions or any other act which required a favorable decision of the Commission for their realization, insofar as this was not obtained previously, a fine of from one thousand to five thousand wages shall be imposed;

II. If foreign legal persons normally carry out commercial acts in the Mexican Republic, without previously obtaining the authorization of the Ministry, a fine of from 500 to 1,000 wages shall be imposed;

III. If acts in contravention to that which is established in this Law or in its regulatory provisions in the matter of neutral investment are carried out, a fine of from 100 to 300 wages shall be imposed;

IV. In case of omission, late fulfillment, filing of incomplete or incorrect information in respect to the obligations of registration, report or notice to the Register on the part of the obligated subjects, a fine of from 30 to 100 wages shall be imposed;

V. In case of contrivance of acts with the intention of permitting the possession or disposal of real property in the restricted zone to foreign individuals or legal persons or to Mexican companies without a foreigners exclusion clause, in contravention to that which is provided by the Second and Third Titles of this Law, the offender shall be penalized by a fine up to the amount of the transaction; and

VI.   In case of other infractions to this Law or to its regulatory provisions, a fine of from 100 to 50,000 wages shall be imposed.

For the purposes of this article, wage shall be understood as the general daily minimum wage in force in the Federal District at the time of determining the infraction.

For the determination and imposition of the penalties a prior hearing of the interested party must be held and, in case of pecuniary sanctions, the nature and gravity of the infraction must be taken into consideration, as well as the economic capacity of the infractor, the time elapsed between the date on which the obligation should have been fulfilled and its fulfillment or regularization, and the total value of the operation.

The Secretary shall impose the penalties, except in the case of the infraction to which item V of this article refers and others related to the Second and Third Titles of this Law, which shall be applied by the Minister of Foreign Relations.

The imposition of penalties to which this Title refers shall be without prejudice to the civil or penal liability which shall correspond, if applicable.

ART. 39.

Notaries public shall relate, insert or add the authorizations which must be issued in the terms of this Law into the official file or appendix of the documents in which they intervene.   When they authorize documents in which those authorizations and clauses are not related, they shall be sanctioned in the manner determined in the corresponding notarial laws and in the Public Brokerage Law.

TRANSITORY ARTICLES

FIRST TRANSITORY.

This Law shall become effective on the day following its publication in the "*Diario Oficial*" of the Federation.

SECOND TRANSITORY.

The following shall be repealed:

I.   The Law to Promote National Investment and to Regulate Foreign Investment, published in the *"Diario Oficial"* of the Federation on March 9, 1973;

II.   The Organic Law of Item I of Constitutional Article 27, published in the *Diario Oficial* of the Federation on January 21, 1926.

III.   The Decree establishing the temporary necessity to obtain a permit for the acquisition of assets by foreigners and for the formation or modification of Mexican companies which foreign partners hold, published in the *Diario Oficial* of the Federation of July 7, 1944.

THIRD TRANSITORY.

The following shall be repealed:

I.   Articles 46 and 47 of the Federal Firearms and Explosives Law, published in the *Diario Oficial* of the Federation on January 11, 1972; and

II.   All general legal, regulatory and administrative provisions which are opposed to this Law.

FOURTH TRANSITORY.

Until Regulations of this Law shall be issued, the Regulation of the Law to Promote Mexican Investment and to Regulate Foreign Investment, published in the *Diario Oficial* of the Federation on May 16, 1989, shall continue to be in force insofar as not opposed to this Law.

FIFTH TRANSITORY.

Foreign investors and companies with foreign investment, which on the date of publication of this Law have assembled programs, requirements and compromises with the Commission, its Executive Secretary or the General Office of Foreign Investment of the Ministry, may submit to the consideration of the cited General Office, the exemption from its compliance, to which that administrative unit must respond accordingly within a period which shall not exceed 45 working days, as from the presentation of the corresponding petition. Those foreign investors who do not claim the benefit from the possibility of the referred exemption must comply with the previously defined commitments before the Commission, persons and public entities specified.

SIXTH TRANSITORY.

Activities of international land transportation of passengers, tourists and of cargo between points in Mexican territory and the central service of administration of passenger buses and auxiliary services shall be reserved exclusively to Mexicans or to Mexican companies with a foreigners exclusion clause.

Nevertheless, in the activities mentioned, foreign investment may participate in accordance with the following provisions:

I.   As from December 18, 1995, up to 49% of the capital stock of Mexican companies;

II.   As from January 1, 2001, up to 51% of the capital stock of Mexican companies; and

III.   As from January 1, 2004, up to 100% of the capital stock of Mexican companies, without necessity of obtaining a favorable decision from the Commission.

SEVENTH TRANSITORY.

Foreign investment may participate up to 49% of the capital stock of Mexican companies engaged in activities of manufacture and assembly of parts, equipment and accessories for the automotive industry, without prejudice to that which is provided by the Decree for the Development and Modernization of the Automotive Industry. As from the first of January, 1999, foreign investment may participate up to 100% in the capital stock of Mexican companies, without necessity of seeking a favorable decision of the Commission.

EIGHTH TRANSITORY.

Foreign investment may participate up to 49% in the capital stock of Mexican companies engaged in the activities of rendering services of videotext and parcel exchange. As from July 1, 1995, foreign investment may participate up to 100% in the companies engaged in the services mentioned, without necessity of obtaining a favorable decision of the Commission.

Ninth Transitory.

A favorable resolution of the Commission shall be required in order that foreign investment may participate by more than 49% in the capital stock of companies carrying out activities of building, construction and installation of works. As from January 1, 1999, foreign investment may participate up to 100% in the capital stock of Mexican companies engaged in the aforementioned works, without necessity of obtaining a favorable decision of the Commission.

Tenth Transitory.

For the purposes of that which is provided in article 9, and insofar as the Commission shall fix the amount of the total value of the assets referred to in the cited article, the quantity of 85 million new pesos shall be determined.

Eleventh Transitory.

That which is provided in Chapter II of the Second Title of this Law shall be applied to foreign investors and Mexican companies with a clause to admit foreigners which hold trusts on their behalf of real property in the restricted zone, on the effective date of this Law, in all that shall benefit them.

Call toll free and order now!

Order Form

Telephone orders: call toll free: 1-800-529-6394 have Visa or Mastercard ready.

Fax orders: (619) 482-7834

Postal orders:

LAW MEXICO PUBLISHING
539 Telegraph Canyon Road #787
Chula Vista, California 91910-6497

Please send the following books:

_____

_____

_____

Name:

Address:

City: **State:**   **Zip:**

Shipping: Book rate: $3.00 for the first book $1.00 each additional book. Surface shipping may take three to four weeks. Air Mail $4.50 per book.

Payment: Check Credit card: Visa Mastercard

Card number:

Name on Card: Exp. date /